Talking to a Stranger

Lindsay Knight was educated in the north of England, where she grew up, and at St Anne's College, Oxford. She then went into journalism and worked on a range of magazines including *New Internationalist* and *New Society*. She edited MIND's magazine, *MIND OUT*, and wrote for *Cosmopolitan*, the *Guardian*, *Sunday Times* and various medical and social services magazines, specializing in mental health and social medicine.

For the past four years she has worked mainly in television and films, producing Channel 4's health series 'Well Being'. Programmes have included 'The Price of Tranquillity?' on the side-effects of major tranquillizers, and another on Italy's radical psychiatric reforms. She is co-author of *Well Being* (1982), the book which accompanied the series. She is a director of an independent production company, and lives in south London.

Lindsay Knight

Talking to a Stranger

A Consumer's Guide
to Therapy

Fontana/Collins

First published in 1986 by Fontana Paperbacks
8 Grafton Street, London W1X 3LA

Made and Printed in Great Britain by
William Collins Sons & Co. Ltd , Glasgow

For kind permission to quote, thanks are due to
Faber and Faber Ltd for lines from 'Annus Mirabilis'
(from *High Windows*) and 'Talking in Bed' (*The
Whitsun Weddings*) by Philip Larkin; Kyveli A.
Songopoulo, Edmund Keeley and Philip Sherrard
and Chatto & Windus for lines from 'Ithaka' from
C. P. Cavafy Collected Poems translated by Edmund
Keeley and Philip Sherrard; Oxford University Press
for lines from the title poem of *The Onion, Memory*
(1978) by Craig Raine.

Contents

Acknowledgments

So many people have helped me with this book that it is probably wiser not to single out any individuals, but to thank them all. My greatest debt must be to all those un-named individuals who so generously agreed to talk to me about their experiences of therapy. They all gave up a great deal of time to do so, and often some pain in reliving the reason for going into therapy and recalling the experience. I hope they feel the book is in some way worthy of their efforts. I would also like to thank the many practitioners of therapy who again spared a great deal of valuable time to explain patiently to me how they practised, and to answer my many questions.

I would especially like to thank my own psychotherapist who has undoubtedly helped me to complete this book and, I hope, to understand a little more about therapy than when I first started researching this two years ago.

Last but not least, I'd like to thank my family, my friends and my work colleagues for their support, love, sympathy, patience, etc. I know many of them will be almost as re-lieved as myself that the book is finished, and without some of them it might never have been.

I would like to dedicate the book to my parents.

Introduction

'As you set out for Ithaka
hope your road is a long one,
full of adventure, full of discovery.
Laistrygonians, Cyclops,
angry Poseidon – don't be afraid of them:
you'll never find things like that on your way
as long as you keep your thoughts raised high,
as long as a rare sensation
touches your body and spirit.
Laistrygonians, Cyclops,
wild Poseidon – you won't encounter them
unless you bring them along inside your soul,
unless your soul sets them up in front of you.'

C. P. Cavafy, 'Ithaka'

A friend of mine was recently advised by a rather wise old
doctor that she would improve her health one hundredfold if
she stopped reading the newspaper in the morning. Certainly
the daily outpourings of doom and gloom, the accounts of
misery, both individual and collective, and the numerous
causes for concern, whether they be rising unemployment
figures or the proliferation of nuclear weapons, are enough to
affect the strongest constitution, physically and emotionally.

Whether or not today's world is truly more evil or disturbing than at any other time, there does seem to be an
increasing number of men and women, young and old, and

even children, who are suffering psychological distress – depression, anxiety, psychosomatic disorders like ulcers, back pain, and migraines, insomnia, phobias. Nobody knows the extent of the problem, although some American studies have estimated that at any one time over 80 per cent of the population in the United States have some degree of impairment caused by mental disorder. General practitioners in this country reckon that at least every twelfth time their door opens, someone will enter with a problem which is psychological rather than physical, even if they themselves do not recognize that loss of appetite or chronic back pain may be linked, for example, to their marital difficulties.

Some will be offered the chance to talk to their GP about their feelings and the possible causes of the symptom. But the majority will be prescribed drug treatment, usually tranquillizers or antidepressants, and nothing else. There will be no attempt to find out why they are feeling this way or have this symptom.

About 10 per cent of these patients will be deemed by their GPs to be in need of specialist psychiatric treatment, and may well be diagnosed as clinically mentally ill. At least one in ten of us will spend some time as an in-patient being treated for a psychiatric problem. That treatment will almost always involve drugs, such as the major tranquillizers used to treat schizophrenia, or antidepressants for more 'minor' conditions. Whether or not such a patient is given psychotherapy or counselling regularly is a matter of chance, depending on the orientation of the psychiatrist and other professionals involved in their case.

Over the past few years, a growing number of consumers of drugs, and some professionals involved in treatments, have expressed great anxiety about taking them. People become as addicted to minor tranquillizers as to heroin, and coming off them can be more painful. All drugs have side-effects, and psychotropic drugs are certainly no exception:

some of the major tranquillizers cause irreversible brain damage. But addiction and side-effects are not the only reasons for people protesting about their use. Drugs only offer symptomatic relief; they do not solve people's problems, they do not get to the root of their depression or anxiety, above all, they do not help people make sense of their suffering and pain. Talking treatments such as psychotherapy, on the other hand, aim primarily to do that, and thereby to remove symptoms like insomnia or anxiety attacks. Sometimes people know that their depression is a result of their divorce or their redundancy, and want help and support while they learn to cope with such crises. In other cases, there is no obvious reason for the depression, and more work will have to be done by the client and therapist.

Psychological treatments like psychotherapy and counselling are more widely available than ten years ago, but they have certainly not swept across Britain as they have some parts of the United States, where you are considered abnormal if you *don't* see a therapist. And outside the more enlightened metropolitan areas, as one would expect, there are considerable pockets of resistance amongst all classes. 'Talking about your problems to a stranger is almost obscene' was a not uncommon response from a Yorkshireman. 'In Gloucestershire we talk to our husbands, we don't need therapists,' said an acquaintance.

Even among the growing numbers of people sympathetic to the idea of therapy, there is great confusion and misunderstanding about the different types of therapy – what is involved, who can be helped, how long it will take. Many don't know where to turn if they decide they want this sort of help, or what might best suit them. I hope this book will sort out some of this confusion, answer people's many questions about therapy and demolish some of the myths and misconceptions. It is an attempt at a guide to the talking treatments, as they are often called, including psychoanalysis, psychotherapy, counselling, sex and marital therapy, group therapy.

Therapy is often likened by practitioners and patients to a

journey, an inner voyage of discovery – a long hard journey, many told me. My aim is to describe the different guides (that is, therapists) available; some of the maps used (the theoretical underpinnings); the forms of travel (the therapeutic techniques); and the very varied reasons for undergoing such a journey (from severe mental illness to a search for some meaning in life).

The book is largely based on interviews with practitioners and, most importantly, with many individuals who have themselves experienced these different therapies. Not everyone's life has been transformed; no miracle cures are on offer. Several therapists said firmly, 'I don't have any magic wand.' But the majority of people I interviewed felt they had benefitted from therapy, if only through the support they received from the therapist and the opportunity to talk, to 'give sorrow words'. It is a sad, but inescapable, fact that far too many men and women feel they have had no opportunity to talk to anyone about their problems. Nor are these necessarily isolated individuals; they are often married or with large families, but they feel unable to talk to someone or, quite frequently, that no one really wants to listen to them.

Others got considerably more out of their therapy than support. They found that their symptoms disappeared, that they were considerably better equipped to deal with life, even when it appeared to be confronting them with insurmountable difficulties. They were relieved to make sense of their depression, to make the connections between present and past events or emotions. Talking about, and through, your feelings concerning the end of your marriage, will not bring back your partner, but will help you come to terms with reality, grieve for the loss and, perhaps, give you such insight into why it ended that any subsequent relationship will be more successful.

This book is written in the hope that it will encourage more people to consider psychotherapy or counselling as a more effective answer to their problems and unhappiness than blanking them out with drugs or alcohol. I would also stress that therapy and counselling are not esoteric activities for intellectuals or for the very rich (though unfortunately National Health Service resources are very stretched and in some areas it would be hard to find such help on the NHS): they are for ordinary people with ordinary problems spoken in ordinary language.

A British analyst, reviewing a book on Freud for the *Guardian*, said he felt he had truly become an analyst when 'a patient, after quite a long analysis, said that he had not heard me say anything which he could not have heard in his local pub.'

If you are reading this because you are considering therapy for yourself, you have already crossed a major barrier. But you may well be nervous and anxious about what is involved, and worried about taking that first step to see a therapist. Most people I interviewed talked about 'plucking up their courage' for that first consultation, if not the phone call to arrange it. I also understand and have shared those feelings. I started out researching this book as a reasonably objective journalist, observing from outside. But for various reasons, including the stress of writing such a book and covering painful areas which often rang bells for me, I decided to see a psychotherapist. I find it enormously helpful, often enjoyable, and believe that most people, at certain times in their life, would find the opportunity to explore themselves, to make that interior journey, a helpful, stimulating and sometimes salutary experience.

1 What is psychotherapy?

'Give sorrow words; the grief that does not speak
Whispers the o'erfraught heart and bids it break. . . '

William Shakespeare, *Macbeth*

Any talking treatment, like psychotherapy or counselling, is basically a conversation between therapist and patient (or client) aimed at helping that patient understand and then resolve their problem. This resolution may also involve the removal of a symptom of the patient's dis-ease, such as depression or anxiety.

The style of the conversation, the techniques used, the grammar and vocabulary, the complexity of the theoretical structures underpinning the treatment, all vary, often considerably. But the common ancestor, whatever mutations and permutations since, is Sigmund Freud.

He was certainly the first psychotherapist as the term is understood today, but he did not invent, and never claimed to have done, the 'talking cure'. In the fifth century BC, the Greek dramatist Aeschylus wrote of words as 'healers of the sick temper'. Freud himself explained: 'Words were originally magic and to this day words have retained much of their ancient magical powers. By words one person can make another blissfully happy or drive him to despair.'[1]

Nor was Freud the first to point to unconscious processes and the conflicts between thoughts, wishes and feelings. Witchdoctors, shamans, priests and poets have all in their own way recognized some form of inner world, the dark powers within every human being. Psychological conflicts have been the stuff of drama and poetry for many centuries.

Freud's achievement was to draw many of these ideas together, to develop them along with many original ideas of his own and to create a mighty structure of both theory and practice. He was the first person to offer a detailed map of the psyche; to explore the unconscious and its relationship with the conscious mind; to provide a vocabulary for describing psychological processes, techniques for revealing the unconscious and for ameliorating the more damaging results of its conflict.

As psychiatrist and Emeritus Professor of Mental Health at Bristol, Derek Russell Davis, has written: 'Psychoanalysis was remarkable . . . it recognized . . . that the symptoms of mental illness, which might otherwise be regarded as accidental or capricious products of the breakdown of the functions of the brain, have meaning in that they express ideas and feelings derived from experience, or, especially, from the unconscious; and that . . . even the strangest manifestations of insanity . . . as well as of lesser disorders, and slips of the tongue, errors, wit, dreams . . . can be explained in terms of psychological processes.'[2]

The fact that psychotherapy tries to make sense of one's depression or insomnia, that it attempts to see some sort of reason behind sexual hang-ups or anorexia, is what makes it so much more attractive than drugs for many people. It offers insights into what may seem irrational, to human beings who are, for much of the time, rational beings. 'In therapy,' said one ex-patient, 'I was enabled to discover reasons for what I was doing and thinking, I realized that they weren't just a strange accident of fate. Psychological problems don't hit you like a bolt out of the blue, any more than many physical problems do.'

Merrill Berger, a psychotherapist in south London, explained the difference between the actions of drugs and therapy: 'I have a very clear image of what therapy does. The unconscious is unhappy about something and like an animal it rises up and makes the person very ill. The psyche needs to incubate; to draw within itself, for healing. Illness is a cry from the unconscious, especially psychological illness or difficulties. The real tragedy of modern medicine, to my mind, is that at this time there is a true opportunity for true healing but it just doesn't happen.' However, she accepts the need for drugs as well as therapy in some cases.

Carl Jung said that symptoms are attempts to give us clues as to how we could change our present way of life for a better one.

People want to make sense of their misery, as well as receiving comfort and support. Modern medicine offers little in this way, partly because the National Health Service (NHS) is so underresourced, but also because many doctors are not trained, and do not have the personality, to deal in a psychotherapeutic way with these patients.

One excellent opportunity for this type of healing – but too often sadly ignored – is when a patient is admitted after a failed suicide attempt. Anyone who tries to end their life is in some despair, some trouble, but a not uncommon reaction is that it's just another silly girl crying out for help. Jill was in therapy for anorexia when a colleague at work attempted suicide. Jill visited and agreed to sit with her when the psychiatrist arrived for an interview: 'It was the closest I'd ever been to seeing NHS psychiatry at work and I wasn't impressed. He just went on at her about being selfish, what about her two children and so on, nothing about why she felt so depressed she wanted to end it all. She was shaking and crying, he didn't offer her any comfort at all.'

Although more and more people have discovered that a professional therapist allows them to 'give sorrow words' in a way that can be enormously helpful, there are still many other men and women who are distinctly wary of this sort of help, partly through ignorance, but partly because of the stigma attached to any problem labelled psychological. They fear their symptoms or emotions will be labelled irrational. People are generally far more relaxed about admitting to pains in the belly than in the psyche. It is not therefore surprising that so many people, consciously or unconsciously, usually report symptoms of a physical nature to their doctor or GP, such as chronic backache or a nagging headache, rather than depression or sexual problems. The prescription for a drug, albeit tranquillizers or antidepressants, may also appear to be less stigmatizing than the suggestion that some form of therapy may help.

'When my GP suggested I saw a marriage guidance counsellor, I felt he was telling me my backache was imaginary and that I was going mad,' said Mary, a shop assistant who just managed to tell her doctor that she and her husband were thinking of separation. 'I felt so ashamed.'

'A friend suggested analysis, and I remember thinking, "My God, he must think I'm quite crazy, not just depressed,"' recalled Joan, a TV producer now very satisfactorily into her third year of psychoanalysis.

Even when people have themselves selected psychotherapy, they may keep quiet about it. John, a teacher who has had two years of individual psychotherapy, admitted: 'I don't tell anyone at work because they'll think I'm a mental case.'

Such stigma is based on fear. There is the fear that we are appearing weak or pathetic to allow feelings of depression or anxiety to take such a hold. 'Pull your socks up therapy' is sadly not so infrequently doled out by GPs or figures of authority like teachers (or even so-called friends). Linked to this is the misconception that psychological pain is not serious, it is an excuse, sufferers are skiving. But the greater fear is that of madness. 'That way madness lies,' said

Shakespeare's King Lear, a thought which haunts people who are depressed, crippled by a phobia, dominated by uncontrollable jealousy or perhaps just deeply unhappy. The suggestion that they might seek professional help may in some way validate this fear.

It is important to remember how desperately ignorant, how psychologically illiterate, are the majority of people in this country. The most well-educated and intelligent people have no idea of the difference between psychoanalysis and the normal run of psychiatric treatment, for example. I rather suspect that the readers of weekly women's magazines have more idea of how 'talking cures' work, than many middle-class intellectuals.

The woman who phones up a radio help-line about her crumbling marriage may have a sounder understanding of the psyche than the successful businessman who drowns his sorrows daily in excellent claret. (It has taken a long time for the acceptance of the view that excessive drinking can be a symptom of psychological distress which can then lead to addiction.)

It is also important to stress how confused and ill-defined are the concepts of mental illness and mental health. Psychiatrist Anthony Clare, in his book *Psychiatry in Dissent*, gives an amusing account of various attempts at such definitions where mental health is described as '. . . an adjustment of human beings to the world and to each other with a maximum of effectiveness and happiness . . . the ability to maintain an even temper, an alert intelligence, socially considerate behaviour and a happy disposition'.[3]

Too many people make the mistake of equating mental health with happiness. But unhappiness is often a very normal reaction to events, and psychotherapy is certainly not essential for people who are just ordinarily unhappy about their life from time to time. None of us can manage to lead our lives without certain levels of stress and anxiety; being mentally healthy is not a matter of protecting oneself from the hardships of life, but about having the ability to cope with them. With its ever rising rates of unemployment and poverty, the western world today (let alone the human misery of the third world countries) offers everyone the prospect of insecurity and anxiety about the future. Add in everyone's particular circumstances, for example single parenthood or chronic disease, to such generalized worries, and we each have a recipe for some mental distress.

When considering whether help is needed, it should be remembered that it is quite normal and healthy to be upset at certain times in one's life: after bereavement, the birth of a new baby, one's child's first day at school, divorce. Every change or transition in life brings its share of stress or anxiety, even apparently welcome events like marriage or a holiday. It is more unhealthy to deny, or suppress, such emotions at these periods in one's life.

It is when the normal distress, or anxiety, rises to such a level that the individual finds his or her life is seriously affected that help should be considered. This could take the form of chronic insomnia, a phobia which begins to take over or a feeling of being out of control and not living life well. Susan was to all but a few close friends who knew her well a very successful, extrovert, happy woman, with a good career in marketing and a not unenviable social life. She had always been prone to minor depressions, but accepted them and even welcomed them as the joy she was also capable of experiencing regularly seemed to make them worthwhile. But after three months of 'downs', of sleepless nights, unprovoked crying bouts and the feeling that life was not worth living, she realized the need for some professional help and found a psychotherapist.

Susan was lucky enough to have some insight into her psyche and its problems. She had a GP who did not fob her off with tranquillizers but listened to her and agreed that psychotherapy was probably the answer. She lives in a city where private psychotherapy is available, and she was able to pay.

But if she had not had all those advantages, Susan, with all her talent, successful career and good income, could have had a very different experience. She might have been referred to the psychiatric services and commuted between periods of time in a mental hospital or psychiatric unit, and her normal life.

Most people treated for mental illness, whether in the community or in hospital, have what are termed neurotic problems, like Susan's: depression, anxiety, phobias, obsessions. A neurosis is, in a sense, a distortion of normal emotions and/or behaviour. All of us have been depressed, but not to the point where that emotion takes control of us or our life. Most people are afraid of snakes, for example, or spiders, but not to the extent of that fear becoming a phobia. Or some people appear to cope better with depression or crippling anxiety because they have stronger networks of support; if that network begins to disintegrate, a marriage ends, or a parent dies, then that person can no longer cope.

A much smaller number of people (about one in a hundred) suffer from psychotic illnesses, the most common being schizophrenia and manic depression. At times, sufferers can totally lose touch with reality; they hear voices, experience hallucinations or great highs of mania. Some recover, others find their lives are permanently impaired, as much because of the stigma and the very primitive treatment (mainly drugs) as from the illness itself. The label of schizophrenic is a damning one, and prevents others from seeing beyond it to the individual who usually has very 'normal' periods and is capable of working and living with his family. The most apparently normal of us could, for various reasons, experience a psychotic episode. Takers of drugs such as LSD have discovered this. The problems of distinguishing between mental illness and mental health exists, I believe, because it is impossible to mark that borderline. As Anthony Clare explains: 'It is probably a mistake to conceptualize normality and madness as dichotomous, that is to say, as states of mind, inhabitation of one necessarily mitigating against the other. Rather they are best thought of as opposite ends of a continuum, a continuum on which most of us find ourselves positioned in that grey and shady area between the two opposing poles.'[4]

It is that grey and shady area, verging on darkness, which is the habitat of the majority of people in psychotherapy. Their difficulties are as many and varied as their numbers, but there are some common denominators, symptoms such as depression, anxiety, insomnia, sexual difficulties. They often express the feeling that something isn't quite right, or have a general sense of unease. As several people explained, they find that their problems or symptoms are getting in the way of living. They are 'on the verge of a breakdown', 'at the end of their tether'. Perhaps the majority would not be diagnosed as clinically mentally ill (although diagnosis varies considerably from doctor to doctor), but they are certainly not mentally healthy.

Depression

This is the most common symptom, the sign of something wrong in a person's world. Depression prompts people to seek psychotherapy or counselling, and the cause, on the surface at any rate, is frequently some relationship problem: the end of a relationship, a string of unsatisfactory relationships, or the inability to form relationships. 'Depression can mean a whole myriad of things,' explained psychotherapist Jill Curtis. 'Some people are in a total crisis, others seem to have reasonably good and successful lives but just don't feel right. They may be the sort of person who discovers they cannot get rid of these depressed feelings by going away on holiday.'

Similarly, psychotherapist Brenda Moor commented, 'A lot of my clients are materially rich but they have lost the sense of "who I am". Their external world is fine but they feel bad inside. They need to make the connection between the external world with their internal world.'

'I don't consider I was mentally ill – I hadn't lost contact with reality and I wasn't behaving in a bizarre fashion – but I was deeply distressed and on the point of trying to kill myself.' Jonathan is in his mid-forties, a college lecturer, and has now been seeing his psychotherapist for four years. 'I would say, looking back, that I was quite inadequate to the task of being.'

Miriam is a thirty-two-year-old teacher, married with a child. She has been in therapy for just over a year. 'I had to recognize that I wasn't coping in various ways, I often felt very depressed. I had a difficult relationship with my husband; and then an uncle, who had suffered from severe depression for many years, committed suicide. I then had all the guilt to deal with. I do think there's a very thin line between the way I was feeling then, the degree of dysfunction, and mental illness.'

For Miriam, her uncle's illness was a crisis point, it confronted her with her own problems, her dis-ease.

Mary is in her mid-thirties. She can hardly remember a time in her life when she hasn't felt depressed. 'Even as a child I felt lonely and alienated, a failure compared to everyone else in the family. I was the only one of six children of very successful parents to fail the eleven plus. I had my first attack of serious depression when I was fifteen, but I didn't ask anyone for help. I certainly couldn't talk to my parents about how I felt. It may sound strange but as soon as I realized I could kill myself, I had that option, I immediately felt much better.'

A good marriage, three children and a fairly satisfying teaching job were not enough to prevent Mary's depression returning at regular intervals. She never asked her GP to help her, but she has spent time analysing herself and recognized some of the underlying themes. 'Firstly, I didn't, and still don't, see marriage and children as a completion of myself. And my depression has a despair underlying it all, I really have no hope for my life.'

The depression when her youngest child went to school was the worst. 'I just wasn't prepared for the intensity of my feelings, I became fanatically depressed, there was just a great blackness. On the surface I carried on my life as normal but everything churned away all the time underneath. Emotionally I was quite paralysed and I then realized this was an indication I needed help. And I also wanted to change, to come closer to other people, for instance, and felt I couldn't make that change on my own.' She has been seeing an analyst for two years.

Carol saw her first psychotherapist when she was a teenager in the United States: Her teenage years were troubled, she was often in conflict with her parents and generally didn't get on at all well with her mother. At university, she saw a trainee psychoanalyst for eighteen months, through the student counselling service. She then came to England and, despite an interesting and quite successful career in teaching, things were not right. 'I went through yet another period of being very depressed. I felt that nobody loved me, nobody cared, there was no meaning to life. I thought I'd never feel better and though I never did attempt suicide, it sometimes seemed like a possibility. I was often in that frame of mind.' She chose to go into psychoanalysis and has been seeing her analyst for over six years.

Like many of the women I interviewed, part of Carol's depression was linked to her single state, her feelings of isolation and failure. 'I felt forlorn, only half a person and often very lonely. I felt something was lacking in my life, that as no man had chosen me as his mate, I was worthless and unwanted.'

Some people seek psychotherapeutic help for specific problems or difficulties; they recognize the sources of their depression. Jane had been married for twelve years when she discovered her husband was having an affair with one of her friends. Confronted with her discovery, he admitted that this wasn't the first time. Jane was devastated by the knowledge and they stopped talking to each other. 'It was as if our whole relationship had been founded on a lie. I felt completely on my own, that I was the only person this had ever happened to, nobody could possibly understand. I did tell a few close friends what was happening and how I was feeling but since they hadn't had similar experiences themselves, they couldn't give me much understanding. I felt I was a lunatic and going insane. My life was completely turned upside down. I felt absolute despair, just like falling down an abyss, everything was out of kilter, and I couldn't cope with the most mundane everyday tasks.' She was clearly heading for a nervous breakdown when a friend recommended marriage guidance counselling. She has been going for over a year.

Deirdre, at forty in her second marriage and fairly contented in her personnel job, recognized that something wasn't quite right in her marriage but felt it was more to do with her. 'I'd had individual psychotherapy before, and knew enough to recognize that my relationships, especially with men, often followed the same, at times destructive, pattern. I wanted to sort this out before my marriage was seriously at risk of failing.' She is in her seventh month of group therapy.

Louisa is thirty-nine and works in advertising. To the outsider, she is a successful and contented career woman who has quite recovered from her divorce five years ago. And, indeed, she says she is often very happy but increasingly aware that she has never quite faced up to her feelings about the divorce and her mother's death a few years earlier. She chose psychotherapy because she hoped that by talking through the loss and grief, she might at last lay some ghosts and gain peace of mind.

Anxiety

Anxiety is another common symptom among those people who seek psychotherapeutic help. Marian, who came to academic life quite late, in her mid-thirties, became tremendously anxious, often to the point of panic, when she had to speak in public. 'It was obviously hindering me at work, as my job involved some teaching, so I consulted the university counselling service.' She saw a psychotherapist for just over a year.

Phobias and obsessions

Phobias and obsessions are frequent symptoms, sometimes with an underlying depression. Julie became agoraphobic, afraid to move outside her house, when she became divorced. She was unemployed at the time and her agoraphobia made any chance of finding another job impossible. 'I was completely a prisoner in my own house. As soon as I stepped outside the garden gate, I had a panic attack.' She went to her GP for some tranquillizers and he referred her to the local hospital's psychology department. She was treated for several months with behaviour therapy (see Glossary).

The most common obsessional behaviour is the compulsive ritual of hand-washing. Michael developed this in his early teens; he was terrified of germs and would wash his hands after touching anything at all. After years of misery, his wife threatened to leave him and that crisis stirred him into asking for help. He has been seeing a behaviour therapist for a year.

Physical and psychosomatic problems

People with depression or anxiety often understand that there is something wrong psychologically and appreciate the offer of psychological help. They might recognize, for example, that excessive tiredness or constant headaches are the body's warning signals that something is psychologically wrong.

Other people, consciously and unconsciously, deny there is any link between their migraine, say, and their unhappy marriage, or their back pain and sexual problems. Depending on the sensitivity of their doctors, they may undergo years of exploratory tests, even operations, before psychological therapy is considered. In such cases, psychotherapy may be seen as a last resort, a last-ditch attempt to treat an apparently intractable condition impervious to all that modern technological medicine has to offer.

Doctors are increasingly recognizing the very strong link between mind (psyche) and body (soma). (Hippocrates recognized it centuries ago.) Psychological factors, often stress and depression, can trigger, or at least influence the course of, physical conditions. These psychosomatic illnesses are still a very controversial issue in the medical world – a minefield, commented one psychiatrist – but a few illnesses are accepted as largely psychosomatic, such as migraine, asthma, stomach ulcers, hypertension, ulcerative colitis. In the case of stomach ulcers, stress or depression trigger off a biochemical response, converting a psychological problem into a physical one. These physical problems are serious and have to be treated, for patients with untreated ulcers can bleed to death. Anorexia, which some would describe as the classic psychosomatic disease, is too often fatal.

No one should assume that psychosomatic diseases are imaginary or that the person is malingering. It is common knowledge that if you're 'run down' you are more vulnerable to 'flu, say, or an accident; that events like divorce, bereavement, change of job, make us more vulnerable to the physical effects of stress. Psychological techniques such as relaxation and meditation are used to treat people after heart attacks or with chronic pain. It has also been suggested that certain personality types are more prone to cancer and heart disease.

Psychological treatments may be especially useful and educative in these conditions because it has been suggested that those people who suffer from psychosomatic disease are 'alexithymic' – that is, they are not psychologically minded, they have a more constricted emotional life, with very little ability to fantasize or describe their emotions. Women are less likely to be alexithymic.

Freud treated many patients who had symptoms of hysteria, but this is far less common nowadays. But there is a small group of people who suffer from 'hysterical conversion' – conditions such as blindness or loss of sensation or some instances of crippling back pain, where there appears to be no physical reason to explain the physiological evidence. Once again, this has to be taken seriously and treated, because the person is truly suffering, but clearly if the cause is totally psychological, then only psychological treatment can help.

Nicholas Spicer is an analyst whose patients frequently include those with seemingly untreatable physical complaints, especially stomach and skin problems. He explained, 'This makes sense to me and my way of working because so many physical problems are symbolic. I would say that a skin complaint, for example, reflects the fact that that person's inner and outer world are in conflict. Centuries ago, people talked about the body in a more symbolic way and we still retain some of that when we say – "his heart is broken", "he can't stomach the woman he is living with".'

Many of the people who receive psychotherapy because, initially at least, of physical symptoms, arrive through the NHS. Dr Andrew Macaulay, psychiatrist and psychotherapist at St George's Hospital in south London, explained, 'You have to be pretty sick to get psychotherapy on the NHS, it's such a scarce resource.' So many of these patients have been treated for a long time and have run the gamut of specialists, tests, in-patient treatment.

Philippa is thirty years old and works with physically and mentally handicapped people. Only a few weeks into a new and apparently exciting job in a centre in London, 'My back went.' She had previously given up nursing because of back trouble, but this time the pain was appalling. She spent several weeks flat out on her mother's floor and was off work for six months. 'I felt very ill indeed and nothing seemed to help. I went back and forth to hospital for tests and treatment, and spent some time eventually in a rehabilitation unit, supposed to be one of the best in the country, but my back didn't improve.'

Philippa didn't appreciate that there might be a major psychological component to her problem, though she did realize that whenever she was under stress, her back was the place that showed the strain. (This is not unusual for hundreds of thousands of working days are lost every year through back pain and psychological factors are often involved.) 'I was terribly anxious that I had some dreadful progressive disease which the doctors hadn't discovered. I read everything I could on the back, I was quite desperate as nothing seemed to make me feel better. I was eventually referred to the psychiatrist, who came round once a week, because I was so weepy.'

When she saw the psychiatrist, Philippa asked him for help in accepting the pain for she believed she would have to live with it forever. He began asking her about her family and her relationships and the tears started to roll. He suggested she might benefit from talking to a woman and after a session with a female clinical psychologist, Philippa realized that talking and bringing things out were helpful. The psychologist referred her to psychotherapy on the NHS.

Anorexia

Anorexia nervosa and similar eating disorders have claimed great numbers of sufferers, mainly women, over the past ten to fifteen years. Anorexia is often flippantly called the slimmers' disease, but most of the practitioners who treat this condition now agree that although dieting may initiate the illness, the underlying causes are psychological. These are usually listed as fear of puberty, certain relationships within the anorexic's family (often a close relationship with the mother), low self-esteem.

Feminist therapists Luise Eichenbaum and Susie Orbach stress in their book, *Understanding Women*, that 'in anorexia, bulimia (bingeing) and compulsive eating, what we see are women trying to change the shape of their lives by trying to change the shape of their bodies.'[5]

Increasingly, psychotherapy and family therapy are seen as effective ways of treating anorexia, once the individual is eating sufficient food to avoid death. NHS treatment, whether in-patient or out-patient, will usually include therapy, and some private therapists specialize in dealing with such eating disorders.

Four years – and two 'disastrous' relationships – after leaving university, Joanne realized she didn't weigh as much as she should. Her GP gave her a month off work and some vitamins. Joanne didn't get any better or any happier. 'I gradually realized I was anorexic. I was just eating enough to stay alive, I didn't have any illnesses or infections and I thought I was perfectly all right. I worked in the health service but no one ever commented on my state. My boyfriend tried to persuade me to see a psychiatrist and eventually I went to one privately, but I never went back. I couldn't be honest to him.

'Nothing in my life was working out, I wasn't happy in my job, or with my boyfriend, but I just soldiered on from one day to the next.' Then she telephoned a self-help group for anorexics and went along to a group run by one of their counsellors. 'I went along with three other women for about three months. The first shock, of course, was that when I first arrived and saw the others, I thought to myself, "I must be sitting here because I'm as thin as they are," I didn't get much out of it, I wanted more than a quarter of the counsellor's attention. Also I didn't like her approach, she only talked about food and goals, it wasn't right for me.'

A few months later, Joanne began to feel quite ill, pains across her chest, a build-up of nervous tension. 'For some reason something twigged and made me admit to myself that I wasn't well and at last wanted some help.' Through an ex-boyfriend, whose present girlfriend was also anorexic, she contacted a psychotherapist.

Who is unsuitable?

Most analysts and psychotherapists I interviewed stressed their wariness of, if not total unwillingness to treat, people who have been diagnosed as psychotic – that is, suffering from illnesses such as schizophrenia or manic depression. Some therapists argue that such individuals cannot benefit from therapy and would agree with Dr Andrew Macaulay who explained, 'I think psychotherapy should not be offered to most schizophrenic people because it may make their condition even worse, it can stir things up.'

Nevertheless, there are differences of opinion among therapists, both in the private sector and the National Health Service. If someone has been diagnosed psychotic and wants psychotherapeutic help, then it is worth pursuing and investigating the possibilities in the area.

Some form of counselling, usually a less intense experience than individual therapy, is more likely to be on offer. Brian Thorne, a counsellor in Norwich, said, 'I and my colleague would certainly not rule out people with a serious mental illness. But in such a case we would obviously have to work with the other professionals involved, like the psychiatrist.'

A number of therapeutic communities, or residential centres offering psychotherapy (like Arbours in north London) are willing to treat psychotic patients with psychotherapy. Family and group therapy might also be possibilities.

Margaret had her first bout of mental illness, diagnosed as manic depression, when she was twenty. Over the next few years, she regularly experienced times of terrible depression followed by periods of elation. 'I saw my illness as something which was uncontrollable, beyond understanding. It was alien, something from outside, which descended on me from time to time.' She explained that she was in the grip of a very serious delusion. 'I was fascinated by ice and felt that I was responsible for all the ice in the world. It made me excited and frightened at the same time. One day, during the Falklands campaign, there was a news item that an ice breaker was being converted into a hospital ship. I felt this was a message for me and immediately took the train to London, to the Ministry of Defence.'

She assumes that she must have been behaving rather strangely, as the police picked her up and took her to the Samaritans, who in turn took her to the emergency clinic at a London teaching hospital. She was admitted to a ward where the emphasis was on psychotherapy.

Margaret has now been seeing a psychotherapist for several years. 'It has helped me to change the image of my illness, and so of myself. It's no longer so alien, I know that the illness comes from within me and is related to me and the way I live my life. It's not exactly controllable, but I can be responsible about taking the drugs they prescribe, though I know they only help a bit of me.

'I was able to talk about my delusion, my fears. I had always thought that when someone went away, it was my fault, that I'd turned them into ice. It was such a relief to talk about this. You see, madness is a loss of understanding. You don't understand yourself and if no one helps you to, if you're left high and dry, then that loss of understanding is with you for the rest of your life, you're a cripple. Straight psychiatry had divided me into the sick and the well Margaret. Psychotherapy helped me to see they were different aspects of me and it's important to strengthen the well bit of me. I may never be cured but the pain and the anger is healed by therapy and I do feel a much better person.'

Psychotherapy is more commonly used with people diagnosed as psychotic in the United States, though it is still recognized that the therapists should be well trained and experienced to work with these patients. There has not been a great deal of research into its effectiveness but a recent book, written by two American psychologists, Bertram Karon and Gary VandenBos, has gone some way to remedy this situation.

Psychotherapy of Schizophrenia: the Treatment of Choice is based on their study of first admission mental patients in Detroit, all 'acutely ill and clearly schizophrenic'. A selected group was treated with just intensive individual psychotherapy; a second group was just treated with drugs, and a third with a combination of psychotherapy and drugs. The psychotherapy-only group did better on five out of the eight tests applied by conventional researchers, including better overall functioning and less thought disorder. This group also spent far less time in hospital than the others and, explain the authors, 'were able to live their lives more like human beings in a wide variety of ways'. The drug-only group did worst and were twice as likely to be readmitted to hospital.[6]

Most therapists stress that the greatest danger lies in treating a patient who is on the verge of a psychotic illness. In his book *Individual Psychotherapy and the Science of Psychodynamics*, psychoanalyst David Malan explains: 'The problem for psychotherapists is to distinguish between those patients who will react to an interpretative approach with relief and those who will react with increased disturbance . . . During many years at the Tavistock Clinic, I have accumulated a long list of patients in whom this question arises; and, even being wise after the event, I have found myself quite unable to distinguish between these two possibilities. I am constantly being surprised by patients whom I would not expect to break down, who do break down, and those whom I would expect to break down, who don't.'[7] He points out that whether or not a patient becomes overtly psychotic, suicidal feelings or other 'disturbed phenomena may at some time call for admission to an in-patient unit. This is not necessarily a disaster; and the process of holding the patient in this way, while she passes through her most disturbing feelings, may constitute an important stage in her therapy; but it *can* be a disaster if it results in therapy being interrupted.' Fortunately, he says, many mental hospitals around London are more willing nowadays to share responsibility with a psychotherapist.

Some analysts and psychoanalytic psychotherapists prefer not to treat people with addictions to drugs or alcohol, or with eating disorders, such as bulimia. Explained one such therapist, 'I've just had such wretched failures. It's very difficult to compete with food or alcohol. Just like prescribed medication, drugs and alcohol prevent someone from facing up to reality, which is what psychotherapy aims to do and they artificially alter that person's mood. It can also be quite justifiably argued that people with specific and often intractable problems need more support and back-up services than an individual psychotherapist can offer.'

Some agencies, such as ACCEPT in west London, do offer both individual and group psychotherapy to problem drinkers. Therapy is often used with alcoholics and drug addicts in residential units also, both NHS and private.

Psychotherapy's critics, of whom there are many in establishment psychiatry, argue that psychotherapists, and in particular analysts, only choose a very select group of patients known as 'yavis', that is, young, attractive, verbal, intelligent, successful. It is certainly not necessary to be middle-class and well educated to benefit from psychological therapy or counselling. For obvious reasons, this type of person figures largely among therapists' clients, but there is increasing evidence that working-class, or less formally educated, people can and do benefit, and that they are beginning to find such help, especially in the NHS. Dr Joseph Berke, reviewing in the *British Journal of Psychotherapy* (Winter 1984) the study mentioned earlier of psychotherapy of schizophrenia carried out in Detroit, comments that a highly significant feature of their work is that it has been done with economically underprivileged minority groups, especially poor, Detroit blacks. 'This gives the lie to the old adage that only the middle classes can use therapy while working-class people only respond to drugs and electroshock,' he comments.

'People coming for psychotherapy do not have to be educated or too articulate,' explained Ruth Schmidt, a psychotherapist and psychiatric social worker at the Paddington Centre for Psychotherapy, a NHS unit in west London. 'They need some capacity for insight and they must understand that they won't have all their problems solved by psychotherapy. Nor should they be too fearful of what therapy is about. What is really important is a high degree of motivation, and some capacity for change.'

Motivation was stressed by every practitioner I met. On the other hand, some people are persuaded or pushed to seek this type of help and having resisted furiously, they begin to discover how useful it can be. One of the problems about writing a guide like this, and attempting to give advice, is that generalizations are almost impossible.

There are always exceptions to the rule, and most psychotherapists do not lay down rigid guidelines about suitability and unsuitability. But as one psychotherapist said to me: 'Each therapist has to draw their own line.' Since the personality of the therapist and his or her relationship with the patient is central to the treatment and its outcome, the therapist must feel reasonably secure with each patient and have some confidence that therapy can help.

2 Answering the critics

Interviewer: 'How is your analysis going after twenty years?'
Woody Allen: 'Slowly.'

The decision to have psychotherapy or counselling is never taken lightly. It is a major step for anyone to seek such help because it means confronting the fact that they have some problem or difficulty which they cannot sort out themselves. It may well mean having to accept the uncomfortable truth that changing your job, or moving house, will not get rid of your depression. Or that a bottle of pills will not remove your migraine or chronic insomnia.

This decision may also run counter to your belief that therapy is a self-indulgence for rich neurotics. Or, however desperate you are to try anything, you may wonder whether it really 'works'. This chapter will mainly address itself to some of the many criticisms made of the talking treatments.

Why professional help?

People often ask this question: some because they think one should just 'pull oneself together'; others because they find the idea of paying people to listen to their problems and innermost secrets quite alien, if not abhorrent. It may seem less strange if one realizes that the relationship between therapist and patient is central to most psychological therapies (and certainly all the ones this book is concerned with). Put simply, psychotherapy is using people to treat other people.

Some people might find it unnatural to build up dependence on someone who is in many respects a total outsider, quite divorced from the rest of your life. The idea is, of course, that that dependence should be worked through and should disappear. Unlike friendship, the goal of therapy is eventually to part. The concept of the objective outsider is a key to any success psychotherapy may achieve, and an answer to the question, *why isn't a close friend good enough?*

'It's good to speak to someone so impartial and uninvolved. My counsellor allows me to be miserable and cry uncontrollably without trying to cheer me up, like a friend would do.'

Most people, however loving and caring, have their limitations as far as friends and relatives are concerned. In a sense, superhuman qualities are called for in the therapist.

'Everything pours out when I see my therapist. I've talked about my childhood and my family in enormous detail, and learned to understand it all. I could never be so amazingly honest with a friend or lover. I would always feel I was boring them, or that they weren't really listening. I really do have to be able to say absolutely everything, however shocking.'

A vital quality in any therapist is to be non-judgmental and to keep their own feelings, values, experiences quite separate from the way they work with what the patient tells them. They should not become emotionally involved, and do not react when something said reminds them of their own experience and feelings. They vary in the extent to which they offer any information about themselves; the very traditional psychoanalyst, for example, will still see him or herself as the blank screen Freud described.

'I know my therapist will never judge what I am saying, or rather will never appear shocked. Also she never feeds into the sessions her own problems and hang-ups.'

Friends and lovers may too often advise rather than just listen. Whether the advice is sound or not, psychotherapy and counselling are based on the belief that it is better in the long run to make up your own mind and be responsible for your own decisions and actions. Thus many practitioners work in a way that is termed non-directive.

'The support of an expert, somebody who knows that this kind of thing happens to a lot of people, who has talked to many other people with the same kind of problem before, is worth a lot more. They are less biased and have come into contact with a wider range of people and emotions. Your friend may well tell you what they think you want to hear and not what they actually believe. They tended to make me feel my marriage break-up was all my husband's fault and nothing to do with me. I learned, quite painfully at times, in marriage guidance, that of course I had contributed a great deal to its failure.'

Finally, but very importantly, a therapist should, and usually does, offer the sort of secure, trusting relationship good parents offer their children. This is especially important for people who did not have such relationships in childhood or who have failed to achieve good relationships in adulthood. In *The Heart of Psychotherapy* George Weinberg comments:

> As psychotherapists, we will see a great many patients who have never been listened to. Their parents paid attention only when they liked what was being said, if at all . . . One thing that power quite often corrupts is the readiness to listen . . . Many of our patients would be quite different today if only someone, some adult, had taken the time to hear them out . . .[1]

As Dr Weinberg and other therapists stress, everyone under-estimates how rare it is to find someone who is a good listener and who has the ability to communicate that 'I hear what you are saying and it matters'. They emphasize the healing quality of being listened to and of having what you say 'reflected' back skilfully by the therapist, who, in doing this, shows he has 'heard' the often deep, underlying feelings behind what has been said. A good therapist not only listens to the patient's words but also to the emotional undertones (which may clash considerably with what is being said) and notes facial and bodily expressions, the non-verbal clues. For example, someone might say they are very happy their son is getting married, but the fixed smile and slight tenseness around the shoulders may belie this.

The art of listening is clearly important when the patient is telling the therapist what may have been a long-held, and shameful, secret, for example, that he is homosexual or had an incestuous relationship as a child. 'We are releasing the person to reconsider it in a whole new light by countenancing his presentation of it, by merely listening,' writes Weinberg. 'Whatever our impact, we encourage the patient to explore new territory. And he comes to think of us as a comrade on his journey to places he has never visited before.'[2]

'A comrade on his journey' may sound romantic, and will undoubtedly bring a sneer to the faces of those who remain sceptical about psychotherapy. But central to the psychological therapies is a belief in every individual's worth, his or her autonomy and 'specialness' and his or her right to be taken seriously. For some, the psychotherapeutic encounter may be the first time such rights have been met. So the good therapist, for the whole of the time he sees each patient, shows that person respect, caring (however painful the process may seem at times), often warmth and empathy. The fact that he or she is a professional, trained and paid to listen, does not preempt caring. A well-respected analyst said some of the best advice he could give to anyone considering therapy would be to find a therapist who is a 'human being', someone who seems warm, not detached and aloof. 'No matter how much craft a therapist learns, he is lost if he suppresses the power to feel distressed, helpless, or to feel exhilarated, or even loved by a patient,' writes Dr Weinberg.[3] It is the professional training which enables the therapist to control such feelings so that he does not reveal them inappropriately to the patient.

Self-indulgence?

The view that psychotherapy is self-indulgent is typically British, fuelled in part by our ambivalence about some American attitudes. It also reflects the stiff upper lip attitude to any problem which is emotional or mental, rather than physical. It means that we generously dig into our pockets to raise money for cancer research, or kidney machines, but that mental health charities' appeals too often fall on deaf ears.

Such attitudes add to the despair of many. 'I'd never have thought he was suicidal,' say the work colleagues of a man who hanged himself. 'They always seemed so happily married,' say apparently close friends of a couple in the middle of a particularly acrimonious separation. Maybe some Americans overdo the 'let it all hang out' approach but the British have honed their emotional cover-up to such a fine skill that it can aggravate the problems.

Most people that I interviewed were pretty desperate by the time they saw a therapist, especially if they had been on an NHS waiting list for several months. Some had tried to kill themselves before they had therapy, and many others reckoned that they would not be alive today if they had not received therapy.

'I don't think I'd still be alive without my therapist,' said Carol, a young woman who was anorexic during her teens and made two or three suicide attempts. 'She has become one of the best friends I've ever had. She listens, and she is very wise, she is *not* a surrogate mother. I wouldn't like her to fuss over, or pamper, me.'

Like many other people, Carol was at pains to emphasize that therapy is not an easy, painless process. 'I've been through some very unpleasant sessions talking about my past. I know it will only work if I am honest, but it hurts.' 'Of course it is very therapeutic and cathartic to pay someone to listen to you,' said a woman who had two years' psychotherapy, 'but you are also finding out the horrors about yourself, you discover you're not everything you're cracked up to be. Perhaps it hurts so much because you gradually come to this self-knowledge, the therapist doesn't tell you. But only through this, accepting the dark side of yourself, can you begin to change. Therapy has taught me that my own salvation lay within me alone, no one else can help. It makes the whole experience a very burdensome one.'

'It can be very hard work, and some weeks I just don't feel like going,' explained Jim who is at the end of his first year of therapy. 'I often think it would be a lot easier to forget my problems by drowning them in the pub, but I know they'd come back again.'

Analysis is perhaps the most harsh of any psychotherapy because the analyst has to take such an apparently detached, objective viewpoint.

'It was often humiliating, painful, irritating, frustrating. I went to my analyst and expected her to be a magician, to take all my problems away with the minimum of pain on my part,' said a man who had Freudian analysis for seven years. 'Then I gradually realized I had to deal with the pain, with her help and support. But the more aware I became of my negative contribution to my life and other people's, the more ashamed I was of my behaviour in the past.'

'There is no pretending in analysis,' said another ex-analysand. 'You explore such primitive thoughts and fantasies, you go into every session naked.'

Partners and friends of people in therapy may criticize it because they are scared of how it will affect *them*. Wives and husbands are especially nervous because they feel, sometimes rightly, that they will be discussed and because they fear it may end their relationship.

Bill had psychotherapy for his depression for two years. 'My therapist warned me early on that it might be quite threatening to my wife. But in fact she was wonderful about it all, very supportive and interested.'

For James, it was less easy. 'What was difficult was that my wife went into analysis as well and, at the simplest level, that meant we both felt each was ratting on the other. We coped by not talking about it. I didn't want to know about her analysis, I was too busy struggling with my own.'

Jill is in her second year of therapy. 'I'm quite amused by men's reactions. I recently started a new love affair and after I'd told him I saw a therapist, he looked very anxious and asked me if I talked about him. I felt like telling him that was a very arrogant assumption but decided not to hurt his feelings.' Lavinia explained: 'My analysis did change my family. It's bound to if one person goes into therapy, it changes the balance. My father was especially horrified, he felt very threatened initially. But then he realized it was helping me. I think it also helped my parents' relationship. I talked more to them about my childhood, asked them questions, it opened things up and allowed them to talk about things they hadn't talked about before. But my two brothers remained very aloof from the process.'

Michael saw the psychotherapist for three years. 'My wife resented some of the ideas I brought home from my therapy. It undoubtedly upsets the balance of a relationship because the minute you start doing something about your own inadequacies, it highlights the other person's, too. Previously we had sort of balanced out each other's failings. On a more basic level, she just didn't understand what therapy was all about. She assumed that I took specific problems to my therapist, like our row the night before. She didn't realize that more often, I was talking about my unconscious, my dreams, rather than crockery throwing.'

But Michael's wife, who now believes that his therapy helped both of them, said, 'He used to come back after every session with the impression of being easier to live with. He was more easy-going because it was as if he saved things up for his therapy sessions. I now feel grateful to his therapist because Michael is so much less moody.'

Bill said that 'because of the way I changed and opened up, therapy cemented our relationship'. Similarly, a woman said of her therapy, 'It has undoubtedly helped me in my relationships with other people. If you like yourself better and trust yourself, then you like other people more too and are much nicer to be with.' Several people said therapy had made them less selfish and more prepared to take responsibility for themselves and other people. James, after several years' analysis, explained, 'I'm much less self-centred now. I became ready to be a father during my analysis. I could at last accept such a huge responsibility.'

If a marriage ends because one partner is in analysis, or because the couple have marriage guidance counselling, the therapist should not be blamed. The relationship's problems may have been aired, and resolution of them may have proved impossible. But a good therapist should help the people concerned to break up in the least painful manner.

On a larger scale, it would seem very likely that therapy and counselling may prevent serious illnesses, whether mental or psychosomatic, though there is no definite proof. For example, studies here and in America have revealed considerable suffering, mental and physical, among people who are divorced. Divorce may cause a greater emotional and physical toll than the death of a spouse. Divorced adults have very high rates of emotional disturbance, accidental death and death from heart disease, cancer, pneumonia, high blood pressure and cirrhosis of the liver (which is, of course, linked to a high intake of alcohol). It may well be that marriage guidance counselling or therapy can ameliorate such effects.

Many of the people who go into therapy feel lonely and isolated from other human beings. An American analyst, Rollo May, has said that psychotherapy is something that occurs when civilization disintegrates. In a similar vein, critics liken therapy disparagingly to religion, seeing it as a sort of emotional crutch. Perhaps some therapists set themselves up as priests or confessors, but I have not met any. Of course, part of the process of therapy involves the patient becoming very dependent on their therapist but that dependence should be worked through and ended if the therapy is to be successful. 'Therapists shouldn't have grateful patients who send them Christmas cards,' said a psychoanalyst. 'Such grateful patients are those people who haven't yet resolved their dependency on us. Someone who has had successful therapy will not talk about it but will get on with living a well-adjusted life.'

But there are those people who still seem obsessed with therapy or analysis, who talk as if they belong to some sort of secret society. For some of them it has not been successful because they long to return to their therapist or analyst, and feel everything else pales in comparison.

Dependency is quite at odds with the aim of therapy, which is to help people realize and accept and cope with the fact that they are on their own and that no one else can solve their problems. 'This doesn't mean you cannot aim to achieve maturely dependent relationships with others,' explained Sue Llewellyn, a psychologist and therapist, in *Changes* magazine, 'but simply that the ultimate responsibility is yours.'[4]

Undoubtedly therapists (especially analysts), and certainly

their professional organizations and institutes, must take some of the blame for the criticisms, fears and suspicions their work attracts. Over the years, in Britain and abroad, there has been considerable in-fighting between different analytic schools, the most well known being the split between Freud and Jung. Their defensive attitudes with regard to each other seems to have led to a general defensiveness with those outside the charmed analytic circle.

Nor does the arcane, not to say obscure, language help the cause. Of the 'great masters', only Freud is a pleasure to read. Even the most devoted of their followers admit that Jung and Melanie Klein are hard work.

Therapists are themselves aware of the need to put their house in order. Consultant psychotherapist Sidney Bloch, in a lecture given in 1982, said: '. . . if psychotherapy is to be taken seriously, its practitioners have a responsibility to cease their feuds, be more honest about what they can and cannot do, be more modest about the state of knowledge of the subject, and inform the public intelligently and accurately about the nature of their activities.'[5]

He remained optimistic that the feuding will end. In my experience while writing this book, I have found every therapist, whatever their school, very approachable; no one refused to talk to me, and many spent hours of precious time explaining their work to me. I feel that among many therapists, there is a change, a desire to be more open about their work, to be more open towards colleagues working in other areas of therapy. I did, however, find that many psychotherapists, and even more analysts, were still firmly sticking to the view that no one should call themselves a psychotherapist unless they have undergone years of their own therapy or analysis. From my own and other people's experiences, I feel that it is too restricted a view, not least because of the very limited resources of the NHS. The little research that has been done on this aspect of therapy shows that, whether or not a therapist has undergone personal analysis or therapy, it makes very little difference to his or her effectiveness as a therapist. In fact, some American research has demonstrated that with some groups of patients, non- professional volunteers who are carefully supported and supervised by professionals can be very effective therapists.

How effective is therapy?

Some psychoanalysts have made tremendous, and un-justifiable, claims for the effectiveness of their work, which has not helped the standing of therapy generally. Analysis and psychodynamic psychotherapy have attracted many critics and, in this country, one of the most vocal is the behaviourist Hans Eysenck. He particularly attacks psychoanalysis and Freud, but his criticisms, which others love to quote, attach themselves to all psychotherapy.

Eysenck, who most recently published his views in *Decline and Fall of the Freudian Empire*, argues that Freud was not a scientist and that psychoanalysis is basically unscientific.[6] Ergo, analysis and analytic psychotherapy are quite in-effective in relieving anyone's distress.

Not surprisingly, his book has met with a spirited res-ponse, from therapists and their patients. Psychotherapist Morton Schatzman, reviewing the book in *New Society*, writes that 'Eysenck's debunking of the therapeutic efficacy of psychoanalysis is so tendentious and biased in its choice of evidence – precisely the charge he levels against Freud's writings – that misleading conclusions result.'[7]

What is most misleading is Eysenck's conclusion that there is no proof that psychotherapy of the analytic type works. He is at least twenty years behind the times in this. There have been several studies, in this country and the USA, which show that psychotherapy is effective. What they do not show is that any particular type of therapy is more effective than any other, or what it is about therapy that makes it effective. Eysenck and others make great claims for behaviour therapy. In fact, the research shows it to be effective with symptoms like phobias or anxiety, but psychodynamic therapy is equally effective with other symptoms, like depression. 'There is no one royal road to the alleviation of psychological problem,' writes psychotherapy researcher David Shapiro.[7] Psychologist and researcher Sue Llewellyn comments: 'It also appears from research literature that it hardly matters what you say as long as you do say something.'

Therapy is not, it is true, as effective as many of its practitioners would like. Many people remain distressed after therapy. Their depression or their phobias remain. Time and time again, I found that therapists stressed their limitations. Time and time again they would say: 'I don't have a magic wand.' No therapist can treat someone successfully without the individual patient or client being prepared to work hard, endure pain, accept reality. Freud was very modest in his aim, 'to turn neurotic misery into ordinary unhappiness'. A marriage guidance counsellor, echoing his sentiments, said, 'Helping my client to accept the ordinariness as well as the extreme pleasures of marriage is part of my job.'

Psychotherapists and researchers stress the need for more work to be done into matching the right therapy with the right person and problem. Anthony Storr believes that psychotherapists are best at treating people who are 'the inhibited, the frightened, the shy, the self-distrustful, the fragmented, the over-dependent, and the over-controlled. They are far less successful with those who lack control over their impulses and who "act out" their emotional conflicts.'[8]

Psychiatrists are among the most vocal critics of psychotherapy. They seem to ignore the question marks hanging over the physical treatments they use for psychological problems; many people have challenged the effectiveness of drugs like minor tranquillizers, or electro-convulsive treatment (ECT) – in plain language, electric-shock treatment. Some people remain on tranquillizers for years, others return again and again into mental hospitals for the same treatments. As well as their questionable success, drugs and ECT can damage people, much more seriously than even the most incompetent or exploiting therapist. Minor tranquillizers are addictive and may cause brain damage. The major tranquillizers often do cause brain damage and many other unpleasant side-effects. ECT can lead to serious loss of memory and other impairments of thought processes.

Critics also seem to ignore what patients themselves say about the usefulness of therapy. Almost without exception, every patient I interviewed said they had benefitted in some way from the therapy or counselling they received. They did not always know why, and many certainly did not care about their therapist's theoretical standpoint or professional training. But they frequently referred to the 'special relationship' with the therapist and the help they felt they had received in making sense of their world and their difficulties.

Perhaps therapists underestimate the importance of this special relationship, although for the patient it is often one of the most valuable ingredients. Patients might choose therapy because they are having some difficulty in their relationships with other people, or because they feel estranged, out of step with the rest of the world. The therapist helps by providing at least one reasonably satisfactory and trustworthy rela-tionship from which should develop more 'real' relationships later.

Dr Sue Llewellyn found in her research into how patients and therapists perceived the value of therapy, considerable difference between what patients and therapists rated as most valuable. Therapists were more likely to have reported the helpfulness of gaining insight, whereas patients were more likely to have stressed the importance of solving problems and gaining reassurance.

Obviously the attitude and needs of the patient are crucial to the outcome of therapy, whether or not it is to be successful. 'We have to remember that most people come to a therapist asking for their pain to be taken away,' said Glenys Parry, psychologist and psychotherapist. Some want it taken away as easily and painlessly as possible, others want to unearth the root cause. Sue Llewellyn concludes that when therapy is effective, it may be because patients are helped to adapt and change the ways in which they previously made sense of the world. Patients develop *their own* new ways of making sense.

'It's like a stepping stone to better things,' said one man after several years of therapy. 'It's certainly not your salvation. People should realize that you may still be stuck with the same life at the end of it, but you can deal with it better, you have a better understanding, and you may be able to change sufficiently to change that life.'

3 The theory behind the practice

'There is a great deal of unmapped country within us which would have to be taken into account in an explanation of our gusts and storms.'

George Eliot, *Daniel Deronda*

'The Child is Father of the Man.'

William Wordsworth, 'My Heart Leaps Up'

Learn your theory as well as you can but throw it aside when faced with the uniqueness of the human soul, said Carl Jung, one of the great influential figures in analytic thought. Knowledge of theory is no prerequisite for therapy; in fact, most practitioners would prefer that their patients do not walk in armed with a textbook on Freud or Jung. But I write this chapter on the assumption that some people have very little, if any, knowledge of the basic theoretical under-pinnings of psychotherapeutic practice, and that they might like to have a passing acquaintance with the major figures – Freud, Jung, Melanie Klein and others – before deciding which route to take.

Freud

Many critics dismiss Freud as old-fashioned, passé and sexist, but he was undoubtedly a genius in his time, whose ideas have permeated western culture so completely that now it is hard to imagine how revolutionary they must have at first seemed. He himself developed and radically altered some of his beliefs right up to his death, and always recognized what hostility and disgust they would arouse. Despite the many breaks and factions within the analytic movement, and the proliferation of psychotherapies, the key concepts and some of the techniques which Freud developed, still influence most therapists working today.

Freud qualified as a doctor in Vienna in 1881, then worked for some years in neurophysiology. His earliest work was on the diseases of the nervous system. In 1885, he spent some months studying in Paris with Jean-Martin Charcot, the world-famous professor of neurology and the director of the Medical Centre, Salpêtrière. Charcot was then using hypnosis to treat, and apparently cure, conditions, such as hysteria and paralysis, with no physiological cause. He argued that hysteria was not an imaginary state but a neurosis.

The idea that psychology might offer an explanation was a revelation to Freud who came from that Germanic tradition of medicine which was firmly embedded in physiology and mechanism. Freud wrote that Charcot's hypnosis experiments gave him the 'profoundest impression of the possibility that there could be powerful mental processes which nevertheless remained hidden from the consciousness of men'.[1] Charcot also hinted at an idea which Freud would later expand upon, that an apparently physical condition like paralysis, which had no physiological explanation, might be 'the result of ideas which had dominated the patient's brain at moments of a special disposition'.

That our behaviour is somehow influenced by ideas or feelings of which we are totally unaware, is an essential insight at the very heart of analysis and psychotherapy. And the essential technique which Freud went on to develop is to uncover and deal with those unconscious events and emotions.

On his return to Vienna and private practice, Freud began using hypnosis with his neurotic patients, and developed its cathartic use: the idea being that once hypnotized, a patient could recall the exact time and occasion of the origin of the symptoms. Then, the symptoms should eventually disappear.

However, Freud was not actually very good at hypnotizing people. In the book he wrote in 1895 with the physician Breuer, *Studies on Hysteria*, he writes: 'I soon began to tire of issuing assurances and commands such as "You are going to sleep! . . . Sleep! . . ." and of hearing the patient as so often happened when the degree of hypnosis was light, remonstrate with me "But doctor I'm *not* asleep."'[2] So he then attempted to persuade patients, without hypnotizing them, into recalling long-forgotten or repressed memories, and eventually just encouraged them to talk freely about whatever came into their minds.

This *free association* is now the Basic Rule of analysis and analytic psychotherapy. It was, though it may not appear so in our relatively uninhibited climes, an outrageous idea, to speak without repressing any material whatsoever. As David Malan explains, it was 'the first essential step that led to the possibility of Man's looking at his true nature – something that had never been done before in his history'.[3] Free association was, as Paul Kline in *Psychology and Freudian Theory* terms it, the 'mental X-ray' which reveals the unconscious mental processes underlying symptoms and behaviour.[4]

Through free association, Freud aimed to make the 'unconscious conscious' and to discover the links between present symptoms and past experiences. He called free association the 'ore from which, with the help of some simple interpretive devices, [the analyst] extracts its contents of precious metal'.

The unconscious

As Freud developed the practice of psychoanalysis, he also worked out the theory on which this was based. Psychoanalysis is both the method of treating psychological disturbance and a theory about the workings of the human psyche.

The key to all this is the unconscious, that part of the mind whose contents remain almost totally inaccessible – except at certain times of creativity, or through experiencing a psychotic illness such as schizophrenia – or through psychoanalysis. Charcot and his colleagues had postulated the theory that the split, or dissociation, between the conscious and the unconscious, was a symptom of mental illness. But Freud came to believe that it happens in us all, as a form of defence used by the conscious mind against being overwhelmed by unpleasant memories and emotions. These defences may somehow allow people to function satisfactorily for many years, at least on a conscious level, but then may break down under certain circumstances, for example after bereavement or divorce. It is as if such events stir up the psyche and wear down the defences. So neurotic symptoms, such as depression or panic attacks, or psychosomatic symptoms, such as back pain or migraine, are signs that all is not right in the unconscious.

It is as if the unconscious is a battleground, with, on the one hand, the forces of the motivational drives (or repressed instincts) in conflict with those, on the other, of repression. Neurotic illness brings the scene of battle nearer the conscious mind than previously.

Psychoanalysis is termed 'psychodynamic' because of Freud's analogy with nineteenth-century physics. 'Just as dammed-up (repressed) water has to find an alternative outlet,' writes Freudian therapist Michael Jacobs, 'so sexual drives (libido) which are suppressed or repressed by the conscious mind have to find outlets, such as through neurotic symptoms.'[5]

Repression is the force which originally pushes certain experiences out of consciousness and it is resistance which keeps them out of consciousness.

Sex

If people know anything about Freud, they know that he thought sex was important: his name is practically synonymous with that activity, and he and his followers are frequently blamed for the 'permissive society'. He was certainly responsible for revealing the significance of sexual drives within every human being, but his views are usually simplified to the point of caricature.

Borrowing again from nineteenth-century physics, Freud conceived our motivational drives as forces of energy, fuelling our desires and emotions, conscious and unconscious. For him, the major source of energy, the most significant drive behind every human being, was the libido. He also believed that this functioned according to the 'pleasure principle', aiming for immediate gratification and the relief of painful tension.

In a paper written in 1910 entitled 'Wild Psychoanalysis', Freud complained that people had wrongly assumed his concept of sex was confined to the physical act, whereas, he said, it was much nearer 'love', with the stress on making mature relationships with the opposite sex. He also recognized the existence of other motivational drives, such as aggression, but explained that all his patients' conflicts arose over their sexual desires and fantasies. Certainly the majority of today's psychoanalysts practising in this country have taken on this broader concept of sexuality, that conflicts arise over problems in childhood relationships as much as, or rather than, over suppressed (because unacceptable) desires for sexual gratification.

Defence mechanisms

Defence mechanisms are those unconscious processes which help every individual deal with unacceptable aspects of him- or herself, often lying just below consciousness. Most defence mechanisms are normal, and useful; we all share the need to suppress unpleasant memories; but to deny them completely may cause problems. A mother, for example, who will never admit her feelings of anger towards her own children or husband, may turn that anger inwards and become depressed.

Repression was the first defence mechanism described by Freud. It is the totally unconscious forcing of unacceptable material back into the unconscious. Other defences include denial; projection (externalizing unacceptable feelings and then attributing them to another person: 'my husband is to blame for everything that is wrong with our marriage'); reaction-formation (going to the opposite extreme to hide unacceptable feelings, for example, hate becomes love, so the husband who cannot accept his true feelings of dislike for his wife becomes totally devoted to her). Another form of defence regularly seen in doctors' surgeries is the conversion of unacceptable emotions into physical symptoms. Freud saw this constantly in his numerous cases of hysteria (this is far less common today).

Some analysts argue that a defence mechanism, like sublimation, is a very useful one because it allows for the unacceptable instinct to be expressed in an acceptable form. For example, aggression is sublimated in certain sports, and the 'Oedipal' drive to compete with his father may result in a man achieving enormous success in his career. Freud argued that civilization, with all its artistic and scientific striving, is the result of sublimated sexual and aggressive drives.

The aim of psychotherapy is to undo clients' unsatisfactory defences, those of denial or projection, so that the repressed material, feelings and wishes frustrated in earlier life, can be revealed and dealt with. Thus the analyst makes sense of the symptoms.

Perhaps Freud's greatest contribution was that he taught

us to take neurotic symptoms seriously, arguing that they have a sense and a meaning for the individual sufferer, however deeply embedded in the past. Yet even today, many psychiatrists who deny the analytic way of working persist in viewing symptoms as senseless and irrational.

At first, Freud believed that neurotic symptoms were always a defence against real-life memories, dark secrets, the skeletons in the cupboard. My patients suffer from reminiscences, he once wrote. These traumatic memories remained, he claimed, in the unconscious and were converted into neurotic symptoms. But he gradually arrived at the belief that these memories were not real at all, but patients' fantasies and unfulfilled wishes, usually of a sexual nature. Clearly, he argued, not every hysterical or neurotic middle-aged Viennese lady could have been seduced in childhood, something which became a recurring theme in his treatment of hysteria and neurosis. (There is now a dispute raging in psychoanalytic circles because an American, Jeffrey Masson, claims that some unpublished letters of Freud's show that he in fact suppressed evidence of real sexual abuse of children and then went on to invent his theories of traumatic sexual fantasy. Janet Malcolm has written a witty and readable account of this dispute, *In the Freud Archives*, if you wish to know more. Without agreeing with Masson, some analytic psychotherapists stress the fact that some of the disturbances they have to deal with do emanate from the real, not fantasy, experience of incest.[6])

Linked to this discovery of suppressed wishes is another major discovery of Freud's, that of infantile sexuality, an unheard of idea in the Vienna of the late nineteenth century.

Freud had already realized the lasting influence of childhood in most people's lives; through his self-analysis, he discovered what an unexpectedly great part is played in human developments by impressions and experiences of early childhood. The child may be father of the man, but the child remains in some part in the man's unconscious. Thus, in our adult relationships, said Freud, we often repeat our infantile attachments and conflicts. A simple example is the man who marries someone identical to his mother, and his friend who marries the complete opposite of his. This tendency to repeat childhood patterns often lies at the root of patients' problems.[7]

On infant sexuality, Freud writes: 'A child has its sexual instincts and activities from the first; it comes into the world with them; and, after an important course of development passing through many stages, they lead to what is known as the normal sexuality of the adulthood.'[8]

Freud believed that at every different stage of infant sexuality, pleasure is obtained from different erotogenic zones. At every developmental stage, the libido (that is, the basic sexual drive) could become fixated, resulting in mental or emotional problems later on. Anal fixation, for example, might show itself in miserliness (the miser is unconsciously holding on to the symbolic value associated with faeces at the childhood anal stage) or an obsession with order. Incomplete sexual development might lead to fetishism (fixated desires for objects like high heels, rather than real women) or, most controversially, homosexuality (inversion or the turning in of the libido on an object like oneself). Analysts have to try to unravel the points of libidinal 'arrest' so that the individual can move on through the remaining development stages. Understandably, a homosexual may be very reluctant to enter analysis with a strictly Freudian analyst unless he or she wishes to become heterosexual. (But today, in this country at least, few psychoanalysts work with such strictly held views of Freudian theory, as I will explain later in this chapter.)

From the ages of three to five, every child learns to differentiate between, and often becomes anxious about, the two sexes, which is that stage of life famously dubbed by Freud as the Oedipal phase, after the Greek myth of Oedipus who unknowingly killed his father and married his mother. Put simply, the child may develop a passionate attachment to the parent of the opposite sex, and feel tremendous rivalry, even hatred, towards the other. Dennis Brown and Jonathan Pedder write:

> The Oedipal complex has, unfortunately, tended to become one of those frozen clichés of psychoanalysis which can easily be ridiculed if taken too literally and concretely to mean that every child wishes to murder the same-sexed parent and have intercourse with the opposite sexed parent. Children do not have exactly an adult's concept of either death or intercourse, but certainly they may wish their rivals (parents or siblings) out of the way so as to enjoy greater intimacy with mother or father. This period of childhood is undoubtedly a time of passionate love and hate, rivalry and jealousy, the outcome of which can have a decisive effect on later character formation.[9]

Freud saw this Oedipal stage as the first major conflict in every individual's development and often the major cause of neuroses. For example, if a child's 'rival' parent or sibling does disappear, through death or divorce, the child may feel it is his fault, that he has killed or sent away the parent concerned. Just as a child's view of reality can become distorted, so it is with someone who may be diagnosed neurotic.

The inability to come to terms with and accept the Oedipal feelings, and the ambivalence towards parents, is said to be the primary source of neurosis. It usually means that it is hard, if not impossible, to form proper emotional relationships with others in adult life, and especially to give and receive love freely – difficulties so frequently presented for treatment to therapists by their patients.

If a boy's Oedipal love for his mother is denied then, as an adult, love and respect become split from sexual desire. So much so that a man can only be sexually satisfied with women he despises and does not love, like prostitutes. This could be one way in which sexuality can be affected by unresolved Oedipal conflicts.

Freud's model of the mind

As Freud developed his ideas on the working of the mind, or the psyche, he also worked out its 'framework' or 'structure'. He had always believed in the idea of different psychic levels (like different floors in a building) but his final structural model introduced the now familiar concepts of the id, the ego and the super-ego.

The id was described by Freud as a seething cauldron of excitement:[10] it is that part of the conscious mind which contains the primitive, instinctual desires and drives, dominated by the pleasure principle. The id can be seen as the very primitive child within us, not yet tempered by the restraints of civilization. But for society's sake it is clearly vital to control the id, and the two controlling aspects of the mind are the ego and the super-ego.

The ego gradually differentiates from the id as the child grows. But during childhood the ego is still very vulnerable and any separation, especially from a parent, can be traumatic and affect future adult relationships. If there have not been such traumas during childhood, by adulthood the ego should be strong enough to withstand the inevitable stresses, the separations and the losses involved in all important relationships. The ego is concerned with the individual's self-preservation; it mediates between the pressures of the id and the pressures of the real world. It is the 'grown-up', rational, controlled part of us. An aim of psychoanalysis is to strengthen the ego. Freud wrote: 'Where id was, there shall ego be.' So in fact, far from Freud believing that the id, with all its sexual drives, should run rampant, he recognized the need for its control.

The super-ego functions in a way that is also largely unconscious and is often likened to the conscience or a parent figure. It is concerned with moral feelings, right or wrong, and is built up from an individual's absorption, from childhood onwards, of the moral views of parents and other authority figures like teachers. But the difference between ego and super-ego is that the ego is concerned with reason and reality, and the super-ego with feelings which may have been distorted from early childhood experiences. So just as the id has to be controlled, so also has the super-ego, otherwise a person may be overwhelmed with feelings of, say, misplaced guilt.

Dreams

The unconscious is normally inaccessible to the conscious mind except, Freud discovered, through free association and through the interpretation of dreams. He called this technique 'the royal road to a knowledge of the unconscious'.

He believed that defences are lowered during sleep, which therefore allows some unconscious material to slip through the net of the ego into dreams. If the analyst can decipher that material (because it is usually like some coded message or jigsaw puzzle with pieces missing), then he has managed to reach into the unconscious of his patient. Just as neurotic symptoms were distortions of the unconscious, said Freud, so, in a similar way, are dream contents: '. . . the dreamer can no more understand the meaning of his dreams than the hysteric can understand the connection and significance of his symptoms.'[11]

Freud recognized that the unconscious often expressed itself in dreams through symbols. Some were universal: the most well known, for obvious reasons, are that a snake represents a penis and a receptacle, such as a box or bottle, the vagina. But he also warned that a knowledge of such symbols was not enough to interpret dreams well. Interpretation had to involve the patient's free associating about the contents of the dream, including the symbols, because everyone's experiences and environment were different. If a snake charmer dreams about his snake, it might mean he was worried about his employment prospects, rather than his sex life.

Free association and the interpretation of dreams were the basic tools of Freud's work, and remain so for many analysts and psychotherapists practising today. Freud expected his patients to lie on a couch, rather than sitting face to face: a throwback to his days of practising hypnosis and because, as he admitted himself, he did not like being stared at all day. Furthermore, looking at one another 'kept the transference from mingling with the patient's associations imperceptibly'.

Transference

Using, or rather analysing and working through, the transference is the other crucial component of psychoanalysis and psychodynamic therapy. Freud first recognized the phenomenon of the transference in a case of his colleague, the physician Joseph Breuer. When Breuer was treating with hypnosis a patient known as Anna O., whose symptoms were associated with forgotten memories, especially of her intense relationship with her father, he was alarmed to discover that she was developing intense erotic feelings for *him*. She developed a phantom pregnancy and revealed her passionate feelings for Breuer by throwing her arms round him. She herself ended her analysis and Breuer apparently failed to connect her attachment to him with the causes of her illness.

Freud, however, soon realized that far from being a troublesome side issue of psychoanalysis, transference was central to his work. He realized that patients transfer feelings, not always sexual but the whole range of feelings one human being can feel for another, all the time on to their analyst. He explained in *Five Lectures on Psychoanalysis* that every patient 'directs towards the physician a degree of affectionate feeling (mingled, often enough, with hostility) which is based on no real relation between them and which – as is shown by every detail of its emergence – can only be traced back to old wishful phantasies of the patient's which have become unconscious. Thus the part of the patient's emotional life which he can no longer recall to memory is re-experienced by him in his relation to the physician; and it is only this re-experiencing in the "transference" that convinces him of the existence and of the power of these unconscious sexual impulses.'[12]

He likened transference to a 'false connection' the patient made between a person who was the object of earlier, often sexual, wishes and the analyst. But it was vitally useful to the therapist because there before his very eyes were past conflicts revived and reenacted. And in the transference, the patient is *repeating*, rather than *remembering*, unconscious desires and feelings. In *Remembering, Repeating and Working Through* Freud wrote: 'For instance, the patient does not say that he remembers that he used to be defiant and critical towards his parents' authority; instead, he behaves in that way to the doctor . . . He does not remember having been intensely ashamed of certain sexual activities, and afraid of their being found out; but he makes it clear that he is ashamed of the treatment on which he is now embarked and tries to keep it a secret from everyone.'[13]

By interpreting the transferred emotions, rather than reacting to them, by accepting or denying love, for example, the therapist helps the patient to understand the past emotions, and to come to terms with them. This interpretation will clearly involve tracing the emotions back to their origin, for example to the relationship with parents.

Freud believed that the transference was stronger and more successful if the patient knew as little about the analyst as possible. Following on from this behaviour, some analysts and psychodynamic psychotherapists today insist on presenting themselves as a 'blank screen' (Freud's own expression) or mirror. It is just as if the analyst was a white screen onto which the patient projects the film of his emotions. (Although others now believe that showing genuine concern and sympathy is important.)

Of course, as Freud himself recognized, transference occurs in all personal relationships. We superimpose our feelings and expectations from the past on to people in the present. A common instance is the constant reenactment of the child/parent relationship. If you had a punitive, harsh father, and were never able to show your anger towards him, you may react to every figure of authority, however benign, as if they were like your father. You will display *inappropriate* anger. Or, again common to everyone's experience, when you fall in love, you project on to that person false expectations and assumptions of their personality (often related to how you saw your parents), rather than falling in love with the real person. Marital breakdowns often occur when the real person does not live up to the fantasy, and there is no way of resolving that transference. We all tend to repeat past relationships in the present; the most obvious being the fact that so many people choose a partner very similar to a parent.

'Transference is clearly an everyday phenomenon,' writes American therapist George Weinberg. 'I used to teach the fourth grade, and when I would walk behind the children while they were copying something from the blackboard, certain of them would hunch over the instant I got close, as if they half expected me to whack them for a mistake. By their reactions to me, I could tell which children were beaten and which were not. Transference appears not just in what our patients tell us but in their every act.'[14]

Transference can also be a worrying phenomenon because it can give the analyst tremendous power over the patient, and, to those few who are unscrupulous, chances of, mainly sexual, exploitation of that patient. The dangers are obvious, as are the disastrous consequences. If the problem which takes you to the analyst in the first place is incestuous feelings for your father, say, then if your analyst becomes your 'father' and shows sexual feelings towards you, there will be no resolution of the original problem. I deal with other issues around transference in other chapters.

Freud attracted many critics in his own time, and many since. Some would argue that he elevated the importance of the individual and his or her gratification over society's well being, but in fact he stressed the need for strong interpersonal relationships and intersocial ones, whilst at the same time commenting on the harsh repressions of society: 'Our civilized standards make life too difficult for the majority of human organizations. We ought not to exalt ourselves so high as completely to neglect what was originally animal in our nature. Nor should we forget that the satisfaction of the individual's happiness cannot be erased from among the aims of our civilization.'[15]

Perhaps Freud can be compared to a father, fondly contemplating his errant child, in his relation to the human race. He, more than most, recognized its weaknesses (he had after all devoted his life to observing human beings) and at times revealed a gloomy and pessimistic view of men and women. But at the same time he contributed to our understanding of mental illness by arguing that there was no significant dividing line between the mentally sick and the healthy; we are all on some continuum and may move up and down it more than once in our lives. He said that the difference between neurotics and normal people was only a matter of degree. We all 'entertain a life of phantasy in which we like to make up for the insufficiencies of reality by the production of wish fulfilments'.[16] The neurotic person escapes from painful reality through his symptoms, the more creative person can transform reality through art or writing.

'Today,' writes Freud, 'neurosis takes the place of the monasteries which used to be the refuge of all whom life had disappointed or who felt too weak to face it.'[17] Thus we return to his rather modest aim for psychoanalysis (modest in comparison to the endless claims of later individuals), 'to turn neurotic misery into ordinary unhappiness'.

He also wrote in *Five Lectures* that 'you can regard psychoanalytic treatment as no more than a prolongation of education for the purpose of overcoming the residues of childhood.'[18] He saw the past as inescapable, controlling us like a puppet-master. Analysis could help individuals to regain some of this control.

In Britain today, only a very small number of practising psychoanalysts would define themselves as orthodox Freudians (their true home is now the United States). The two main groups within the British Institute of Psycho-Analysis follow the views of Melanie Klein and the 'objective-relations' school (which incorporates the ideas of Balint, Fairbairn, Winnicott and Bowlby among others).

Melanie Klein

Melanie Klein and the object-relations theorists all place far more emphasis on the importance of relationships with other people than did Freud. They see these relationships, especially with parents or parent figures, as playing a significant and vital part in every individual's development. Both Kleinians and the object-relations group base their work to a considerable extent on observing children, in analysis, play and other activities. Klein was a pioneer in this field and she analysed children as young as two years old. She believed that so many adult problems were linked to neurotic infant fantasy that the only solution was to incorporate child analysis into the education system. She stresses the impact of internal (that is, unconscious) over external reality. Klein believed that the ego – that part of the mind or psyche which roughly corresponds to the conscious, and is concerned with rational thinking, and external perception – develops in a child's first six months. (Freud placed it nearer three years old.) She also had a concept akin to the doctrine of original sin, that children were born with an aggressive drive and a knowledge of sexuality. Both combined to colour the developing internal fantasies, which Klein believed through her work with children, to be so incredibly powerful and rich, that they remained with every individual throughout their adult life.

Julia Segal, in a usefully down-to-earth guide to Melanie Klein's theories and practice, *Phantasy in Everyday Life*, explains that 'the earliest phantasies are of incredibly dangerous, unnamed, seemingly unnameable dangers and powers of perpetual bliss, of fusion with the loving and wonderful world for ever, of being suspended in total horror for ever, of disintegration into a million painful fragments . . .' If this sounds rather bizarre, as many claim Klein's ideas to be, Julia Segal continues, 'Looking at the roots of phantasies in infancy can make sense of the unrealistic enormity they often have. For a week-old child being angry with the mother or her breast . . . for not preventing all pain, for actually inflicting . . . the discomfort of a wet nappy . . . is being angry with the whole world.'[19]

These 'phantasies' (the analytic term implies a more meaningful phenomenon than the fantasy of make-believe) usually involve the mother, the all-important figure according to Melanie Klein, whom the child both loves and hates, wishes to destroy and fears will destroy it. She coined the term 'introjection', which is the internalizing of images of important 'objects' (namely, significant emotional figures such as mother) and it is these internalized images which have such a powerful effect on the developing psyche. These phantasies are not necessarily based on real-life experiences – that is, an individual's internalized image of his or her mother may be far more to do with the infant's early unreal fears and desires about the mother than the way in which the mother actually behaved towards him or her. However, argue the Kleinians, the feelings those phantasies arouse *are* real and so they have to be dealt with, and resolved, if they are causing psychological disturbance.

Obviously we all recognize such unreal, internalized ideas up to a point. We carry round quite false expectations of certain people's behaviour, for example. But if most of our beliefs, and therefore our behaviour, are based on such distorted views, then problems and symptoms like depression may arise.

One of the most crucial stages for a young child, according to Melanie Klein and her followers, is that period when the child begins to recognize its 'separateness' from its mother, a discovery which is both exciting and terrifying. At the same time, the child is also realizing that it can feel both love and hate towards its mother, rather than having to 'split' her into the 'good mother' and the 'bad mother'. Most people will usually manage to work through the emotions of this time, but a problem arises when the child's phantasy of its omnipotence, say, and its ability to destroy its mother (or father) appear to have been fulfilled in reality. That is, when a mother goes into hospital for some time, or dies; when the father leaves for no apparent reason, as far as the child is concerned; or the mother appears truly destructive, by battering or threat of suicide. Then the child will believe, unconsciously maybe, that the death, or illness, was its fault, and that therefore it can never risk such a close relationship again. This may cause depression or phobias in adult life. Similarly, the death or loss of someone close in adult life can trigger off memories – and repetition – of these internalized feelings.

So for Melanie Klein, the source of psychological disturbance is distorted fantasies often connected to enormous guilt. The inner world is far more significant than the external environment, and there is a limit to how much good mothering can change such phantasies, as they develop before the child can make rational judgments about its mother's or father's behaviour. It is a gloomy view of human development; however, as Anthony Storr suggests optimistically, if a child manages to traverse the difficult passage of separation and ambivalence, and then manages to make really satisfying relationships with real people in the real world, 'the internalized images lose their emotional charge', perhaps only to be reactivated at the time of someone's death.[20]

In analysis, Kleinians aim to reach the very primitive layers of the unconscious which were 'laid down' in the first year or two of infancy, in the hope of releasing the patient from early fixations and repressions. They place great stress on working with the transference, and recognize that the therapist becomes, for the patient, numerous figures and objects (breasts, penises, dolls) which people their phantasies. The hope is that, through interpreting the transference and unconscious material like dreams, the distorted, stereotyped images from the past will be replaced by more realistic and also less painful images. You may re-experience through regression the loss of your mother at the age of three, and then learn through analysis that she died from cancer, not as a result of any act of yours. That enormous guilt once removed, you may then be able for the first time in your life to form a truly loving and mature relationship.

Object-relations theory
The external reality, as much as the internal phantasy, of loving relationships is the stuff of object-relations theory on which many Freudian therapists in Britain today base their work. Melanie Klein did not depart from Freud in her views

on the importance of instinctual drives, and very much developed the rather pessimistic idea that aggression is innate. But object-relations theorists such as Ronald Fairbairn, John Bowlby, and D. W. Winnicott, argue that aggression is not innate but always a response to threat, and that the main motivational drive is to make relationships with other people and, through that, to become an autonomous human being, to develop the real 'self'. There is a drive for contact with another human being right from birth (and not merely to gratify basic needs like food and warmth).

So clearly this group, like Melanie Klein, stress the importance of good, strong bonds between parents, especially the mothers (somewhat to the irritation of some feminists, Bowlby and others still placed the emphasis on the mother, rather than the father). It is a very major step away from Freud's view of human nature which, for many people, seems to be too centred on the individual and his or her gratifications.

For this group of analysts, mental health depends on the quality of the object (person)-relationships begun in early life. There are three main stages of a child's development: the first, from birth to one year of age, is one of almost total dependence on the mother. The way in which a mother responds to the child's basic needs will affect how he feels about those needs thereafter. If he denies them, for example, he might separate the sexual from other parts of his personality. It is the stage where basic trust is established in other people.

In the second stage of development, the child is becoming more aware of being separate from his mother and other important people around him. There may be conflicts between him and his mother as he begins to assert some independence, by overeating, for example. And if there are problems at this stage, they may lead in later life to his developing difficulties over separation and loss, which might cause depression.

The third phase, from three to five years old, is the time of the Oedipal conflict, which object-relations theorists accept as a concept, whilst stressing the importance of the whole relationship with the parents, not just the sexual element. Following the classical Freudian line, they would agree that many neurotic disorders, like phobias, result from problems at this stage.

Thus these early stages of childhood, and notably the relationship throughout with the mother, must provide basic strengths for the individual to survive and lead a satisfactory adult life. There is considerable stress placed on the mother, or sometimes an acceptable mother substitute, which is questioned by feminists working in this field. Winnicott, a paediatrician turned psychoanalyst, coined the phrase 'good enough mother' and made the comment that 'There is no such thing as an infant, meaning, of course, that wherever one finds an infant one finds maternal care, and without maternal care there would be no infant.' He wrote about the 'true self' and the 'false self', which is created as a form of protection against deep feelings of insecurity. The mother plays a vital role in providing the secure, nurturing environment in which the true self can develop. Winnicott believed that 'what we do in therapy is to attempt to imitate the natural process that characterizes the behaviour of any mother with her infant. It is the mother-infant couple that can teach us the basic principles on which we may base our therapeutic work.'

Similarly, John Bowlby, whose work revealed the problems arising from the separation of mother and child, saw therapy as providing an important corrective experience for someone whose earlier experiences had been deprived in terms of good personal relationships. When a patient discovers that this time the important figure, the therapist, will not fail him as his parents did, then the process of recovery may begin. Bowlby said therapy provides a secure base, a temporary attachment figure, from which the patient could explore him- or herself and relationships.

Luise Eichenbaum and Susie Orbach, two feminist therapists, stress this aspect of therapy in their book *Outside In . . . Inside Out*, explaining that the 'concept of nurturance within the therapy relationship . . . is the cornerstone of feminist psychotherapy'. Their views are based to a considerable extent on those of the object-relations theorists, but obviously with some major adaptations from feminist thought. These are discussed in Chapter 5.[21]

Michael Jacobs in *Individual Therapy in Britain* explains that the aim of object-relations-based analysis is 'the ability to think, feel and act for oneself, to explore, to experiment, take risks and above all to become one's "self".[22] Harry Guntrip, another leading member of this group, saw the real drive as being to become a person, the true self. In some ways, this goal is again widening out from Freud's 'ordinary unhappiness' and is not so very different from the views of Carl Jung, Freud's great friend turned opponent.

Carl Jung

A large number of British psychotherapists and counsellors subscribe to the theories and practice of Carl Jung, the Swiss psychiatrist who was originally close to Freud, sharing many of his ideas, and who then broke away completely in 1913. This break was mainly because Jung could no longer accept what he saw as Freud's excessive emphasis on the important role of sexuality in human development.

Jung's ideas are not easy to grasp; he does not write well, let alone with Freud's elegant clarity. He said himself: 'Nobody reads my books,' and 'I have such a hell of a trouble to make people see what I mean.' Rather than refining concepts, he was constantly elaborating them to the point almost of incomprehensibility. This, plus his stress on the spiritual and the supernatural, has meant his views are frequently dismissed as fey and unscientific. Critics have commented that the Jungian theory is more like a metaphysical system than a school of scientific psychology. But then many critics argue that no analytic school is truly scientific. No, Jung's major problem for someone considering therapy is his inability (and many of his followers share this) to articulate his theories in a clear and readable fashion. It is sad because his ideas make fundamental sense for many people. You may decide from the following account whether you are one of this group. But it seems to be the case that Jungians and Freudians are born and not made.

Anthony Storr comments that if he had to summarize the essential difference between Freud and Jung, it would be that Freud 'undoubtedly attributed supreme value to the orgiastic release of sex, whereas Jung found supreme value in the unifying experience of religion'.[23]

For Jung, analysis was a spiritual quest, a religious experience, its aim being to achieve the integration or wholeness of the personality. Jung called this process 'individuation'. It is strikingly different from Freud's rather modest goal of turning 'neurotic misery into ordinary unhappiness' and helping his patients to adjust to their world, to love and work. Jung showed little interest in people's external world, their interpersonal relationships. For him, analysis was totally an inner journey, reconciling the opposites of the psyche; it was nothing to do with improving a person's marriage or parental relationships.

'This is one reason why the *Collected Works of Carl Jung* discourage the average reader,' writes Anthony Storr.[24] 'Unless he is exceptionally persistent, he is unlikely to find anything which seems remotely connected with day-to-day problems, neurotic symptoms, sexual difficulties . . . it is frustrating to open one of his books and to be confronted with a discussion of "The Visions of Zosimos" or a disquisition upon the meaning of the Trinity.'

But Jung's ideas do have considerable appeal, not least

because many people value the spiritual; they profoundly disagree with Freud's view that religion is 'the universal obsessional neurosis of mankind'. Readers will also find Jung's thoughts more positive, less reductionist, more forward-looking (he was far more concerned with the present and future than the past) and enjoy working with myths and symbols.

His views on the causes of neuroses, on man's alienation from his primeval roots, fascinate many people. It is not surprising that Jungian ideas were taken up by members of the growth movement and the alternative societies of the sixties. He believed that neurotic symptoms appeared when people felt 'stuck', had ground to a standstill, psychologically, when their life seems to lack meaning and significance. Such feelings usually come in middle age – Jung was fascinated by the mid-life crisis – usually after, according to Jung, the drive of sexuality has waned and the basic needs of mating and producing children have been met. Analysts and psychotherapists always mention such a category of patient, the person who may not have specific symptoms like depression, but a general sense of meaninglessness about their life, a dis-ease.

Such feelings arise, according to Jung, because this person has lost touch with that vital layer of the unconscious he called the 'collective unconscious'. This contains the past experiences, the inherited wisdom, of past generations of the whole human race. It is what Anthony Storr calls the 'myth-creating level of mind' which manifests itself in regularly recurring trends or symbols. Jung's *archetypes*, as he called them, are common to all cultures and times: the wise old man, the earth mother, the ideal man and woman, the child, the hero.

It is a difficult and controversial concept. Simpler, perhaps, to accept that every individual's personality has many aspects, such as the masculine and feminine, the warm and the cold, the loving and hating, the adult and the child, the thinking and the emotional. When these aspects become unbalanced, when, for example, the intellectual is over-emphasized at the expense of the emotional, then something is wrong and it will appear in some symptom or feeling or unease. This is likely to happen in middle age because the early years of adulthood are inevitably emphasizing sexuality, achieving in a career, domesticity, perhaps at the expense of the spiritual.

Jung was constantly returning to the theme of man's alienation, his estrangement from himself. In an interview he said, 'We must give time to nature so that she may be a mother to us. I have found the way to live here as part of nature, to live in my own time. People in the modern world are always living so that something better is to happen tomorrow, always in the future, so they don't think to live their lives. They are up in the head. When a man begins to know himself, to discover the roots of his past in himself, it is a new way of life.'[25]

So the aim of Jungian therapy is to help the individual get in touch with those roots, and the unexpressed or unfulfilled parts of himself; to become whole again. The main route is through the analysis of dreams – not, like Freud, to discover the suppressed desires of childhood, but to reach the healing powers and energy of the unconscious, the real self. Patients were asked to confine their free associations strictly to the dream images themselves. Jung believed that neurotic symptoms were not wholly bad because they revealed that the unconscious was compensating for some lack of balance in the conscious world. Just as the body is continuously keeping the physical symptoms in balance, so the psyche too, Jung believed, is self-regulating.

Almost any attempt at summarizing Jung can make him sound pretentious and woolly, though all the accounts of him as a person make it clear he was not. Dreams were interpreted quite literally, through the analyst's 'translations' of the symbolic language. 'To my mind,' Anthony Storr writes, 'the importance of Jung's description of the process of individuation and the experience of the self lies in the fact that he recognized that, for many intelligent, able people, the attainment of Freud's goals of "honour, power, wealth, fame, the love of women" are not enough.'[26]

With some patients, Jung developed a technique known as 'active imagination', encouraging them to draw or paint their dreams and fantasies, or to recreate them in words, as poems, or even through dance. Some Jungian therapists still use this, as do many people working in the field of mental health: art therapy is widely practised in mental hospitals and day centres. Partly because of this emphasis on the healing powers of creativity and the importance of mobilizing them, Jungian analysts and therapists do attract patients from the arts, music, literature and the media, along with people and patients who embark on therapy as a way of exploring and developing the self, as much as a process of removing troubling symptoms. Jung wrote: 'What the doctor then does is less a question of treatment than of developing the creative possibilities latent in the patient himself.'[27]

Another major contribution of Jung to understanding humankind was his work with people suffering from psychotic illnesses like schizophrenia. Freud worked mainly with neurotic patients; Jung worked for some years in a mental hospital, almost solely with psychotic patients, before going into private practice. He developed his ideas of the unconscious, especially of the collective unconscious with its symbols and archetypes, from studying the delusions and fantasies of these patients. Through making the first attempt to apply psychoanalytic thought to insanity, he found meaning in the apparently most deluded and incoherent ravings and fantasies. He was probably one of the first psychiatrists to stress the continuum from 'normal' through 'neurotic' to 'psychotic'.

Yet Jung's theories and practice were less rooted in the 'medical model' than Freud's and, even now, some Jungian groups do not insist, for training purposes, on a background in medicine or related subjects.

One such therapist, whose very varied career included car maintenance and jazz, commented that Jung treats human beings with more respect than the average psychiatrist. He certainly treated analysis as a dialogue between two human beings (though it was very important to him that the therapist should have received personal analysis as part of their training); he did not use a couch and was less passive, less the blank screen, than the traditional psychoanalyst.

However, just as the Freudian school (especially in the UK) has absorbed into itself the ideas and techniques of many other psychoanalysts, so the largest Jungian institutes in London (The Society of Analytical Psychology) and elsewhere have moved closer to the Freudians, Kleinians, and object-relations school. (Cynically, I wonder if such a convergence is not partly self-preservation, on the lines of there being safety in numbers to deal with the very strong opposition to psychoanalysis.) So SAP members do use a couch, do work with childhood material and have developed their work with children, which was never an interest of Jung's. The couch is used partly because there is more emphasis on the need to regress in order to repair the damage wrought in early childhood, but also to free the creative and imaginative processes.

Recently, a much smaller group of Jungians, led by Dr Gerhard Adler (who was one of the original founders of the SAP and was himself analysed by Jung), broke away and established the Association of Jungian Analysis which could be said to practise more closely to Jung's original work. 'We felt that the SAP had become too eclectic,' explained Gerhard Adler. 'We wanted to place Jung's teachings back into the centre of our work.' Thus AJA therapists tend to see patients less frequently (perhaps twice a week rather than four or five times); they do not automatically use a couch; and some concentrate on dream analysis and working with the patient's creativity, through paintings or poetry. 'But I have no intention of saying one type is better than another,' stressed Dr Adler. 'There is no such thing as orthodox Jungianism.'

4 Psychoanalysis: the first psychotherapy

'It is the onion, memory,
that makes me cry.'

Craig Raine, 'The Onion, Memory'

'Analysis is a journey into the crevices of one's mind, which
are inaccessible by any other means.'

London psychoanalyst

Psychoanalysis was the first, and many would say foremost,
psychotherapeutic treatment. Its influence has far exceeded
the strength in numbers of its institutions: in Britain, for
instance, there are only between 300 and 400 practising
analysts (including the analytical psychologists which,
strictly speaking, are what the Jungians are called), the
majority to be found in the north western parts of London.

They are seen by many people as some sort of secret
society, a cabal. More than other therapists, analysts are
feared, and thought a threatening and subversive group. One
young analyst who lives in south London (some miles from
the charmed circle of Hampstead and its analytic environs)
said she had stopped telling people the truth about her job as
they either cracked stupid jokes (calling an analyst a 'shrink'
somehow cuts them down to size and weakens their magical
power) or, more commonly, are downright hostile and
offensive. 'It took me a very long time before I could admit to

my friends and work colleagues that I was in analysis,' said Janet, a young housewife who had five years' psychoanalysis. 'It felt like some hideous dark secret. When I did talk about it, everyone was constantly asking me what it was like. It was as if they thought I was into witchcraft. They had so many fantasies about what went on.'

They assume, for instance, that patients lie on their analysts' couches and talk endlessly about nothing but their sexual fantasies (and perhaps even act them out, say those with the most prurient minds). They ridicule the observations of Freud and others who, as I explained in the previous chapter, uncovered in the unconscious some very primitive desires, instincts, passions, 'unthinkable' thoughts and wishes.

But analysts are regularly confronted with feelings of pain and suffering which most people would recognize, and have often experienced. The problems which patients bring to their analysts is the stuff of daily dramas and soap operas: unsatisfactory marriages, frustration and despair over an unfulfilling job, depression, anxiety. 'There's nothing very dramatic or exciting about what goes on in analysis,' said an ex-patient. 'Sometimes I have felt my analyst plumbed the depths of my unconscious, other times I've taken very trivial, day-to-day problems I wanted to talk about.'

Some people have likened their analysis to 'growing up'; for the first time, they have confronted certain aspects of their personality, good as well as bad, and eventually became more autonomous, fulfilled individuals. The analyst allows them to grow up by providing certain secure boundaries which they may not have experienced in childhood. The insistence on the analytic hour and the regularity of the sessions can seem absurd until one realizes that many analysands were never given such security and consistency by their parents.

Analysis is not a quick, efficient way to treat symptoms. It is like approaching a physical ailment with a change of diet, a new lifestyle, rather than with surgery. Analysts do not promise to 'beat the blues' or bring you instant happiness. It is a slow, tortuous process.

Psychoanalyst Dr Andrew Skarbek commented: 'I think it is very important to realize that analysis can be a marvellous experience. It can make one's life more meaningful, but it is not always the most effective treatment of symptoms.'

However, several ex-analysands told me that not only had symptoms been removed, but they did not believe it could have been done any other way. Dr Pat Gallwey, a Kleinian psychoanalyst and psychiatrist, said: 'Of course I intend to treat and remove symptoms, that's why patients come to me in the first place. I am a doctor, there's nothing airy-fairy about what I do.' He cited the case of a woman who came to him suffering from very serious bulimia nervosa (bingeing on food and then vomiting): after two years' analysis her symptoms had gone but she realized there was much more the matter in her life in general.

Where analysis differs from other psychological treatments is that it aims to explore in great depth the causes for the symptoms. It may not be able to alter basic character structure, nor will it always prevent depression or compulsive behaviour occurring again. But, explains Anthony Storr, its success may depend on 'the patient feeling that he is no longer at the mercy of what I must still continue to call his psychopathology, but able to experiment with his own nature and make creative use of it.'[1]

However well a house is built, the rain will continue to fall and beat down on it. But the more solid the structure, the more weather-proof it will be. And after analysis, the 'house' understands that the rain falls willy-nilly, and doesn't just pick on that particular roof.

Analysis attracts critics partly because its aims can sound insubstantial, pretentious, even naive. The obscure, arcane writings of psychoanalysts do not improve the public's level of understanding, yet, as recent television plays have shown, the words spoken between analyst and patient are ordinary, everyday, even banal. 'I am very concerned that people should know analysis is not an intellectual joust,' said George, who went into analysis depressed and disturbed about his homosexual way of life. 'It is hard for the outsider to imagine that over the years, talking about one's dreams, emotions, very ordinary worries and dilemmas, builds up and connects, gets woven into a whole, so that a whole part of you is exposed and realized, and some very profound things are understood.'

'It is also as much a matter of life and death as *Emergency Ward 10*. I don't think I would be alive today if I hadn't been helped in analysis.'

Which helps to answer one of the popular criticisms of analysis – that it is navel-gazing self-indulgence. The commitment of time and money alone means it is rarely a decision taken lightly, rather more out of some measure of desperation.

Who goes into analysis – and why?

The time and money required for analysis lead to the majority of patients being middle-class professionals. But, as every analyst I interviewed stressed, there is no reason why someone who is working class shouldn't benefit from their treatment.

Nor is a high level of education important. 'A certain level of intelligence is far more important than education,' said Gerhard Adler. 'Some people come along, having read the whole works of Jung. But that's no use. Technical terms are a sort of abbreviation for the analyst, we don't usually use them with the patient.'

'High educational achievement is only a minor hindrance to successful analysis,' remarked analyst Nicholas Spicer.

'Some of the patients who have used it to best advantage are the ones with the least formal education. They don't read books very much. If people read too much, they can use their intellect to build up more defences. Or they're having to battle their way through other people's ideas before they discover their own.'

Most therapists would say that patients need a degree of introspection, the ability to articulate one's feelings, and an average level of intelligence, so that they can reflect and describe these emotions.

The motivation to work, to confront painful issues and to change, is constantly stressed by analysts as an important factor in the outcome of treatment. 'Curiosity is vital,' said Dr Andrew Skarbek. 'It is important that someone coming into analysis genuinely wants to understand themselves better, why they are so angry, why they can't succeed in their career, why they always seem to have such bad relationships with the opposite sex.'

The difficulties and symptoms which propel people towards analysis are no different from those which take so many of us to our GP, a marriage guidance counsellor or the gin bottle. 'All sorts of people who have personal problems come to consult psychoanalysts,' explains *Guide to Psycho-Analysis in Britain* published by the Institute of Psycho-Analysis. '(Some) will be suffering from depression, or from the inability to work, love or enjoy things. People may come with obsessions, phobias, and irrational anxieties; they may wish to do something about their homosexuality, their perversions, addictions or psychosomatic illness. Most people who seek an analyst's help are sensible, sane, intelligent people. Some will be very near or fully into the delusions of insanity; others may be delinquent. Perhaps the one feature necessary to all is a deeply felt wish to understand and do something about themselves.'

'I see a lot of people who are simply unhappy,' explained

Nicholas Spicer. 'They may or may not have symptoms like depression. And usually, but not always, their unhappiness is linked to their personal relationships.'

Deborah's story is like many I have heard. At the age of thirty, she was very successful in her career as an academic, but she was single and felt she had never experienced any very good relationships with men. She had suffered from periodic bouts of depression since she was a young teenager. 'I felt forlorn as a single woman. You are made to feel this, as if, being single, you are lacking something because you haven't been chosen by a man. I felt worthless and unwanted, and often very lonely. I hated being on my own. I don't think I would ever have seriously attempted suicide but the thought certainly crossed my mind. There seemed to be no purpose or meaning to my life.'

She had spent some years in the United States, so the idea of seeking help from an analyst was less alien to her. As a teenager, she had undergone some psychotherapy, which had helped. But this time she decided on analysis because it seemed more intellectually exciting. 'I loved the thought of exploring my dreams, unravelling the past.'

Like Deborah, Betty, a nurse, had tried individual and group therapy for some years. As a child, she had been a school-phobic and as an adult suffered from other fears and phobias. 'After the psychotherapy, I still felt very screwed up, very neurotic. My relationship with my mother had always been poor, and that upset me. I was horribly up and down and showering my neuroses all over the place and all over everyone I knew.'

'I don't know why, but I just felt that analysis might help me. I felt I wanted something deeper, more of a commitment to change, I think I was trying to do something more thoroughly than I had before.'

Julia is a music teacher who decided on psychoanalysis, never having tried any sort of therapy, because several of her friends seemed to have been helped by it. 'I had suffered a whole series of losses in my early twenties – serious illness in the family, a love affair which went badly wrong. I felt I was always choosing the wrong sort of man. My depression went on for several months and I knew I wasn't making any headway on my own. It was getting in the way of living.'

George is a journalist who, in his twenties, was very involved in the encounter group movement. 'At that time, I was very prejudiced against analysis. I thought it was fuddy-duddy and old-fashioned.' He led encounter groups and was obviously a powerful figure for members. 'But I was really very unhappy about myself. I was gay, very promiscuous, and had never experienced a really satisfying relationship. I began to question encounter groups because there was I, the leader, and I was the one who needed therapy. I spent a couple of years with a psychotherapist then decided to try analysis because I felt that only by probing deeply into my unconscious could I sort out my emotions and my behaviour. I also chose analysis because I thought I needed some discipline in my life.'

After relationship problems and depression, the most common reason for having analysis is a general sense of unease, of meaninglessness, dissatisfaction with life. It can be more worrying than a specific problem like a phobia, or a sexual dysfunction, because the solution is very unclear. 'I couldn't quite put my finger on what was wrong,' said one analysand. 'I seemed to have so much: a reasonable marriage, children, a career, yet none of it meant anything any more. From the bit of reading I'd done on psychology, I knew that psychoanalysis might help because it believed that feelings like mine had their causes buried in the past, perhaps my childhood. It's like Wordsworth said, "thoughts that do often lie too deep for tears".'

Such feelings of emptiness are often linked to self-destructive impulses, nothing matters any more. Geoff, for example, seemed to his friends to have everything: a thriving business, an enjoyable hobby of motor racing, plenty of money, plenty of women. 'It seemed like I got anything I wanted but I never had any sense of satisfaction out of it. So in searching for fulfilment, if you like, I was taking greater and greater risks with my life, driving even faster on the race track, being provocative and risk-taking in business, and in relationships with girlfriends. I know now that my behaviour was a lot to do with needing constant excitement, a good fight. I felt empty the whole time, unfulfilled, worthless. Whatever goal I set myself, I achieved but it meant nothing. I was never depressed but I didn't know who I was, having cut myself off from my working-class background and acquired some of the trappings of middle class success.' After several years of Freudian analysis, he now looks back and recognizes that he was suffering from 'a very poor and damaged sense of myself.'

A Freudian analyst agreed that such feelings of emptiness, the sense that 'something is missing', are well suited to analysis because they signify that something went wrong very early in that person's life. 'Only via analysis can we reach far back into the unconscious to discover and work through the original trauma.'

Analysts will treat people with phobias or obsessions, but recognize that there are other, more direct methods of treatment, such as behaviour therapy (see Glossary). Nicholas Spicer has been seeing a patient who is terrified of travelling on the London Underground: 'Analysis is obviously not the only, or even the most suitable, way of dealing with such a problem. There could be several practical solutions, travelling by car or bus, which I might say are equally appropriate. One man who came to consult me, came only once. I suggested travelling by car as a first-level solution to this problem. That was what he decided and he – and I – regard the "therapy" a success. But if such an individual is prepared to spend time and money to understand why he has developed such a phobia, then I can help. Some people with phobias are very resistant to analysis, to thinking in that symbolic way which it demands. At first, my patient was very resistant to the idea that his fear of the tube door closing reflects his fear of being caught in a marital relationship, where "the doors have closed and cannot be opened".'

If thinking in such terms, talking about the 'as if-ness' of life and the symbolism of a symptom such as a phobia, seems absurd then psychoanalysis is probably not the therapy for you. Anyone considering analysis must be ready to think about their problems in psychological terms. In comparison, it is not surprising that 'creative types', writers, artists, musicians, will often turn to analysis when they are having problems with work, the dreaded 'creative block'. They value the insights gained and the release of potential, which is so much a part of Jungian theory. As one Jungian analyst explained: 'These creative people are beginning to get the idea that Jungian analysis is especially appropriate for them. They want our help to discover, uncover, new sources of creativity within them. I hope I can help them, and all my patients, realize that the powers of the unconscious are immense, but that we are mostly unconscious of such powers.'

One of his ex-patients is Michael, who writes plays and novels. He first approached the analyst because he wanted to write about analysis, he thought it might be an interesting intellectual exercise. 'My analyst knew immediately, I discovered much later, that writing about it was just my cover; in fact, I was very dissatisfied with my work, I felt second-rate and worthless. I was nothing like as happy or as complete or as fulfilled as I wanted to be.'

At least 50 per cent of analysts' patients are themselves training to be analysts or psychotherapists. James is a doctor who chose analysis with the aim of becoming an analyst himself. 'But that wasn't the only reason. I did need help too, like most people in my position. It's just that trainees often deny they might need analysis for themselves as individuals as well as for their work.

'I knew there were things in my life and personality that I just wasn't coming to terms with, I kept coming up against the same blocks, repeating the patterns, the same mistakes, in relationships, for example. I had tried yoga and buddhism but I felt analysis might be more appropriate because it did not involve a philosophy alien to my own culture. I felt more affinity with Jungian theory because it seemed less reductive, more about expanding one's potential.'

Although analysis offers the patient a very secure relationship during analysis, it also does assume a certain ability to cope day to day. The analyst can appear to be harsh and uncaring; they will never, for instance, offer reassurance, friendship, their home telephone number.

'You get very frustrated in analysis,' said James, 'you go in expecting tea and sympathy, and you get neither. I would sometimes ask her about specific problems, a row with my wife, something at work, and then I'd realize that when I did this, it was a way of avoiding getting in touch with something deeper, and more painful. The worst time was when a very close friend committed suicide. I saw my analyst that night, desperately wanting reassurance, love, a shoulder to cry on. She just said, "So what does his death mean to you?" I felt rotten at the time, but she was right. I needed to acknowledge my feelings of guilt, and also anger towards him. Gaining that self-knowledge is a long, hard grind.'

Analysis is not intended to comfort or console. When some of Freud's followers began to veer towards this, he strongly criticized them. Their aim, he wrote, 'is to make everything as pleasant as possible for the patient, so that he may feel well there and be glad to take refuge there again from the trials of life. In so doing, they make no attempt to give him more strength for facing life and more capacity for carrying out his actual tasks in it. In analytic treatment, all such spoiling must be avoided. As far as his relations with the physician are concerned, the patient must be left with unfulfilled wishes in abundance. It is expedient to deny him precisely those satisfactions which he desires most intensely and expresses most importunately.'[2]

'It's like opening up old wounds which haven't healed well, cleaning them up and letting them heal again,' said one analysand.

Analysis will undoubtedly 'stir things up', and the person who is socially isolated, has no network of support (though, sadly, is someone who might benefit from the insights gained), may do badly because they cannot cope with their pain in between sessions with their analyst. This is obviously not just true of people suffering from psychotic illnesses. For anyone who feels like this, a form of psychotherapy which is less exploratory, more supportive, is recommended. (See Chapter 5 for a case example of how someone with manic depression was treated by analytic psychotherapy within the security of a hospital ward.)

'The healing power of psychoanalysis lies then in the hoary dictum "know thyself",' writes Joel Kovel. 'Why this should be a less than tumultuously popular theory is not hard to see. For the attainment of knowledge of this sort requires tempering of the self – and tempering entails a fire, not merely the fire of repressed wishes, but the first of such wishes played out in an actual, if highly unusual, relationship with another person . . . the fire, in short, of human enthralment. Enthralment, moreover, with someone who is pledged not to gratify the wishes set free . . . because such gratification favours repression.'[3]

'You have to realize that you may lose some defences which have taken a lifetime to build up,' explained a patient after some years of analysis. 'You must be careful about entering analysis. Many people do not realize how vulnerable they are.'

Do I have to lie on a couch?

The couch is probably the classic symbol of psychoanalysis, with its sexual overtones and the suggestion, the threat, of being controlled, taken over.

'I was determined not to lie on the couch,' recalled James, after a seven-year analysis with a very orthodox Freudian. 'I walked in and sat opposite her on a chair. I can remember thinking, how can I talk if I can't see her face and work out what's going on in her mind. It took me almost eighteen months before I realized that seeing her face was a distraction. I was there to find out what was going on in my mind, not her's. Even so, the first time I lay down on it, I felt very self-conscious. It seemed such a clichéd situation.'

'Using the couch is a way for the patient to come closer to their inner self,' explained psychoanalyst Dr Malcolm Pines. 'He does not then have to engage in social dialogue, put on his social facade. Certainly some patients cannot tolerate this and then I sit next to them, not behind, and they can see me.'

Caroline has just started couch analysis, after several months of discussing her anxieties about it. 'I had been flirting with the idea for ages, and my analyst prefers to use the couch. There was obviously a sexual component in my reluctance to use it. If I'm honest, my fear was of letting go. We analysed these feelings first.'

When she had been using the couch for a few sessions, she became quite depressed. 'Now that we are not talking face to face, I can't perform. I can't use my charm on him or any of the other tricks I've learned to use with people, being witty or flirtatious, my defences are useless. I'm afraid he will discover and dislike the real me.'

Many analysts nowadays will give their patients the choice

of using a couch or not, though they would always prefer it was used. A Kleinian analyst explained: 'Of course I understand the fears of losing control or being seduced, and I admit it's a very strange situation altogether. But it does facilitate free association, and so leads to a greater depth of material, especially from early childhood. Seeing me is a constant distraction.'

After three years' analysis, Bill agreed. 'The first year I was not at all relaxed using the couch, but then I began to close my eyes, free associate, it was often rather pleasant. I think it helped. Once I felt better about it, I made rapid progress.'

Kenneth Lambert, a Jungian analyst, suggests the use of the couch to most of his patients. Sometimes they take naturally to it. Sometimes, discussion and analysis are called for as a preliminary to the patient's use of it. His experience suggests that its use makes it easier for patients to relate to the 'more primitive, infantile and imaginative processes of their psyches' and to find means, including words, with which to express and communicate their experience to their analysts. 'Most patients have tried all they know in terms of conscious and directed thought and action. The horizontal position, or indeed a loose and flexible use of the couch, can activate the more imaginative, intuitive and holistic capabilities of patients, by comparison with their rational and aim-directed side.'

Dr Lambert is a training analyst of the Society of Analytical Psychology, the original Jungian society in England founded forty years ago, and no doubt many members of that society would agree with him. However, other Jungians tend, like Jung himself for much of his lifetime, to favour the patient's using a chair, thus hoping to stress the equality of patient and analyst. Dr Lambert explained that he would take the equality for granted but stressed that, at the beginning of an analysis, the relationship 'is more asymmetrical for the purpose of the treatment though, as time goes on, it becomes more symmetrical.'

Lavinia, an artist in her early thirties, had a Freudian analysis for about four years and, after a gap of two or three years, saw a Jungian. 'It was very different in many ways. I can sum it up by saying that the Freudian was an anonymous figure behind the couch, and the Jungian made herself much more available, sitting opposite me on a chair. I am more and more convinced that for me, the use of the couch was counterproductive. It slowed up the process of analysis because I found it so inhibiting. It took me longer to build up any trust in him.'

The attitude of the analyst

Lavinia's first analyst was a very traditional Freudian, taking a very objective and detached stance which, for some months, she found cold and difficult to relate to. This aspect of psychoanalysis is often the hardest to accept. One has to realize that it is the strangest of relationships, like no other (Anthony Storr has likened the analyst and therapist to a secular priest.) Storr writes: 'During the time of the therapy, the therapist puts himself at the patient's disposal and re-frains from talking about himself. This feature of psychotherapy is difficult to match outside the confessional.'[4]

Naturally Freud set the ground rules. He wrote that 'the doctor [sic] should be opaque to his patients and, like a mirror, should show them nothing but what is shown to him.'[5] He also likened the analyst's position to that of a blank screen on which are projected the patient's fantasies and emotions.

Almost without exception, the analysts I interviewed believed that it was in their patients' best interests not to know anything about them. So consulting rooms are usually rather characterless, or else a reflection of a universally civilized and cultured personality (books on shelves, pictures on the wall) but no photographs of spouses or children. The same is true of many psychotherapists.

We go back to that 'major therapeutic tool', the transference, when we look to the main reason for the analyst's attitude. If the patient knows too much about his therapist, then he will not have so many fantasies about him and such fantasies are very useful to the therapist in understanding the patient. Anthony Storr recommends that no personal photographs should be in the consulting room, because explicit reminders of the therapist's life outside may well inhibit the expression of feelings of love, hate, envy, anger towards the therapist. If the patient is a woman and the analyst male, she may have a fantasy about marrying him. This fantasy would never become explicit if she knew he was already married. 'Exploration of such a fantasy,' explains Dr Storr, 'may lead on to all kinds of discoveries about the patient's wishes and fears in regard to men which would greatly aid her understanding of herself and her difficulties in relationships.'[6]

So the fantasies about the analyst are an important source of information for him or her. If the analyst remains relatively anonymous, the patient will 'transfer' to him or her images from the past, misconceptions about people's expectations of, and attitudes towards, that patient.

Another essential part of most analyses is the patient's regression to a more infantile, primitive state. He or she has to feel very secure within the analytical relationship to allow this to happen. A Freudian analyst said: 'It's a highly emotionally charged situation which should never be mixed up with an ordinary relationship. Otherwise we would never reach the patient's unconscious fantasies and conflicts, their dream-world. There would not be the same level of regression.'

'There is always a wish to know more about your analyst,' explained a trainee analyst, 'to get more into their lives. But it's very important to have those boundaries set, you feel safer and more secure, safer to explore feelings and thoughts in more depth. Sometimes you feel very trusting of them, sometimes not. It's not anything to do with them, it's very much a reflection of one's own mental state. The traditional boundaries help in that. And I do find that analysis is at its more helpful when it is very intense.'

The analyst obviously has her feelings and fantasies about the patient, that is, the counter-transference. Another Jungian trainee commented: 'People can make me very angry and when I first started, I had to guard against too much identification with patients. One woman I remember, about my age, everything she said made me think "that's just like me". If I had told her that, we would have moved onto a different level, a cosy chat, sharing experiences.'

One of the strictest rules of analysis is that there should be no sexual involvement with patients (although inevitably one hears of sad exceptions). Apart from the obvious infringement of professional ethics and the exploitation of the patient's vulnerability, such involvement would impede the aim of analysis: to lead someone out of dependency on the analyst, to self-sufficiency and taking responsibility for themselves.

Nor would 99 per cent of analysts mix socially with patients. Gerhard Adler said: 'I would never accept invitations from patients. I think it embarrasses them to meet outside. A patient needs his fantasies about his analyst, the transference must not be confused. If an analysis ends successfully, there is then a kind of symbolic friendship.'

Another aspect of analysis which can appear absurd is the strictness of timekeeping, the regular pattern of meetings. In no other relationship would one meet with such reliability and professionalism in this way. 'The analyst is a fixed point in the patient's world,' explained Dr Pat Gallwey. 'You try to be consistent in basic things, time, place, style of work, dress. I once wore a light cotton jacket instead of my usual dark one and it really disturbed the work with one patient. The main way I understand my patients' theories and feelings are to see how they relate to me. I would not call myself a blank screen, I hope I convey a sympathetic and alert interest in them.'

Analysts are hard taskmasters on themselves; they would never reveal their own personal difficulties to their patients, however troubled they are feeling. It would undermine any confidence in them. One analyst I met went through a very painful divorce without ever missing a session or revealing anything to her patients.

Howard, a journalist, was in Kleinian analysis for five years. He defends analysis against its many critics. On the rigidity of its practice, for instance, he said: 'Life is full of meaningless rituals. The boundaries set by analysts have good reasons, I believe. Most rituals we take for granted. We don't bat an eyelid when someone asks that ridiculous question on meeting a friend, "How are you?" and doesn't even wait for an answer. Many people seem to have a stake in attacking analysis, especially if they are a bit shaky psychologically themselves.' Most analysts are not cold, detached, remote Dr Strangelove figures. Caroline accepts that she knows nothing about her analyst's life but 'I like the fact that he recognizes we are two real people, we get on well as a man and a woman. I find that is fantastically reassuring.'

Gloria, on the other hand, found her Kleinian analyst very cool and very self-contained. 'She even once went to sleep, which made me furious. She told me I was boring. But on the whole I found it reassuring that she didn't care. I could talk to the "blank screen". She didn't feed her own political views, or personal hang-ups, into the situation. She very rarely gave any opinions on anything.'

Research has shown that patients do better if they perceive their therapist as warm and sympathetic. Writes Anthony Storr: 'They are more likely to perceive him in this way if he is genuinely warm and sympathetic and not afraid to show his feelings in his tone of voice. If the therapist tries to protect himself from entering into his patient's feelings by being detached, he will cut himself off from an important avenue of understanding what the patient is feeling. The therapist has to walk a tightrope between over- and under-identification with his patient.'[7]

Jung wrote: 'If the doctor wants to guide another, or even accompany him a step of the way, he must *feel* with that person's psyche . . . Feeling comes through underprejudiced objectivity. This sounds almost like a scientific precept, and it could be confused with a purely intellectual, abstract attitude of mind. But what I mean is something quite different. It is a human quality – a kind of deep respect for the facts, for the man who suffers from them, and for the riddle of such a man's life.'[8]

'Jung made no judgments,' explained Peter Mendelssohn, a Jungian analyst and honorary secretary of the AJA. 'What I'm doing as an analyst is listening to what the person brings to me, without judging. I accept that the reality, for example, of the patient's impossible marriage, is the reality, for that person, of his psyche and that is what I have to deal with. You have to accept both the good and the bad in someone, which isn't always easy. I'm human as well. But when I do become angry with people, and I have done, I hope that that anger can be instructive, we can talk about it.'

So what happens?

Analysand: 'It felt very strange at first, and it is sometimes very hard. I don't always want to do it, other times it's very enjoyable. Sometimes there's nothing to say, at other times, a whole gamut of feelings spills out.'

Miriam is thirty-two, a teacher, who has been in analysis with a Jungian analyst for almost seven years. 'I go five times a week, to a block of flats in north London, take a lift to the fourth floor, am welcomed by my analyst, a rather smart, shortish woman in her early fifties.

'I lie on a couch, on my side so that I can look at her when I want to. If I've had a dream the night before, I usually talk about that first. She will ask what I feel about it, and I'll describe my feelings about the different bits of the dream. She may say what she thinks about the dream or she may leave it. I recently had a dream about having lunch with her. She said it seemed like I now felt I could have a good relationship with my mother (the fact that we don't is one of the problems that took me into analysis in the first place). I might then talk about a letter I'd received from my mother, what annoyed me about it, or perhaps I would tell her the latest irritating habit of my husband's. I sometimes sit and moan about his messiness, not doing the dishes, that sort of thing. Again she may comment, perhaps relating it to my feelings about my mother and father, or she may not.

'Sometimes I just lie there silently, not knowing what to say or why I'm there. Once, two or three months went by with my not saying anything. I'm still not sure what was going on. I do know that I resented the money ticking away. It's a common feeling among analysands to feel you're not getting enough out of it, coupled, on the other hand, with the expectation that your analyst has all the answers.

'My analyst does a lot of interpretation, especially of my dreams which I find very difficult. Sometimes I'm feeling lazy, I don't want to do any work so I'm happy for her to interpret.'

Freud described psychoanalysis in a very clear, matter-of-fact way: 'Nothing takes place in a psychoanalytic treatment but an interchange of words between the patient and analyst. The patient talks, tells of his past experiences and present impressions, complains, confesses to his wishes and emotional impulses. The doctor listens, tries to direct the patient's process of thought, forces his attention in certain directions, gives him explanations and observes the reactions of understanding or rejection which he in this way provokes in him.'

For most analysands, their analysis is a very slow, undramatic process, peeling off the onion skins of memory, occasionally hauling something from the unconscious, a flickering memory or emotion. 'Freud likened analysis to an archaeological dig,' said Jim, who had six years of analysis. 'That's just right – the pace, the care taken. Just as separate bits of pottery are unrecognizable until together they make a jar of some kind, so in analysis you gradually piece together through dreams, ideas, emotions, free association, yourself, how you are now and how you might change, or perhaps decide to accept yourself unchanged.'

'The quietness and lack of drama was a surprise to me,' said Mark, a writer who saw a Jungian analyst for three years. 'I'd once had a girlfriend who was being analysed and I recall that she seemed to spend most of the time in tears, whether with the analyst or outside. I'm not very demonstrative so I was worried about that. I'd also been to a sort of fringe therapy session where everyone let themselves go and screamed and all that. I could never have joined in. But analysis provides you with a different sort of emotional outlet. The analyst goes at the pace of the analysand.'

The analyst also sees people with very differing temperaments. Roger saw a Freudian psychoanalyst for seven years. It was his decision, but he was very equivocal and aggressive when he first went. 'I walked in and told her there were some problems I had to deal with, but others, like my very promiscuous behaviour, I did not want to change. She quietly said, "But I think that's just what you do want to deal with."

'She was very good, she had a hell of a job with me, in the first year I often wouldn't turn up. But gradually I appreciated the regular tempo our sessions provided, it was bloody reassuring, like the backbone in my life which was very chaotic at the time. What was very important for me was that she focused not on what the world was doing to me, but on what I was doing to my world, with my life, and what the consequences were. We concentrated on my inner world, there were no excuses for me.'

Free association

Talking about whatever comes to mind, or free association, is the basic rule of analysis, but it is not as easy as it may sound. Dr Andrew Skarbek explained: 'Very few people are able to talk freely straightaway. They continue to put up resistance. But once they realize I am not an all-knowing guru, who can bring about magical changes in their life, the analysis really begins as we become partners on a journey into the unknown.'

It takes most people several months to feel any ease in free associating; it is, after all, the opposite of how most people have been encouraged to behave, to edit and censor before speaking.

'Sometimes I'd just lie on the couch and look at the ceiling. I came to know every crack in it, and I would free associate about what the cracks reminded me of: a place I'd been on holiday, a castle somewhere abroad. Childhood stories,' recalled Geoff. 'There are no boundaries placed on what you can say to your analyst, so it's exciting and frightening at the same time. You need to have a lot of trust in your analyst before talking without checking yourself.

'I explored very primitive thoughts and fantasies, I remember talking about my dreams of shitting, what shit meant to me. I could never talk about that to friends. There were lots of faecal images in my outpourings. I thought I was shit, basically. It often wasn't a pleasant experience for me. It could be humiliating, painful, irritating. The more I became aware of my negative contributions to my life and other people's, the more I felt ashamed and humiliated.'

The gaining of this self-knowledge and self-awareness is perhaps more painful because it is through self-discovery, rather than what the analyst says (which could then be dismissed as someone else's opinion). 'Talking to someone about yourself can be very cathartic,' recalled Dan, an artist who was in Jungian analysis for two years. 'But it hurts too when you are finding things out about yourself that you hate, the horrors, the dark side of your character. It wasn't my analyst who told me but slowly I came to know myself better. I think an analysand is like a blinded person, with very little or no self-knowledge. Analysis takes away the blindfold, that's what it's all about, but it's really hard to realize you are not everything you've cracked yourself up to be. I came to understand that I was still very like my family, a boneheaded, bourgeois, unliberal lot of people. And I had pretended to myself I was so different. I also recognized how critical of people I was, as a sort of defence against admitting how worthless I really was.

'The first port of call for my analyst was to put me in touch with the bits of myself I didn't know. It taught me to stop projecting my ideas and fantasies, to stop blaming other people for my faults. I realized I had inherited a general terror of women, the family view that women can never make up their minds and have to be protected by males. Even if I don't change that much, I do at least recognize all this unliberal stuff in me.

'I believe that analysis helps you to break the programmed loop most of us are on. I believe we are all like a cassette tape, we spend the first half of our life recording and the second half, playing it back. So you never change, except through analysis.'

Everyone's fear about analysis is that it will uncover some

'terrible dark hole', some awful secret, tucked deep down in the unconscious, as one ex-analysand explained. 'In truth,' she continued, 'it is usually more a succession of rather pathetic little discoveries about oneself, a coming to terms with a series of losses.'

Often it is an emotion, or emotions, surrounding some event, which have been suppressed, rather than the event itself. So, for example, someone remembers their parent's death, but seems to feel no emotion when recalling it, explained a Freudian analyst: 'Our early life is that integral part of us which colours the emotional quality of our life for the rest of that life.'

Early on in the analysis, the analyst may have suspected that a major part of the patient's difficulty is linked to, for example, his mother's death. But the analyst has to wait for the patient to feel and understand this in his own time.

Bill is a photographer who was in analysis for about three years. He had a seven o'clock appointment three times a week. 'I found it very difficult at first. I usually wanted to talk about recent events and problems in my marriage which was one of the reasons I was there in the first place. But she was perpetually, in a very gentle way, turning me back to childhood experiences. After about six months of this, often feeling at sea and wondering what on earth I was doing there, I began to realize that my unease, my constant anxiety and fear of life, all that was something to do with my father and his death when I was twelve.

'I discovered that I had never really acknowledged his death. It had happened when I was at boarding school and I hadn't felt able to talk about it, or show my grief. I could then trace back to that time a sadness that had become a part of me, my character, how I presented myself to the world. In the analysis, I did find myself re-experiencing some of that grief and it hurt, but there was no dramatic catharsis as one imagines there will be, it was quite a gentle experience. I did cry a lot in those three years, but never in front of my analyst. When I started, I had been terrified I would find out something unspeakable about myself, it wasn't like that at all. Just an interminable haul through a series of little discoveries. Rather sad really.'

After a year or so of analysis, Bill had 'an extraordinary opportunity' to return to his old school, and test out what he had discovered with his analyst.

'I had been there when my father died. They had dealt with that in the most unfeeling way. I went round with an old friend, who had also been there with me, and I told him how I had felt as that small boy and we got very drunk together. My analyst didn't ask many questions when I told her about the visit, but she then knew I was beginning to make the right connections.

'Then we began to discover a sort of subtheme, a more complicated and earlier grief, related to my parents separating and my father leaving home when I was very little. My analyst would occasionally guide the talk, she'd move the tiller now and then. She might say, "Did you ever feel like . . .?" She suggested to me that small children often feel very responsible, and therefore guilty, when a parent leaves. I realized this was true of me, I had a sort of conditioned response, a perpetual fear of people leaving me. I learned that I have to stop being the "me", that is, that young, deserted boy always looking for someone to replace my father. I had always sought after and admired figures of authority. I had also resented them.

'At first this realization that I had to change made me very short-tempered. I was removing some constraints which no longer seemed relevant to the way I wanted to lead my life. There was a feeling, for a time, of losing part of my personality and having nothing to replace it with. That takes time.'

Like most analysands, Caroline's difficulties were rooted

in her childhood and her relationship with her parents. 'I am the oldest of four children. My father and mother never really talked to me. They're both quite impossible and manipulative. I was always the family failure, I truanted from school, but they never asked me why, they just sent me back there. I had my first serious depression when I was fifteen and my younger sister had a breakdown soon after. My parents didn't even seem to notice.'

She married and had two children, then resumed her career as a journalist on a provincial paper. Periods of depression were a regular occurrence but 'it never occurred to me to get help, probably because my parents had been so unconcerned. I thought it was my problem, my fault.'

After a particularly bad patch, something happened which triggered off Caroline's decision to have analysis. 'My car broke down in the country one day and I phoned my mother to ask her if she would pick me up. She refused because she was going out to lunch. I said nothing to her, I can remember sort of freezing emotionally. But later I wept and wept, quite out of control. I then talked it over with a very close friend, who had always nurtured me, and then I realized my mother's coldness that day highlighted how she had always been. I knew then I had to sort out all the feelings awash inside me. I chose an analyst that another friend had recommended.'

Initially, Caroline felt much better. She had someone to listen, help her unburden herself. Then, as with so many analysands, the process changed, became more painful, as she freed the unconscious and re-experienced childhood memories. 'I feel it all very intensely, like a raw wound. It's not so much that I've dug up new memories, they had always had an extraordinarily strong hold over me, but that the emotions attached are that much more powerful.

'The other day I recalled to my analyst that when I was a little girl, my mother never kissed me good night but she always kissed my sister. And I wouldn't ask to be kissed. Just like now, when I'm hurt, I withdraw into myself. I recently found out that my mother was not able to breastfeed me, and I realized that must have seemed like an early rejection too. I think our attitudes to food are very closely linked to our early experiences. And though I'm not anorexic, I always stop eating when I'm feeling depressed. It's another form of withdrawal from life.'

The pain of analysis often comes through what another ex-analysand termed the 'plugging into the childhood needs' as they are re-experienced in the relationship with the analyst; those needs are transferred on to the analyst. Only through feeling and understanding them – and their distorting effect on one's adult life – can they be worked through and put into perspective.

Caroline explained how the relationship with her analyst affects her: 'I was always seen as the family scapegoat, the ugly, stupid one, and so, naturally, I'm afraid that my analyst will also reject me, as so many other important people in my life seem to have done. I have a lot of dreams about him, which we discuss. Often they are about my being a ragged outsider, a waif, watching him and his family from a distance. I dream he hasn't bothered to see me – that is, treat me – and I'm a ragged, half-dressed urchin. It will be some time before I can allow myself to trust him and believe he won't reject me.

'At the moment I'm in a very regressed, babyish stage with him. He says I've been painfully honest, but that I have not yet allowed myself to experience the real feelings of grief and anger which are bottled up inside me. I'm still afraid of that, afraid of what it would mean for our relationship.

'I do find him very warm and caring, which for me is very important. And I'm very dependent on him, I feel depressed or bad-tempered on the days I don't see him. He's very strict about time-keeping, it's hard for me to leave him after an hour, however I'm feeling. I know I have such feelings of deprivation, it's going to take a long time to work it out.'

Eventually, she will discover that she can show her anger and that her analyst will not reject her, he will still be there for her. She is already finding herself able to express her love for him, her neediness, and unlike her parents in the past, he has not abandoned her.

Transference

Anthony Storr in *The Art of Psychotherapy* writes that transference 'is the most important single factor in therapy . . . what the therapist tries to do is to understand and interpret the patient's attitude to him, and by this means to help the patient understand his difficulties in relationship with others.'[9] It is a marvellous opportunity to discover how one is in relationship to others, especially those to whom one is close, without value judgments being made. In group analysis or therapy, there is a certain transference within the group, which means projecting feelings onto other members of the group as well as the therapist.

Anthony Storr relates the case of a woman patient who had attempted suicide and came to be assessed for psychotherapy. In the middle of talking, she suddenly broke off and asked him, 'Can't you say something? I'm doing all the talking . . . I can't bear the silence.' He wondered aloud what she might be reading into the silence and she replied that if he did not talk, she did not know what he thought of her. 'What do you imagine that I might be thinking?' She replied: 'I think you might be finding me boring, or that you are criticizing me.' He then explained that it sounded as if she always approached people with negative assumptions, as if she never expected them to find her interesting or likeable. She agreed that this was indeed the case. This particular girl had lost her mother when she was very young, and had never managed to get on with her father. She had not had enough love in early childhood to acquire any sense of being loveable, or even likeable. He went on to discuss how, if one does not like oneself, one is apt to make the assumption that no one else will like one either, and thus approach other people with suspicion and hostility.

In cases like this one, Storr explains, the patient's developing, changing relationship with the therapist will be the crucial factor in helping her. 'Just as negative attitudes derived from the past will at first colour the patient's attitude to the therapist, so positive attitudes achieved during the process of therapy will be, in most instances, transferred to people outside the consulting room.' The case of the woman illustrates negative transference which can then be changed to positive transference, that is, the initial assumptions of rejection and hostility are changed into a feeling that the therapist is emotionally very important to the patient. If this change does not take place, the negative transference is not resolved, then the therapy is unlikely to be effective.

Dr Pat Gallwey said: 'Transference is the experience, within the relationship with the therapist, of the patient's past, especially their infancy and childhood. It is essentially their stereotyped images of the past, that is to say, what has stayed with them. It is very important because it amounts to a reliving of the relationship with a nurturing parent, even sometimes with the mother's breast. On the other hand, patients often experience me as an inanimate object, like a toy in the cot. Transference gives you some idea of the past in the present, it helps you sort order out of confusion. People often have the mistaken idea that analysts think they know it all. We are also in the dark. The analyst's job is to construct theories about what the patient is experiencing, to try and feel through to possible meanings. All the time a good analyst is waiting for the next association, going over material in his mind to see if it supports or refutes the way he is understanding things at the moment.'

A young trainee Jungian analyst explained that she is often treated as the patient's mother or father. 'Or else patients develop fantasies about me, like a woman at the moment is doing who is a very similar age to me. She says that I'm very together, that obviously everything is easy for me, I have no problems. So we can discuss and work with these feelings. It's a projection of her feelings about her parents, she always felt excluded by them. She told me one day that they even had a secret language, they spoke Welsh which she had never learned.'

This same patient has the common fantasy that her analyst will take her over. The analyst commented: 'She sees me as her very possessive mother and with her and other patients, I have to be aware of the "possessive mother" in me, the wish to do things for my patients, to help them get better rather than helping them through time, and with pain, to help themselves make sense of their internal world. When a patient makes me feel angry, I have to look at this emotion and understand that this is how they may have made their parents feel, or that they are getting at me for what their parents did to them.'

Marjorie, a doctor in her late thirties, has been in psychoanalysis now for about eighteen months. She explained how looking at the relationship with her analyst, the trans-ference relationship, has helped her greatly in understanding, and slowly coming to terms with, aspects of her personality. 'It's rather like making the unseen enemy, what's going on in one's unconscious, visible. The feelings I've displayed towards my analyst have shocked me, I hadn't realized how envious or competitive I could be. Sometimes, for instance, I have felt he was out to denigrate me or undermine me, that if I succeeded in, say, work, he would be unhappy. I am amazed that such intense feelings are coming from me. Or when I have suspected him of sexual feelings, they are actually mine, he is the blank screen, displaying no feelings at all.

'You see your emotions in magnified form in the analyst's

room. I often think, oh my God, I must have been behaving like that all my life, I must change this behaviour.

'Some of the time, I am reliving my traumatic relationship with my parents, and it took me a long time to talk about that. Part of you knows what the transference is all about and that your analyst isn't any of the things you project on to him. But another part of you feels he can be the "persecuting mother" or alternatively "a very loving partner".'

Sidney Bloch, a psychiatrist and psychotherapist, explains that the transference can become quite 'convoluted and involved and come to dominate the therapeutic relationship. The therapist's function is then to interpret the resultant "transference neurosis" which is a transitional state between the original neurotic condition with which the patient presented and normal psychological functioning . . . the roots of the basic neurosis are clarified through the interpretation of the transference neurosis.'[10]

James felt 'an enormous, but also very ambivalent, attachment' to his female analyst, 'just as I had for my mother. I was very much in the business of transferring my childhood feelings for my mother onto my analyst.' In the same way, he tried to play childhood games with her. 'I was very spoilt by my mother. I was the oldest boy and very pretty as a child, with great golden curls. People had always commented on this and I can vividly recall sitting in trains, watching an adult unwrap a bar of chocolate and knowing that if I gave them a certain look, I could get a piece of chocolate. I could be very seductive. I can still remember feeling that my analyst was very lucky to have such a star patient, my fantasy was that she went around saying, "I've got James in analysis." It was all of course a defence against my essential feelings of worthlessness. This delusion that I was somehow favoured.'

Interpretation

James explained that 'we often repeat childhood experiences, or emotions, throughout our adult life, and in the relationship with the analyst. It's a bit like an action replay, and you begin to understand this as the analyst interprets it back to you.'

Anthony Storr explains that interpretation falls into three main categories: making sense of symptoms; tracing connections between events, symptoms and personality changes which are not immediately obvious; and pointing out discrepancies between what a patient says he feels and what his description of his behaviour indicates he actually does feel.'

Interpretation is rarely a dogmatic statement. The analyst will gently push the patient towards insight, and may make a number of hypotheses. 'It sounds to me like . . .' or 'don't you think small children feel . . . about their mothers?'

For James, there was a childhood memory which he recalled more than once with his analyst. 'I was only about three or four, and my mother and I were in the park. I was throwing stones into a lake to drive some swans out of their nest on an island in the middle. My mother slapped me and dragged me away. Of course, I didn't appreciate then that swans could be dangerous and attack human beings, I just thought my mother was punishing me because it gave her pleasure.

'I gradually realized that, in many ways, I was still that three-year-old child, discovering I wasn't omnipotent, feeling overwhelmed by the world, feeling very deprived and behaving in all sorts of bizarre ways to get instant gratification.'

Not that James's understanding was instant. 'Alas,' comments Sidney Bloch, 'the magic interpretation does not exist. There is no single formulation uttered by the therapist which will lead to the patient's cry of "Eureka!" and his complete acquisition of insight. On the contrary, the themes that crop up in therapy – via free association and corresponding interpretations – are explored and studied time and time again using a variety of approaches. What is baffling and obscure to the patient . . . requires elaborate and painstaking work until clarification is reached.'[12]

'We come back to the same theme in all sorts of ways,' said Marjorie, 'but I'm never bored. It's as if there's a certain driving force that is always bringing you back to what you have to deal with now. It's like chipping away at a block of stone to produce a figure over a long period of time.'

Anthony Storr writes: 'Analysts are conceived of as persons whose function is to penetrate beyond appearances, who never take anything at face value, who read a hidden significance into the most trivial utterance. Of course there is a sense in which this can be true, in that prolonged practice in observation of others does lead to psychotherapists making connection between overt utterances and underlying preoccupations which are not obvious to those who are unused to thinking in this way. But great novelists, like Proust, are at least as observant.'[13]

Charles has seen two analysts but has never completed an analysis: 'I was eager intellectually but not ready emotionally.' He was always late for his sessions, and occasionally didn't turn up at all. 'I always had a good excuse, mind you.' Inevitably, they spent a great deal of time discussing his behaviour and it became clear to him that his lack of punctuality (which was also common in other areas of his life) related to his fear of dependence and of losing control.

Dreams are frequently source material for the analyst's interpretation. Jungian analysts may ask their analysands to write down their dreams in a dream book. Different theoretical outlooks are reflected in analysts' attitudes to dreams. One woman had a five-year analysis with a Freudian, then, some years later, saw a Jungian. 'Both analysts used to talk about my dreams and I found it a very helpful way of making progress. But they had very different ways of interpreting dream material. My Freudian analyst saw my dreams as the stuff I was repressing because I was inhibited; whereas the Jungian talked of the symbolism in my dreams, the symbolic aspects of myself and my life. But whatever the vocabulary applied to dreams, at the very least I found them a good vehicle for understanding something about myself. They are the clearest illustration we have of our unconscious. They can't be controlled by the conscious mind.'

She remembers a vivid dream towards the end of her second analysis: 'I dreamt I was in a large house. I somehow knew it was mine. Underneath it there was a very strong metal foundation. My analyst interpreted this as meaning that the house was me and now I, through therapy, had a strong personal foundation. It signalled that I was now almost ready to end the analysis.'

Does analysis help?

Many ex-analysands spoke of their dread of their analysis ending. 'I still miss analysis three years later,' commented one man. 'It was a lovely feeling – if something was nagging you, or you had a particularly strange dream, you had someone to discuss it with. I believe there is a great satisfaction in understanding yourself. You can never talk to anyone else in quite that way, that depth. I miss the intimacy, the peacefulness. Of course there were also times of frustration and anger, but they are not my over-riding memory.'

Another man said he had felt ambivalent about ending. 'On the one hand I wanted to get on with my life, spend more time with my family, not be so wrapped up in myself any more. On the other, I could go on doing it forever, it was the most amazing experience.'

'I found it very helpful to talk about feeling angry, or my

feelings about the loss of lovers, for example, because outside there is very little opportunity, even with close friends, for such discussion,' said a woman who had both Freudian and Jungian analysis.

Everyone I interviewed said analysis had helped them in some way, though inevitably there was some ambivalence and criticism. A couple of people said it sometimes felt very 'contrived', 'like wandering around in your head'. One woman said: 'I sometimes think it's a whole load of nonsense, but I still go back the next day and realize how much I'm getting out of it.' Another said that sometimes she is aware of the 'essential absurdity surrounding this strange relationship'.

Mary had a Kleinian analysis for five years, and has very mixed feelings: 'I could never get over the contrivedness of it. You go to this stranger's house, lie down on a couch for fifty minutes, go back to being a child. I often felt she was up to something. She would talk about "breasts" like Kleinians do – the good breast, and so on – and I felt such images were very forced. I felt she was force-feeding me. It was wrong to have her forcing her psychological theories on me.'

But Mary does admit that the analysis helped her in some ways. 'I think I probably got less worried and anxious about things, more accepting, which helps me cope with my children. I think I'm more self-contained, don't let my neurotic feelings spill over other people any more, I'm more self-sufficient. So perhaps it was worth doing. I did go back for a few sessions two years after finishing, as I had some personal problems. Then I wondered whether I could ever manage on my own again. It is a bit like separating from mother.'

Although most people emphasized the fact that their analysts spoke in everyday language, and didn't use jargon or technical terms, one or two, like Mary, were very aware of the theoretical structure creaking in the background. 'My

Freudian analyst once had the audacity to suggest I felt penis-envy of my brothers,' recalled Anne. 'I admit there are some theories you feel are right and it's a relief to hear them, but that certainly wasn't one of them. I was also very resistant at first to some of his ideas about childhood, about loss and anger, that my depression might be internalized anger linked to early childhood events and feelings. But now I have my own child, I'm more prepared to accept that we are strongly influenced by early childhood, perhaps even pre-birth.'

She had a Freudian analysis for four years and two years later saw a Jungian analyst. 'I experienced my Freudian analysis as a very isolated experience, very much apart from the rest of my life. We focused on me, the individual, to the exclusion of everyone else. My Jungian analyst was very different. She encouraged me to see myself and my difficulties in a wider context.'

Obviously analysis helps on different levels. First, there is the simple fact that 'there is the enormous healing value of just having someone listen to you regularly, understanding and accepting you.' This ex-analysand also said: 'At last I was allowed to talk about my emotions. This is an area which is terribly neglected, we live in such a heady, masculine, highly organized world, which too often seems to have no time for our emotions.'

And there are the lasting benefits of gaining insight and self-knowledge which often lead to the disappearance, or at least control, of symptoms such as depressions or delinquent behaviour.

'My experiences were very helpful and very clarifying,' Anne continued. 'They shed light on why I behaved in a certain way. They opened up family myths which I had never questioned, like the idea that marriage is the only answer for a woman. I gained far more insight into my childhood upbringing and my relationship with my parents. This is very much linked to my attitudes to men, and I began to understand what I had wanted, and now wanted, from them, and how I presented myself to them.'

In practice, this means that after four years' analysis, she was far more confident, rarely depressed: 'I could put my heart into work, even though I still hadn't found the man of my dreams. And I could imagine life without him, without marriage, and valued my independence.' She did marry several years later.

Michael, a writer, commented: 'Analysis "growed" me up. I gained far greater self-knowledge, often quite painful, like the acceptance that I'm only a B-stream writer – but I'm happy with that now. It hasn't rid me of all my periods of depression or insecurity, but I accept that my salvation lies within myself. I've had to accept my dark side. I now honestly believe that I'm responsible for everything I do and am, I would not have accepted that before. I don't think I've changed a great deal, but I'm just more prepared to accept what I am and what I have. It hasn't made me much happier, but I am more productive, conscientious, generally function much better. I went into it wondering why I wasn't a superstar and came out wondering why I was such a little plonker. At least I can build on that, it's a much better position to be in. That's what I mean about growing up.'

Lavinia remarked: 'Yes, I have changed. Not my basic personality but many of my attitudes have. I don't allow problems to get in the way so much any more, I work through them. The effect is that I feel more happy and confident, much less depressed than I used to. It's given me a belief in change, a more optimistic viewpoint on life because I, myself, have seen such changes happening in me.'

John said: 'There is support given, though not directly. To all the emotions within me that I had found so unbearable, my analyst said, "let us look at these feelings, these fantasies" so that made me feel it wasn't all so terrible. Problems now no longer seem so insurmountable, so overwhelming. Now I feel I can go through anything, I'm not so afraid of life.'

Several people felt they owed their lives to their analysis. 'It gave meaning to my life,' they said. 'It meant it was worth going on living.'

'There is no doubt analysis saved my life,' said James. 'One way or another, I know I'd be dead by now if I hadn't done it. It put me in touch with myself, confronted me with my very self-destructive tendencies, what I did to other people. I have accepted some of this and I have made changes. There is no doubt my life is enriched.'

Most markedly, James's relationships, especially the most personal ones, were much improved: 'I learned that love is coming to terms with ambivalence. You see the other person clearly and you accept them as they are. Before I went into analysis, I had made a firm decision not to have kids. I thought the world was too awful a place. One of the most tangible payoffs was that I changed my mind and we now have two children. I became ready to be a dad, to make such an optimistic statement and to accept my responsibility. It loosened me up to trust another person, my wife, enough to get her pregnant.'

For George, who had been unhappily homosexual, analysis made a dramatic change; he is now happily married with a child. 'For anyone teetering on the brink, trying to decide whether analysis would help, I would say try it. Obviously some gay people are very happy about that, and that's fine, but there are also those who like me, did not feel easy about it but didn't know how to change. But they are understandably afraid of aversion therapy or of being lectured to. I have discovered that, for me, homosexuality was an escape route, an acting out of deep emotions. Some people turn to alcohol.

'Not that my analyst pretended to have any magic formula, she takes on everyone as an individual, unique and different.

'My friends all said I seem a much nicer person, a better friend. So it isn't self-indulgent, either. You become much better equipped to have decent relationships with other people once you have gained a better understanding of yourself.

'I had never had a good relationship with anyone before analysis, so I don't believe that my marriage is just a coincidence.

'The other thing about analysis,' he stressed, 'is that the benefits last. It's almost four years since I stopped seeing my analyst, and I'm still benefitting from it because of the insights I gained. I have never suffered such severe depressions since. I am convinced that I would have eventually killed myself if I hadn't done it.'

Finding your analyst

Analysts and patients alike agree the number-one priority is to find yourself a good, reputable analyst. Theoretical schools come second. Gerhard Adler, for instance, was not alone in making the sort of comment that he would always prefer to send someone to 'a good Freudian than a bad Jungian'. Analysts are well aware of their responsibilities. 'When you are choosing,' said Dr Andrew Skarbek, 'try to see more than one analyst. We can't all work with everyone. You have to realize you are giving a slice of your life to an analyst – and vice versa.'

'There's so much at stake,' said a trainee Jungian analyst. 'You shouldn't go out and just offer your psyche to anyone.'

Many of the people I interviewed had found their analyst through personal recommendation. This seems to be one of the best routes, provided you respect the views of the person making the recommendation. Everyone, whether in analysis or other forms of therapy, strongly advised 'shop around'. Try to meet two or three analysts before making your final choice; a good analyst will respect you for doing this. You may even be prepared to undergo two or three sessions with an analyst before deciding he or she is right for you, but such careful choosing also comes expensive.

If you do not inhabit the heady world where every other person you know has their analyst, or if you just want a more objective view, there are three institutions which can help you. The Institute of Psycho-Analysis trains analysts and has a clinic attached to its premises in central London (see Resource Guide). Its members tend to follow the theories and practice of Freud (though somewhat modified nowadays), Melanie Klein (this group is apparently in the ascendancy at the moment) or the 'object-relations' theorists (Balint, Winnicott and others).

The Society of Analytical Psychology, founded in 1945, is a professional body of Jungian analysts which, its prospectus explains, 'provides a training programme along contemporary Jungian lines' and also has clinics for adults and children. The Association of Jungian Analysts, formed under the aegis of Gerhard Adler, is still small (twenty-five analysts with seven trainees compared with the SAP's membership of around a hundred). But, explained Adler, there is no one line of practice. Some will use pure dream analysis with acts of imagination (such as painting); others, like him, would bring in Freudian or Kleinian ideas if they seemed appropriate.

If you approach any of these bodies, you are fairly sure of finding a reputable analyst with a certain degree of competence (though inevitably one does hear scandalous stories of goings-on between patients and even quite distinguished analysts), but there can never be complete safeguards in such an intimate situation. If sexual advances were made to you, or anything else happened which seemed unethical, then you have some safeguard if that analyst belongs to a professional body which is naturally concerned about professional ethics. There is never any sure guarantee of competence if you have no personal recommendation.

'How can analysts know if another is any good?' observed a

psychiatrist who has undergone three different analyses, with varying degrees of success. 'I'm sure this is why they are so obsessively concerned about training and supervision. I do know they remove people from the courses.'

All three organizations are training bodies and the training is long and intensive. Applicants have to be very committed, not least because most have to pay the fees themselves. No public funds are available for training analysts. Many would-be analysts come from the medical or related professions.

Both the Institute of Psycho-Analysis and the Society of Analytical Psychology insist on a degree in a related subject, possibly medicine or social sciences, and some considerable experience of working in a related field. (The SAP specifies clinical experience in the psychiatric field.) The Association of Jungian Analysts says applicants must be medical practitioners or possess a relevant academic degree acceptable to the professional committee.

Most trainees are thirty years old, or more, with plenty of life experience. All three trainings involve a personal analysis for the training period, as well as lectures and seminars and, after at least a year, one or two cases under supervision.

The Institute, the SAP and the AJA each have a clinic where patients receive analysis at very reduced fees, depending on their means; some do not have to pay at all. All three clinical services are staffed by analysts and professional students under supervision. A few places at the Institute are assisted by the National Health Service. Anyone considering application to this clinic should realize that, if accepted, they will have to visit their analyst there every working day for several years.

As one analyst said, there may be advantages in being analysed by a trainee because they are so carefully supervised and are usually more cautious in their approach too.

If you do not want to attend a clinic, all three organizations will refer you to private analysts. However, there is no full analysis on the NHS except at the Institute's clinic.

How long will it take and how often will I go?

These questions are uppermost in anyone's mind when considering analysis. They are impossible to answer. The general belief, or rather misconception, is that analysis goes on indefinitely.

Despite a marked movement in analytic psychotherapy towards much briefer therapy, analysis still seems to take, on average, four to five years. When discussing the issue of time, it is important to remember that analysts aim to provide far more than symptomatic relief (though, of course, they hope this will also happen). In Jungian analysis, explained Gerhard Adler, 'the real aim is to help a person to be as complete as possible, to find their potentialities, to be in creative and constructive touch with their unconscious.' And, he added firmly, 'Don't you realize, we are dealing with a lifetime in analysis.'

It is some time before you know what you're dealing with, said another Jungian analyst. 'We're not going in with a sledgehammer like some fringe therapies, which aim to solve people's problems over a weekend. People have developed patterns over the years and it can take a very long time to get a new orientation.'

Kleinian analysts particularly work with very early, and therefore very deep, experiences which is another reason for lengthening analyses.

Two other important factors concerning the analyst rather than the patient, according to David Malan, are the pursuit of 'therapeutic perfectionism' and 'a tendency towards passivity and the willingness to follow where the patient leads'.[14] The latter is probably one of the most significant differences between analysis and other forms of psychotherapy, where the goals are clear and limited, and the therapist takes a more directive line.

Inevitably there are exceptions, like London analyst Nicholas Spicer, who has a Jungian orientation but says he belongs to no school except his own. Most of his patients stay between one and two years, although he thinks two years is probably too long. 'I say to people they have every right to expect results. Analysis is costly, and a lot of effort. If after eight to ten visits someone is not seeing tangible results, they should either complain or leave. It's my job to get them out of here. Freud said the time to end analysis is when it seems to be interminable.'

They argue that such frequency allows for the recollection of forgotten memories and feelings, for transference, and for regression, when the patient returns to a very infantile and primitive state. It can be a very intense experience and this requires very regular support from the analyst.

'Just seeing your analyst five times a week gives you a lot of support,' said a trainee Kleinian analyst. 'I feel I can tackle something deeper in myself, however disturbing, because it is contained within such regular meetings.'

Andrew Skarbek said: 'In such an intense relationship, it is vital to have this very close, regular contact. It is a bit like feeding a baby. A patient does get addicted to analysis. At weekends, he has to endure the separation. Meeting five times a week is easier for both of us, it gives one the opportunity to learn and clarify. Something brought into the discussion on Tuesday, for example, may not be clear until Wednesday or Thursday.'

James, who was in Freudian analysis for seven years, believes the regular tempo, the intensity of almost daily sessions, are integral to analysis: 'I feel that most theories and models of practice of psychotherapy treat human beings like a tin drum. But analysis treats you like a Stradivarius. It's the time taken, the very cautious, tentative exploration, the humility of the approach. Like Freud's archaeological metaphor, there is a very careful dusting down of every bit of material you bring to each session.'

Lorraine has been treated by a Freudian analyst and a Jungian. She found both experiences useful, and points out that one of the differences is the frequency of sessions. 'I had to see the Freudian at least four times a week, to keep up the pressure, as he put it. But the Jungian said it didn't matter, perhaps I only needed to go once a week or even less, because the psyche goes at its own sweet pace, it can't be hurried.'

Indeed, Jungian analysts do not require such uniformity of regular sessions, though again there are variations according to individuals and to theoretical groups. Kenneth Lambert, of the Society of Analytical Psychology, explained: 'It depends on every individual patient. If someone's difficulties seem to be based on a serious disturbance in infancy, you probably cannot deal with them unless you have, on a regular basis, four or even five sessions a week, gradually reducing to three or less as the analysis moves towards the end. Only in very special cases do I see someone once a week. They have to be very stoical and the work will be fairly goal-orientated.' He explained that with longer gaps between sessions, a person's defences often strengthen and therefore the work may have to be done again next time. It is like, I imagine, leaving enough time for a wound to grow a thin scab which then has to be ripped off every few days to promote the healing process.

But Gerhard Adler argues: 'Three times a week is ideal, and twice is all right. In the AJA, we believe that the intervals between analytical sessions are very important, they produce new reactions. They are an important part of the analysis, which can be seen like a wave, with peaks and troughs.' He said that working like this does not prevent the transference taking place and it also helps towards inner personal independence.

Anthony Storr writes: '. . . there is no evidence that I know of to suggest that the results obtained by five times weekly analysis are superior to those achieved by less intensive therapy; and something is to be said against very frequent sessions on the grounds that it encourages a too great dependence upon the therapist and the therapeutic situation.'[15]

Time is obviously an important part of the equation when you are choosing an analyst, and the cost of that time. Most sessions are the traditional fifty minutes; there is nothing magical about such a length, the ten minutes gives the analyst time for a coffee or visit to the loo before the next patient. And, as analysis and therapy demand concentration and alertness, any longer would not be productive but tiring for both sides. You may be surprised by the discipline surrounding the session's timing. 'Toward the end of a session, I'm very aware of the clock which I can see (always a very noticeable part of the furniture in an analyst's room), and usually quite concerned about how much time I have. She will make a noise or move slightly, that's the cue to say it's the end of the session, whether I'm in the middle of things or not.'

5 Different types of individual psychotherapy

'Only connect.'

E. M. Forster, *Howards End*

Individual psychotherapy has developed in many different ways and directions since the early days of psychoanalysis, which was, of course, the first psychotherapeutic treatment in any formal sense. Some psychotherapists very firmly base their work on Freudian or Jungian concepts, others have borrowed from the techniques of humanistic therapies, such as Gestalt, or have been greatly influenced in their work by feminism. Another important group are the behaviour therapists who, to put it very simply, see all human behaviour as a learned response which can, therefore, be un-learned.

Each group naturally argues for their own corner and insists they have the Holy Grail of therapy. The in-fighting and academic disputes certainly don't concern the average depressed person who thinks she or he needs a therapist, but it is important to be aware of some of the distinctions and the claims which are made when you are making your choice of therapist. For example, those psychotherapists who work in a very analytic way, will insist that nobody should call themselves a psychotherapist if they have not undergone their own personal analysis for at least three years and also been supervised for a certain length of time. But should you ignore these comments if your friend has just recommended a therapist who has helped him or her a great deal and who has not had that sort of training? And if you cannot afford private therapy, but have been offered some on the NHS, should you reject it because your therapist is a relatively unqualified trainee psychiatrist or nurse?

Certainly one should be wary of the charlatans and quacks who claim to practice psychotherapy and exploit vulnerable people, and their existence is one reason for the somewhat dogmatic stance of various psychotherapy organizations. But there is also a danger that too dogmatic a stance by the therapist makes them insensitive to patients' needs. Professor Derek Russell Davis has practised psychotherapy in Bristol for many years and encouraged the development of a psychotherapeutic mental health service. 'I know the argument that your own analysis makes you alert to your own prejudices, but I also believe it can make you very orthodox in your doctrines rather than continuously sceptical, as therapists should be.'

Dr Pamela Ashurst is consultant psychotherapist in Southampton where she provides a psychotherapy service for a large number of people by using trainee doctors, nurses, social workers and other involved professionals, such as hospital chaplains (under careful supervision from herself and other trained therapists). 'I believe that anyone working as a therapist should try to gain as much personal experience of therapy and training as possible, but I've never been absolutely convinced that a long personal analysis makes one a good therapist if you do not also have the right curative personality.' (She has personal experience of therapy in a group and individually.)

There are three fairly distinct schools of individual therapy available in this country: the psychodynamic (based on analytic theory and practice), the behavioural and the humanistic or growth therapies (see Glossary). The gap between them is narrower than many imagine, especially within the NHS. As one therapist said to me, 'there are as many psychotherapies as there are psychotherapists.'

'Few psychotherapists stick as rigidly to their theories as they claim,' said psychologist Dr Sue Llewellyn, who has recently completed a doctoral thesis on the consumer's view of therapy. 'There is a lot more impressionistic, individualistic work around than people would admit to.'

Good therapists will put their patients' needs first. This may mean, for example, that a psychodynamic therapist would refer someone with a phobia to a behaviourist because that type of treatment is more appropriate. Or it may mean they offer a more supportive approach because the patient is unable to cope with a more analytic, distanced approach.

Inge Hudson is a senior clinical psychologist in a large general hospital in Hertfordshire. She has experienced both group and individual therapy, psychodynamic and humanistic, and mainly practises psychodynamic therapy. 'I believe it is wrong to be too rigid and dogmatic about the types of therapy patients are offered. It is always a question of making the right match between patient and treatment. I think it was Winnicott who said every individual in therapy is on their own individual journey. The theory is useful, but it should never come between the individual patient and his or her reality. Nor should it prevent the therapist being human.'

She believes that behaviour therapy can be the treatment of choice for people with phobias or obsessions. 'But I might well sneak in some psychotherapy during or after as I think, after a certain period of time, the combined approach can be very useful. Agoraphobia, for example, can be seen as a learned way of avoiding anxiety, so behaviour therapy can help you to change that way of behaving. But I also believe that agoraphobia is to do with fears about being separate and independent. So a more psychotherapeutic approach may help the individual talk through these feelings, once behaviour therapy has helped him or her combat the agoraphobia.

'When patients first arrive, whatever the problem, they tend to say, "I think I'm mad or something is terribly wrong with me". While they are having psychotherapy, they say, "now I know I have reasons for that behaviour". It's a great relief for them.

'If people are not so ready to explore themselves or to tolerate the pain entailed in trying to change, then I would offer them a more supportive type of psychotherapy. Alcoholics, for example, need support if they are trying to stop drinking.'

'I am a great believer in adjusting the treatment to the patient,' said Dr Henrietta Santer, chief psychologist for Guy's Health District in south London. Her initial psychotherapy training was in analytic therapy, but she then learned to use behavioural therapy at a London psychiatric hospital. Now she mainly practises cognitive therapy (see Glossary). 'I believe that therapists who only have one style of working to offer patients are in danger of not being able to adjust to each individual patient, as the good therapist always should.'

She gave the example of a woman she had treated for a spider phobia. The woman had previously seen a very analytically orientated psychiatrist who had insisted on concentrating on the patient's relationship with her mother. Dr Santer explained: 'This woman's life had been really interfered with in a major way by her phobia and she just felt, however problematic the relationship with her mother was, that this man was not listening to her, was not sensitive to her major problem, the spider phobia. One of its effects had been that she did not dare have children.'

The woman overcame the phobia after thirty-four half-hour sessions of behaviour therapy. She then told Dr Santer that she would like to talk more about herself and her mother, because she still felt rather insecure about becoming a mother herself and realized that this might be something to do with her own mother. But if she had not been treated first for the spider phobia, she would never have been able to look beyond it to this more deep rooted insecurity about having children.

Psychodynamic psychotherapists

This group includes a wide range of people who, to a differing degree, base their work on the theories and techniques of analysts such as Freud. Many have also incorporated some of the theories on child development. Their aim, like analysts', is to help patients to make sense of their inner world, to understand the usually unconscious conflicts which have caused symptoms like depression or anxiety.

'As therapists,' said Dr Pamela Ashurst, 'we are in the business of helping people to make sense of the predicament in which they find themselves.'

'We look at people's difficulties in terms of their whole lives, it's not just a snapshot view of the present,' explained Dr Glenys Parry. 'Why, for instance, is this person prone to respond to adversity by always seeing themselves as unloveable or powerless? It is about finding some kind of hidden truth about how things are for you as an individual.'

A large number of psychodynamic psychotherapists work in the private sector, and are not therefore as restrained in terms of time as those working in the health service. Some adhere more strictly than others to analytic practice, and this group of therapists, sometimes known as analytic psychotherapists, include analysts who also take patients for less intensive psychotherapy (usually because there are not enough people who can afford full-blown analysis).

The main professional group to which these therapists belong is the British Association of Psychotherapists, formed about twenty years ago by a breakaway group from the analytic institutes. It now has a well-established training course for psychotherapists and many therapists working in the NHS, especially social workers, have done this training. The BAP brochure explains that analytical psychotherapy is 'a form of treatment in which the patient, with the help of the therapist, explores conscious and unconscious thoughts and feelings, and past and present experiences, with the aim of resolving emotional conflicts and personal difficulties.' Trainees choose to follow Freudian or Jungian theory, and are supervised either by members of the Institute of Psycho-Analysis or the Society of Analytical Psychology. Any BAP trained therapist will have been in personal analysis three times a week for at least five years.

Though inevitably BAP members are concentrated in London, a small but growing number are to be found in other towns and cities, specifically in Cardiff, Oxford and Bristol. There can be no major change in the availability of analytic psychotherapists while there is such a strict emphasis on training and supervision by analysts, the majority of whom live and work in London.

Other private centres and organizations offer psychotherapy from therapists trained by means of their own analysis and supervised while training by an analyst. These include the Lincoln Memorial Clinic, the London Centre for Psychotherapy and the Arbours Association (see Resource Guide).

But what, you may well ask, is the difference between psychodynamic therapists who work on strict analytic lines, using a couch, free association, interpretation of dreams, and analysts? Not surprisingly, the answer to that question depends on the person who gives it. One leading analytical psychotherapist said the difference was not worth exploring.

Another said the difference was 'snobbery'. Analysts, on the other hand, who often practise both, tend rather gently, to put down psychotherapy (the 'bastard child of analysis' as one said).

There is a pecking order in the psychotherapeutic world as in any other (so psychotherapists can be equally patronizing about counsellors, for example). 'Analysis is the Rolls-Royce,' one patient was told by a psychiatrist. But any sound car will get you to your destination, the quality of the journey will be different, that's all.

So, whereas analysis may involve sessions five days a week, analytic psychotherapy can be more flexible. Some therapists, albeit reluctantly, see patients only once or twice a week. Inevitably therefore, this type of psychotherapy may be less all-consuming than analysis, which people have described as a long exploration of the psyche.

Also, psychoanalysis is more concerned with the patient's inner world than his or her life outside the consulting room. 'I must never forget that the patient is out there in the real world, having to cope,' said an analytic therapist. 'I am always making links with their real world, their environment outside.' Some therapists may on occasion give practical advice, which an analyst would never do. They may be more directive.

'Instead of waiting for the patient to get there as in analysis, through free association, you steer them a bit more,' said Dr David Sturgeon, a psychiatrist and analytic psychotherapist at University College Hospital. 'We do a bit more interpreting. In analysis, you always want the patient to have his hand on the helm. In psychotherapy, yours is there as well.'

This does not mean that analytic psychotherapy isn't a tough and painful process. Sheila was offered psychotherapy at a London teaching hospital after a year of continuous cystitis, which made her life a misery. It had begun after a close uncle had died of cancer (her father had died when she was a very small baby) and a long relationship with a boyfriend had ended. 'I went all over London being investigated and nobody could find anything wrong. I was convinced I had cancer, especially after one doctor said I hadn't. Eventually a new teacher in the school where I worked noticed I was looking very pale and washed out. She said she had experienced a similar problem and was being helped through psychotherapy. After six months on a waiting list, I was referred to a young woman, a psychiatrist who was training to be an analytical psychotherapist.

'She was very laidback, the classical therapist. It was very heavy and intense in this small room. For a good nine months I was absolutely terrified that she was trying to make me mad. I was quite bewildered and very defensive. Every week I would think it was her way of breaking me down. Once a week was not enough, it made it even more painful to wait so long between each session.

'I would walk in and I'd just talk, lots of free associating. At that stage she didn't do much interpreting. Though she might ask, what do you mean by that?

'After about eight months, she suggested that perhaps it was not the sort of therapy for me. She had her doubts about me. I thought she was just trying to make me ill. It really frightened me; the first time someone had tried to help me and now they wanted to throw me out.

'We agreed to continue. Just before the Christmas break I had broken down in a session and wept, the first time I'd cried for four or five years. I just let go. I'd always before that kept such incredible control. That was the turning point in the therapy. I began to admit something was wrong.'

If you want psychotherapy on fairly strict analytic lines, then you should approach an organization like the BAP, or centres mentioned in the Resource Guide. But if that does not concern you as much as finding a good psychotherapist who will help you to understand some of the reasons for your predicament, from a psychoanalytic perspective, then there are plenty of therapists, in the private sector and the NHS, who can offer such help. They often have a professional training, such as social work or psychology.

Britta Harding was a psychiatric social worker who now works privately as an individual psychotherapist. As well as her initial social work training, she has trained as a group therapist, used family therapy with anorexic patients and their families in a psychiatric hospital, and helped to develop an NHS sex therapy service and training course. Her therapy is grounded in psychodynamic principles but she would call herself 'supportive' rather than analytic, and she has worked with a number of emotionally disturbed people who may not, she believes, have been able to undertake the rigours of more analytical therapy. 'I also believe in the importance of an individual's sexuality, their sexual development can tell you a lot about them as individuals and their psychological makeup.'

Like many therapists, she sees a wide range of patients, from the 'unhappy and unfulfilled who come for peace of mind', to, occasionally, those with a severe mental illness, such as schizophrenia. The latter, explained Britta Harding, need a different type of treatment, mainly support, and a listening ear. She also points to a small, but perhaps growing, number of women who, because of their involvement with the women's movement, had denied themselves satisfying relationships with men and now feel disillusioned and alone.

'I try to understand why people feel and act as they do. In the beginning especially, there is a lot of going back to the person's childhood, to try to make some sense of their feelings, to try to get at the hiccup or knot which is causing the pain. The way someone has coped in childhood very much determines the way they cope now. Parents' attitudes clearly have a great influence; a woman may have little self-confidence partly because, as a child or teenager, she was put down by her mother. And often schools have caused difficulties, especially boarding schools.

'Once we have built up some trust, then we can begin to work on the depression, or whatever has brought the patient to me. I ask them what in their lives do they want to change, how they see themselves in their relationships and in society. We have then to work towards some change. I think change is a key word in therapy. The time needed varies enormously. Some people may feel much better after a few months, others become very dependent. Some come for two years and may return several years later. I warn them all, 'I don't have a magic wand. It is hard work.'

Brenda Moor was originally a teacher who, through her work with young people from very deprived backgrounds, became interested in psychotherapy. 'I knew I was using my intuition anyway and I wanted to work one-to-one. But I was afraid of the damage I might cause through ignorance. So I decided to have my own therapy, as training – and also, of course, for me.'

Her own therapy, and now her own work, straddles the divide between psychodynamic psychotherapy and humanistic or alternative therapy. She also uses dreams, though not necessarily using symbolism for interpretation. But here again she might use Gestalt techniques by asking someone to be the person or object in the dream. 'So I'm aiming to help that client work through the meaning of that dream for themselves.'

Of course, people who need help are often referred to psychotherapists, without any idea of what that means, let alone what type of therapy they might want. I have met many who benefitted from all types of psychodynamic therapists, with *and* without formal analytic training.

Gillian, for example, was widowed when she was only thirty, after helping her husband through years of illness.

She was left with plenty of money, and was therefore able to live in some considerable comfort with her only son. But, after several unsuccessful relationships and, at best, an uneasy friendship with her own parents and her in-laws, she became increasingly miserable and lonely. 'I started eating and became very large, which destroyed the little bit of self-confidence I'd had. I couldn't sleep without taking pills and was drinking a lot on my own. I was scared of going out with a man because I felt I had the effect on people of making them hate me. I became so desperately unhappy that I asked my GP to refer me to a psychiatrist in Harley Street. He was lovely, talked to me for ages and then recommended a psychotherapist he knew.'

The psychiatrist suggested she saw the therapist, a social worker who did part-time psychodynamic psychotherapy, for six sessions. Gillian has now been seeing her for three years and admits it's come to the point of having 'more of a chat' than therapy. 'But I think she saved my life. It was amazing at first, at last there was someone who was there for me all the time, it felt. I could ring her if I was feeling really terrible and she saved me from two suicide attempts. She was someone who believed in me. I could talk to her about sex, she was quite unshockable, and ask for advice with my son when he was acting up. She also gave me the confidence to do something more with my life, to start my own business. I think everyone should have someone like her.'

Many people practising psychotherapy within the NHS work in a psychodynamic way, but, as one sceptical analyst commented, it's a lucky dip whether a patient is offered a trained therapist with some training and personal experience of therapy, or a keen young registrar who has read some Freud and Klein. His particular frustration was with those doctors and psychologists who claim they are therapists by virtue of their professional training, despite the fact that neither training insists on any psychotherapeutic experience, personally or with patients. Again, this may not matter; plenty of people have benefitted from psychotherapy from these untrained professionals who are, or certainly should be, very carefully supervised by their qualified seniors. Pamela Ashurst, for example, holds regular supervision sessions for her staff, trained and untrained, where cases are carefully discussed and inappropriate practices gently sorted out. She explained that 'the cornerstone of training is close and careful supervision, an integral part of my department's work'. Some therapists would argue that because psychotherapy resources within the NHS are so limited, anything is better than nothing. Not many patients are offered psychotherapy now and this would be far fewer if only fully qualified therapists were allowed to practise. And, anyway, who would decide what that qualification should be as there is no nationally agreed training in psychotherapy?

Where the claims of doctors and psychologists about their original professional training do matter is when they set themselves up privately as therapists, not just without any specialist training but also without any supervision whatsoever, and often charge exorbitant sums. A Harley Street address is certainly no guarantee of good psychotherapy.

Types of patients

Not surprisingly, private psychotherapists tend to treat a narrower range of people than the health service; most of their patients are middle class, mainly because of the cost, but also because, on the whole, psychotherapy is more acceptable to that group. But as most therapists stress, and cases from NHS therapists prove, you certainly do not have to be middle class and well educated to benefit from psychotherapy.

Jill Curtis, a member of the BAP and a private psychotherapist, has worked as a social worker in a psychiatric hospital where she also practised psychotherapy: 'That has taught me that you can do this type of psychodynamic psychotherapy with people who have very little formal education. Psychotherapy is all about feelings and we all have those.'

'Obviously we use language and talking,' said Stan Ruszinsky, who works at the Tavistock Clinic and the Institute of Marital Studies. 'And you can argue articulacy helps. But language and being articulate can be used as huge intellectual defences. So with people who do not have such defences, that is, the less educated, often more working class, work may proceed more quickly.'

Another therapist explained that his caseload varies from the odd cabinet minister, academics, consultants, GPs, journalists, trainee social workers, a sales rep to an ex-squatter and four men and women who are unemployed.

'I think there may be some correlation between affluence and the need for therapy,' said Elspeth Morley, a psychotherapist and chair of the BAP. 'The richer you are, the more choices you have, and neurosis could be seen as a function of choice. But if you have no choices, if you are struggling for your existence, very much living day to day, then you may go under totally. You may never receive therapy, but have a total breakdown and end up in a mental hospital or committing suicide.'

Obviously NHS departments and centres offer therapy to a wider range of people. The Paddington Centre for Psychotherapy is an NHS resource for people in that area of west London and is psychoanalytically orientated (the majority of the therapists have had their own therapy or analysis, and have undergone a full training with a body like the BAP). Ruth Schmidt, one of the Centre's psychiatric social workers, explained that patients come from all classes. 'People do need to show a certain degree of motivation and capacity for change. But they don't have to be too articulate.

People need a little stability in their lives for the therapy to help, that is, a roof over their head. That doesn't mean they don't have many other problems, including financial. But there is a tendency in this country to wait before offering any type of help until someone is really desperate, battered or homeless. We would rather try to help before they go over the edge. There is a vast majority of people who are coping a bit, struggling along, rather miserable.'

Like most therapists, Ruth Schmidt finds she sees more women: 'Women are so often more in touch with their feelings. Society has not encouraged men to be like this.'

Some referrals to Paddington Centre feel they are being punished or believe the person referring them (often their GP) believes they are mad. Or they may not be sympathetic to what they consider a 'soft' approach, especially if they are parents with difficult children. Such misconceptions are another reason why psychotherapy is still such a middle-class activity.

Who is not suitable?

People with psychotic illness, such as schizophrenia or manic depression, are far less likely to be offered psychotherapy in the NHS than those with depression or a psychosomatic illness. Private psychotherapists, like analysts, are also reluctant to treat such patients. 'I think psychotherapy can help such people,' said Merrill Berger, a psychologist and analytically trained psychotherapist, 'but it has to be in a more secure setting like a hospital. I do not have close enough links with a psychiatrist to take on patients who are on lots of medication or need medical back-up. People with so little self-protection need more than I can offer.'

'I would always be prepared to see someone, even if they have been diagnosed schizophrenic,' said Jill Curtis. 'I'd like to make up my own mind about whether we could work together. But I would be cautious about anyone with a long history of mental illness.'

Psychotherapists who are also doctors, and working within the NHS, may be more ready to take on seriously mentally ill people. Dr David Sturgeon said: 'Even if someone is psychotic, you still have the person within. It's rather like someone who is diabetic, you know there will be times when they are unwell. Obviously you have to be very careful because you don't want to push them back into a psychosis.' He lists as unsuitable for this type of therapy people who cannot tolerate some level of anxiety or sadness; who in a crisis would immediately rush to the bottle or slit their wrists. 'As a therapist I am always working with people with a low threshold of tolerance, I and they have to be aware that therapy may make the problems worse for a time.'

'I do not work with alcoholics or drug addicts because I believe they need to be in a special unit with back-up services,' said Jill Curtis. 'Every therapist has to draw their own line.'

ACCEPT in west London (and now moving into other areas) provides a therapeutic service for people with alcohol problems, and now also those addicted to tranquillizers. 'I was told you could never do psychotherapy with alcoholics,' said Charles Vetter, founder and director of ACCEPT. 'But once someone agrees to a contract of abstinence, you can carry out very successful therapy.'

Types of problems

People consult private psychotherapists for the usual range of symptoms and difficulties. Depression is one of the most common. 'But that can mean a whole myriad of things,' explained Jill Curtis. 'Some patients are depressed about something specific, like a bad marriage, some come in total crisis, and others are quite successful, quite affluent, but something is not quite right. These are people who have begun to realize their inner world is troubled, that a good holiday is not enough to get rid of their unease.'

Denise is a bright, sparky thirty-year-old who runs a small advertising agency very successfully. She works under enormous pressure, which is one reason she has found therapy so useful. But she initially went to a therapist because of a very common problem; her marriage had broken up.

'I was feeling quite desperate after my husband had gone. A friend who had had the same experience recommended her psychotherapist and I went along, rather reluctantly. For six months I saw her twice a week then once a week for another six months. I then stopped for about eighteen months, but returned because I was feeling so desperate and depressed again. No one will make you see your therapist, least of all her, so you do have to be motivated to go, and to get something out of it.

'The very first time I went, it felt like I was doing a lot of lonely things in my life – I was finding it hard to live on my own, I was starting a business on my own. My major emotion was that of being completely abandoned by the world.'

Denise's psychotherapist is 'an extremely attractive woman, quite tough. She is very strong on sticking up for women which I found very helpful. And at first for me it was much easier to talk to a woman.

'It was strangely easy the first time, I had a specific problem to talk about, all my feelings were near the surface. I was often in floods of tears, I was the "walking wounded", just an open wound.'

Six years ago, James felt that he was 'faced with the total collapse of my personal world.' He had been depressed for many years and had been prescribed anti-depressants. He had several times thought of suicide and had once tried to kill himself with his car exhaust. But having shut himself in the car and the garage, he had panicked and driven the door down. His first marriage had broken up and his second was, by this time, decidedly rocky. 'I had begun to wonder if I would ever make a relationship work, I was bursting into tears all the time, I didn't like myself a bit and I was beginning to think I must be mentally ill.'

His GP referred him to a psychiatric out-patients clinic where he had a 'ghastly' interview with a psychiatrist and a group of students and was told to forget the NHS as he was not an extreme enough case to receive psychotherapy free. He then managed to find a private therapist and has been seeing her for four and a half years. He describes her as a 'quiet, fairly undramatic sort of person, the sister I never had'.

Having done various trainings in the USA and her own Jungian analysis, Merrill Berger explained: 'The great majority of my patients come to me with a life crisis. They're stuck, they don't know what to do next. The crisis may be in their marriage or at work. Some are severely depressed. They feel they just cannot cope and are in great pain. That pain can be a vehicle for change and a richer life. But the attitude in the UK is so anti-therapy, it is not used often enough, especially in the NHS. Therapy is really very good at helping people who are just unhappy.'

Shirley, an attractive and apparently self-confident thirty-six-year-old divorcee, had first had some therapy when her marriage was beginning to end several years before. Though the therapy had not mended the marriage, she believes it was helpful because 'it made me more aware of where I had gone wrong and did enable my husband and I to have a dialogue and part more amicably.' Some years later she contacted the therapist again.

'I was in desperate straits. I had had a series of broken relationships and felt very confused about it all. I had experienced plenty of flings with men but now I wanted a real relationship. It was eluding me. I was still going through the adolescence I had missed as I married so early.' She hoped seeing a therapist might help her break the pattern. She has been going once a week, sometimes fortnightly, for almost three years.

Brenda Moor has many clients who have lost their sense of identity. 'They feel very bad inside,' she said. 'Where can you talk about this internal world if you do not talk to a therapist?' She listed the major reasons people come to her (though the underlying causes may, of course, be different): a broken relationship or series of relationships; 'something feels wrong, I don't know what it is'; a sense of emptiness, not knowing 'who I am'; a recognition of patterns in one's life, and a desire to understand them, for example, a perpetual avoidance of conflict or a constant sense of worthlessness which prevents the individual ever asserting themselves. She is very interested in people who are going through what is termed the mid-life crisis, like the woman in her fifties whose children have left home and whose relationship with her husband is poor and unrewarding. She becomes aware of how much she has given in her life and how little has been given back. 'At this stage people are very aware that their life has an end, they are not in this world forever. There is an urgency about them. And frequently a lot of anger and bitterness about the past.'

Though such depressions can be very serious for the individual involved and their families – and, if untreated, may result in suicide – people suffering from them may not be offered psychotherapy on the NHS even if they ask. Whether or not you receive NHS therapy does depend to a considerable extent on the resources available in your area. In London, there are several specialist NHS psychotherapy centres, the most famous being the Tavistock Clinic, and many hospitals offer psychotherapy. But in other parts of the country, you may be lucky to find a psychologist who offers behaviour therapy to people with phobias.

Inevitably, therefore, psychotherapy within the NHS tends to be offered to people who have apparently more serious, perhaps more life-threatening, problems than desperate unhappiness. They may well be people who might have been refused psychotherapy elsewhere, people who regularly overdose, who appear to have a serious mental illness, perhaps bordering on psychosis. 'We see people who have often been through other agencies like marriage guidance,' said Dr David Sturgeon. 'They have very difficult problems, some quite deep-rooted personality problems, extreme neuroses, behaviour disorders, perversions. Many private individual therapists would not feel able to help them.'

June, for example, a woman in her early forties, had spent several periods of her life in psychiatric hospitals and had a history of heavy drinking. Her desperation is easily understood and she tells her sad, strange life story. 'My mother sent me to a children's home when I was three years old, and my brother came too when he was the same age. She told us our father had been killed during the war and she couldn't afford to look after us. I remember feeling completely insecure and unwanted as a kid. We were always different from other people. We never had school uniforms and never had any money. My mother didn't pay the children's home for us and every Friday night they packed up our things and said they'd send us away if our mother's money didn't arrive the next day. It never did, she spent it all on drink, she drank like a fish. But luckily one of the maids took pity on us and always paid up.'

June says she enjoyed school, 'and would have enjoyed it more if I hadn't felt so different from everyone else. I wanted to stay and train as a teacher but at the age of fifteen I had to leave school and go back to my mother. She didn't want us but we could go out to work and earn money for her.'

When she was twenty, June married and for ten years was

reasonably happy. But then her mother died and depression and desperation were triggered off by this event.

'I didn't seem to feel any emotion when she died and all my relatives turned on me and said I was just like her, that I'd do the same thing to my child she'd done to us.' Soon after, June had a daughter and was terrified of copying her mother, though she adored her child. 'When my daughter was three months old, I slit my throat. I decided that if I was going to be like my mother it would be better to get it over with. But my husband found me and saved my life.'

Then followed a succession of stays in the local mental hospital, where the only treatment she received was drugs. 'No one ever talked to me about the reason for my suicide attempts or my depression. I got so fed up, every time I saw a different psychiatrist, he just gave me stronger drugs. They didn't mix very well with all the gin and vodka I was drinking at the same time. I was regularly taking overdoses because I just didn't want to bother living.' During this time, she also discovered that her father had not died in the war. He had been living in a nearby town, but had made a financial agreement with her mother never to contact them. He did contact June after hearing of her mother's death but, having made two visits, disappeared again. 'Once again I felt a complete failure, totally rejected.'

After several years going in and out of the psychiatric hospital, June was sent to see the consultant psychotherapist in her area. 'I didn't know who she was, I just felt the hospital didn't know what to do with me and sent me to her to get rid of me. I was terrified, but the therapist talked to me, the first time any professional had bothered to. She explained that it was a case of talking the pain and problems out, not blanking them out with drink and drugs.'

It took several months before June felt she could trust her therapist, whom she saw once a week. 'It took me a long time to realize she wasn't going to go away. She was always there for

me when she said she would be. In therapy, I found you go to
the root of things. Sometimes when she explained things, I
thought that makes sense. It was the first time anyone had
ever bothered to make the links between my present problems and my past, the psychiatrists in the hospital had said
there wasn't any link.'

Six years later, and eighteen months since her therapy
ended, June no longer gets depressed and she hardly drinks
alcohol. 'I've so much more confidence. My therapist told me
I could cope, that I wasn't like my mother. In the end I
believed her. I trusted her with my life and she helped me
decide it was worth living.'

Especially in the health service, psychotherapists often
treat problems which are psychosomatic, or people with a
mainly physical problem where there may be some emotional
component. Psychotherapists encourage their colleagues in
medical wards, for example, to consider the psychological
element of their patients' illness; there are sometimes tremendous results. One woman had suffered persistent cystitis
for over a year before she was offered psychotherapy. It was
such a relief to have her problem taken seriously that the
cystitis almost disappared before she had her first
appointment with the psychotherapist. Psychosomatic disorders such as ulcers, persistent back pain, migraines, may
all be helped by a mixture of psychotherapy and physical
treatment. Not that anyone should assume such a problem is
totally without physical foundation, and in many cases, a
doctor should check for any physical symptoms before
advising therapy.

Another woman was referred to a psychotherapist because
she was suffering from terrible panic attacks. Her
psychotherapist explained that she was obviously very
anxious about problems in the family, but that it would take
some time before she could accept the link. 'Psychotherapy is
about facing up to one's difficulties,' he said, 'and that is not

always easy. Some people prefer a physical solution. This woman is just the type of patient who, if her GP had not been sensitive enough to the potential of psychotherapeutic help, could have been taking Valium for years. Sensitive and enlightened doctors may consider psychotherapy when someone cannot cope with an incurable or chronic condition, such as multiple sclerosis or diabetes. Often people's problems seem to have no physical explanation. For example, at a sleep clinic in south London, patients with chronic insomnia or those who sleep too much, have been successfully treated with psychotherapy.

Anorexia seems to be increasingly common, and it is generally accepted that psychotherapy can be a useful treatment, once the person is eating enough to stay alive.

Carol is now thirty-two years old and has been anorexic, to differing degrees, since leaving university. She once went to a meeting of a self-help group for anorexics but she knew she wanted more than that. 'The leader spoke about nothing but food and goals. She just hadn't got it right. I was really depressed as well. So I never went back.' She continued to cope with her anorexia somehow and never went to the extremes of vomiting. 'I controlled it. Of course what I didn't realize at the time was that it was the only thing in my life I could control.'

Therapist Marilyn Lawrence writes in *The Anorexic Experience*: 'I have suggested that anorexia represents an attempt to maintain control. It is a symptom of the fact that the woman regards her life as generally being out of her control. Limiting her food intake and continuing to lose weight are the only things she really feels able to do. She feels part of herself to be "strong", "good" and "worthwhile" . . . So an approach to treatment which focuses on weight gain as a route to recovery must have the effect of making the woman feel an utter failure. As well as loathing her new fat body, she will interpret it as a sign of her own weakness and stupidity.'[1]

About four years ago, Carol became very depressed and had physical symptoms of nervous tension. 'Something twigged, made me admit I wasn't well and, at last, wanted some help.' Through a psychologist friend, she found a psychotherapist and saw her once a week for about a year. 'She was a psychiatrist but worked privately as a therapist in the evenings. I went to her home and we always sat in the same chairs, opposite each other. She never talked about food unless I mentioned the subject. She immediately went right back to my family and my childhood.'

How often and how long?

In psychodynamic psychotherapy, the session usually lasts the classical fifty minutes and rarely more than an hour. Therapists prefer to see people more than once a week, but they are flexible about this and tailor frequency to people's needs and pockets. The duration of therapy also varies enormously and no therapist has hard and fast rules. If a specific problem, for example, within a marriage, is to be dealt with, a few months may be enough. But usually the average is more like eighteen months to two years. However, if you are seeing a therapist within the NHS, you will be fortunate indeed to be offered more than once a week.

Denise's therapist is strict about timing. Sessions are kept strictly to fifty minutes. 'It's hard, we finish on the bloody dot, never a minute over. Sometimes I've felt really angry about that. I used to go at 8 a.m. before work but then it's very difficult to change gear and go into work.'

What happens?

As most people have themselves chosen psychotherapy, rather than been forced into it, there is usually a sense of relief surrounding the first session, as well as the expected anxiety and curiosity about what will happen.

'Once I had made the very major decision that I needed therapy and summoned up the courage to phone a therapist, I couldn't wait to start,' recalled Louise, who had suffered periods of bad depression for several years. 'We immediately started talking about my childhood, my family, and I really enjoyed the first few times. It was marvellous that someone would give me their undivided attention.'

'The first time was quite easy,' said Robert, a teacher who had been suicidal. 'The therapist asked me why I was there and I remember thinking of all that bloody hurt inside me. My eyes filled up and my voice cracked. What a relief to be able to show my feelings to another human being.'

Brenda Moor recalls her first sessions with a psychotherapist and recognizes similar emotions when she sees new clients. 'I didn't know what to expect. I just remember thinking I want to get it right, but what am I supposed to be doing. Now of course I tell my clients, there is no right or wrong way, it's your therapy.'

The initial release of emotion may last for several sessions. Philippa was referred for NHS psychotherapy, to a young psychiatrist, after months of endless and time-consuming tests had discovered nothing physically wrong with her back. She had suffered years of severe back pain and had also been treated with drugs for anxiety. She has now been in psychotherapy for two years.

'For the first three months, I just sat and cried, then talked and talked. All the bottled up guilt and grief poured out of me. I think John, my therapist, could have been anyone during that time, anyone who would just have sat there and let me talk. It felt like a great dam bursting, talk and emotions, tears, I went through my whole life history. Then I remember one day, it was as if I sighed a great sigh of relief and became aware of this man sitting opposite me.

'I have now come to understand that my back problem was a cry for help. He said the burden of responsibility I was always taking on, with my family or friends, or my job as a nursery teacher, was like a rod up my back and my back had gone under the strain. It's a good metaphor.'

Clearly the aim in psychotherapy is that through talking and interpreting, the client and therapist will together find some explanation or meaning for the client's difficulties and symptoms. 'I help people make connections,' explained Brenda Moor.

'I hope I help people make sense of what is happening to them,' said Ruth Schmidt, at the Paddington Centre. 'I try to make things available and conscious to them.'

All psychodynamic therapists will interpret what the patient says, and will work on connecting the present and the past, going back into the person's childhood and family relationships. The analytically orientated will work more with dreams and will use free association. Dr David Sturgeon explained that he does ask patients to 'say exactly what comes to mind', thus using free association techniques. He also, quite unusually for a NHS therapist seeing most patients only once a week, uses the couch unless a patient objects. 'It is difficult to get patients to use the couch, but I do believe it helps to relax them and removes that barrier of having to look at me and trying to interpret my facial expressions.'

Like David Sturgeon, Jill Curtis has undergone her own analytical training and she prefers to use the couch (she sees most patients about twice a week). 'I think the couch is very important. People can float away if they wish and by not having to look me in the eyes, they have a different relationship with me from any other. All their lives they may have tried to please everyone around them, they may constantly be in fear of being judged, they may never have had such freedom to be themselves and say what they want to say. If someone is very distressed, I will move to where they can see me. It always surprises me how many very successful people come and the first time on the couch, they cry so much.'

'It often felt that I was just sitting there and chatting,' said Carol, who saw a therapist because of her anorexia, 'but of course it was more structured than that. I could never talk openly to friends either. For the first few months, she encouraged me to talk about my family, something I'd never really done before with anyone, and the memories poured out. I was very close to my father but since my early teens, I had not had a good relationship with my mother. She was very cold and unemotional towards me. I would show love and affection, would be crying out for it to be returned. My therapist has helped me to work out that that is how my mother is, she does love me but can't show it.

'I also now realize the great pressure that was on me as a teenager to achieve academically at school and socially, to be more upwardly mobile than my parents. To be an adult. I can remember feeling I didn't fit in anywhere, and I still sometimes feel it, despite therapy. I now understand that adulthood was imposed on me too soon and I reacted against this through becoming anorexic, that is, not growing up, becoming little again.

'I found it easier to talk about the past than the present. That was more painful. She would talk about the men I was involved with. She made me realize that I did want to attract men, but I always wanted to control them. There was no way I could open myself up to them, I was so afraid of being hurt. I still behave in the same way sometimes but I do know and understand why, and I don't feel so guilty any more. Therapy has also helped me to improve my relationship with my parents. Now I accept that they don't show their emotions. It still frustrates me but I don't show that frustration now, so I don't hurt any of us by a tantrum. I'm more patient towards them.'

Some psychotherapists rely more heavily on the work of a

particular analyst, perhaps Freud or Jung, than others. Sometimes their theoretical viewpoint may be very obvious; in other cases, people have no idea of their therapist's philosophic slant after several years of therapy.

Denise went to a psychotherapist after her marriage ended. 'I was aware that she was a Freudian as occasionally she would make very obvious and apparently superficial Freudian connections between things, and I would say "don't tell me my problems are to do with my wanting to sleep with my father". We would have little sparring matches.

'She was very intense at first, delving into my childhood, making observations about family relationships.

'It is difficult to understand the therapeutic process, to know what she is doing. It has always been fairly nitty-gritty, like talking about day-to-day events or feelings, for instance, "I saw my family last night, it upset me and I don't know why" – but that's me. I've occasionally taken her a dream or two, and she has been very interested but she has never suggested we do more dreamwork. If I'm not talking, she will ask me what I'm thinking about and I will free-associate. I have done a lot of that. It's quite difficult.'

After about eighteen months, Denise ended the therapy but about two years later, she returned to the same therapist because she had become very depressed again. 'I suppose it was like having to deal with unfinished business. It was more difficult going the second time because, though I was very depressed, I was not so sure why I was depressed. It felt like I was admitting defeat. I'm a great achiever and always want to be a success. I think my therapist's theory is that I stopped my therapy the first time just as we had started to deal with my relationship with my father. I don't know if that is true but certainly the first therapy was different. I tried to hide things from her. And I didn't always want to know the reasons for my feelings or actions. A major no-go area was my father. I have a very close family life, a very strong relationship with my father, and this has had a tremendous impact on my life and the way I have always dealt with men. I think it's made me very hard on them.'

In the first year of therapy, Denise would lie on the couch which analytic psychotherapists prefer to use. 'But I didn't like the disembodied voice coming from behind me so the condition of my going back a second time was that I wouldn't have to use it. I also suspect I did not want to get as deeply involved in the therapy this second time around. This time it has been more like counselling, she is more directive and advisory. This is how I had always wanted her to be. I got involved in a very difficult relationship, with a man who was married, and to my surprise she helped me work through the whole thing. She has given me the confidence to become very involved with someone else, she has been very supportive, there have been so many mini-crises.

'The last six months I have brought her current situations mainly, but we sometimes analyse them in relationship to the past. I find that psychotherapy very quickly switches from the here and now to looking back to the past. We have done a lot of work on my family this time, whereas in the first year it was mainly about me and my husband. I often enjoy my sessions now, we occasionally laugh. Sometimes I can now tell her things which make me laugh at myself, and I realize I've done something incredibly stupid.'

I interviewed Denise while she was still seeing her therapist once a week. Sheila had finished some months before; she saw a NHS analytic psychotherapist at a London teaching hospital, and even several months later, her therapy seemed a more vivid and overwhelming experience for her. Of course every therapist works in their own way, but inevitably the personality of the individual client or patient is a crucial factor in the therapy.

'My therapy took precedence over everything else in my

life, including my boyfriend and career,' said Sheila. 'I believe that if you want to get something out of it, you have to be absolutely dedicated.' Many patients stressed the importance of being motivated if you wanted your therapy to work at all.

'It was physically and emotionally draining,' recalled Sheila, 'but it was also very stimulating and exciting and I miss that. I now feel tremendously restless because I want everything in my life to change as much as I feel I have.'

Sheila goes back to her childhood ('which was very complex and fairly unhappy') to explain how she eventually ended up in therapy. Her father died when she was a baby, and she was brought up by her mother and many aunts and uncles, all in the same town. Her mother remained grief-stricken for years and Sheila was the only child in this family. 'Even at the age of eleven I knew something was wrong. I was very moody and subject to depression. When I went to university, I suffered from terrible depressions. I felt guilty about relationships with men, I couldn't confide in my mother. Life became more exciting in my twenties, but also more traumatic. I would swing from terrific depressions to tremendous elation. I had a year abroad, having lots of love affairs which came to nothing. I came back to England feeling like a lost being.'

At the same time, she thinks she probably covered up most of her emotions because 'I was the sort of person friends always came to for help. I had a problem about asking for help, I had been brought up to be independent and self-reliant.'

About six years ago, a very close uncle, her father substitute, died, and an unhappy love affair ended. Not only did she become very depressed but she also suffered almost non-stop bouts of painful cystitis which no doctor seemed able to treat. Eventually she started in therapy with a young psychiatrist training to be an analytic psychotherapist.

After about nine months, Sheila realized 'how much there was to let go and work through' and started seeing her therapist twice a week. 'That was better for me but still extremely traumatic. I began to get migraines and they continued for about nine months. I spent most of the second year mourning my father for the first time, I spent a whole year in tears. I had bottled it all up since I was three. I didn't recover any actual memories of early childhood, just terribly painful feelings.

'I regressed terrifically. I even started to buy very pretty, almost childlike dresses. When I went home to my mother's, I turfed out all my old dolls from cupboards and cuddled them. I took photos of my childhood for my therapist to see. Her acceptance of all this was very important to me.

'I discovered that I had internalized a lot of guilt. One of the earliest memories I recovered through therapy was that, as a small child, I used to scream all the time. I was quite disturbed. And my mother was in such a state that one day she left me at home with the lodgers and went to stay with the neighbours. I remember sitting on the bed with one of the lodgers who said to me, "Do you realize what you're doing to your mother, you're very naughty. She might die too" (that is, I might "kill" her as I'd "killed" my father). My mother had always given out this strange message to me: "Do tell me if you're bothered about anything but if you do, I might die." So I had always had to keep myself under strict control.

'My mother was a constant theme in the sessions. We have a very intense relationship and she had always put great pressures on me. During the therapy, I began to understand my mother's and family's involvement in my emotions and neuroses. I had been the golden child of the family, there was incredible pressure to perform well all the time. I was also brought up to believe that you cannot have a career and have boyfriends as well. In my family, especially my mother, men were regarded as second-class citizens, and at the same time, they always leave you, as my father had done when he died.

'I used to fill the sessions with so much material that dreams took second place. But sometimes I would take her a dream and she would interpret it for me. She had begun to interpret what I said far more in the second year, after listening and assessing for the first.

'Like so many people, I had a great deal of insecurity and guilt about sex. My mother had never been able to talk about sex, she had always been very possessive about me and jealous of any boyfriends I had. The odd comments she made suggested she thought sex was something pretty dreadful. Typically, when I at last summoned up the courage to tell her I was seeing a therapist, her first question was "are you having some sort of relationship with this woman?" It was an extraordinary question which highlighted her sexual insecurities. But it also touched on mine.

'For over a year before therapy, I had had no sexual relationships because of the cystitis and the pain. I had met several rather seductive women and I really began to wonder about myself and what vibrations I was putting out. I really did go through a period of being very scared I was gay and that my therapist would seduce me. The turning point on that came when one session we had to move into a different room with a couch in it. I immediately saw it as a bed. She sensed my fears and talked about it, saying no woman was going to seduce me and that we had to talk about my fears and sexual insecurities. She never touched me, which I think was correct for me, though I'm sure there can be a place for touching people in a reassuring way in therapy.'

Most psychodynamic psychotherapists base their relationships with their patients on the model of the analysts; they may show warmth, but they reveal little of themselves or their own lives, and do not involve themselves with patients outside the consulting room. This is because the relationship is the key tool of the therapist, so that the patient feels enough trust in their therapist to reveal their most private fantasies and emotions to them.

Denise sees an analytic psychotherapist and still, after four or five years, knows nothing about her. 'She does keep a sort of distance, though she could be warm and, I felt, caring at times. I've not asked her much about herself, I'm sort of curious but not that interested.'

Miriam is the first to admit that she developed enormous dependence on her therapist; the transference was very strong: 'She began to represent everyone and everything that had happened to me, I invested her with great power. It really is the most extraordinary relationship, very unnatural in some ways. That is why one has to look at it as a relationship which itself is the treatment.

'The transference, the relationship between us, was the main instrument she had. She would say to me "we're here in this room, what you say to me now is your life and what it means to you." She became a whole set of feelings, a conglomeration of different people. Sometimes I felt very competitive with her, because she was successful and I was sure, though I never found out, that she must be happily married and have children – the things I didn't have. I never knew much about her as a person. I think that is important because it would cloud things, and that time with her was for *me*.

'But much of the time I felt this enormous trust in her and felt very protected and cared for. I became quite obsessed with her, I would talk about nothing else. Every remark she made I took home and analysed. One day she called me "sweetie", I didn't say anything at the time but it threw up a whole set of reactions in me. I felt I was being patronized, as I felt I had always been as a child and an adolescent. I told her about all this at the next session and we sorted it out. In therapy, I think you get so immersed in the relationship that it's like being in love, you read wrong meanings into everything. She appeared in all my dreams. Twice as a prostitute, all tarted up. Then another time as someone very frumpish. Both these figures are projections of myself, the different sides of me.'

Miriam also developed great feelings of dependence on the hospital where she saw her therapist. 'I began to view it as my real home and I would often drive past it at night to make myself feel better. It made me feel so safe, even the secretaries were always very friendly and caring to me. Very small things, like the secretaries calling me by my first name, mean such a lot when you are going through great pain.

'One day I gave my therapist a plant, in bud. I explained that I wanted to watch this flourish every week as I felt I was flourishing. It was there every session and my therapist told me that her secretary took it home at weekends. She realized its importance and said, "We don't want it to die, do we?"'

Jenny saw an NHS psychotherapist (a young psychiatrist) twice a week. 'He was quite a blank person to me, especially in the beginning, operating in a very traditional manner. He said and reacted very little. He has relaxed more now, but he still won't answer all my questions about himself or react to my more provocative remarks. I do enjoy provoking him and I sometimes feel very hostile to him.' Transference of sexual emotions can be especially powerful, and demands great sensitivity and caution from the therapist. Jenny's father left home when she was only two years old. 'So it's very important to me that my therapist is a male. He is partly a father figure, comfortable and fairly conventional, but he is also a sexual figure, quite attractive enough for me to fancy him. The relationship with him is all-important. I have never had any good relationships with men before.

'I will try to provoke him into rejecting me, as I have always done to men especially, or to be very provocative or flirtatious. I talk to him a lot about our relationship. It's important to me that he seems to like me, he hasn't rejected me, even though he knows all the bad bits about me. I sometimes feel as if I'm transparent to him, also naked and vulnerable. I desperately want him to like and approve of me. I still haven't been able to show my anger with him, I never have been able to show it to any man because I always thought they would then reject me.

'At the moment we are dealing with my flirting with men. I now appreciate that it gives out confusing messages, I have done the same to him.'

After several months of psychotherapy, Jenny started taking much more care about her personal appearance, especially on days when she was seeing her therapist. 'I'd bother much more about my clothes, wearing perfume, and make-up. I wasn't so drab or so manic. There was real magnetism in the room, I started fantasizing about having sex with him, I was always trying to please him, and eventually we talked about this. Sometimes I will walk out of the consulting room feeling we have made love. I know he enjoys our talking about sex too. It can be a really nice sensuous experience and it has extended into the rest of my life. I feel more turned on by men, at last I realize I do have a libido.

'It's also so helpful to talk about sex to him. Sex was a real biggy for me, I'd never had an orgasm before I went into therapy, though I had slept with a number of men. The whole area felt taboo, completely closed down inside me. I'd never felt able to masturbate either.

'I explained to my therapist that my first experience of sex had been ghastly. He helped me in several ways to look at this. For a start, he was the first man I'd felt able to have trust in, which meant the sexual aspect of our relationship was very important. It took me ages to tell him how I felt about him, and he said very little. I now realize he was a very good choice of therapist for me, he can be so many people to me: a father, a sexual being. I now understand so much more about relationships. I began, also, to learn about linking those feelings and events with what had happened in the past, and that there seemed to be a dreadful pattern about the men I chose.

'Together we worked out that I felt sex for men was pleasure, but not for women. That went back to my childhood when my mother had a series of failed relationships after my father left. Every time she had a new boyfriend, she'd invite him round and cook him a beautiful meal, steak, chips, strawberries, luxuries we never had. I always felt very jealous and angry about all this, and then the relationship always ended and my mother would be devastated. So I had worked out that for women, sex was giving a lot and getting nothing but pain in return. I think he was right in his interpretation – I feel it when he's not. It just doesn't fit.'

Even therapy once a week can have a powerful effect on a person's life. Dan is a social worker who had three years of psychotherapy: 'People must be aware of the power of therapy. It is only one hour a week, perhaps, but you so often go into this incredible other world during that hour. It can be very disturbing. It can be almost like a mystical experience. I would often feel I couldn't drive home straightaway. I was so upset and so then my psychotherapist would let me sit downstairs. It also had a physical effect on me: first the headaches when I was disturbed by all the feeling and memories it stirred up, and later often incredible fatigue.'

Therapy is also inevitably painful at times. 'I always warn my clients about the pain,' said Brenda Moor. 'You may have to give up some of your old roles. You may discover why you have been hanging on to that lifestyle, that relationship, which has caused such damage, and may decide you can cope without it. But that can be a very difficult time. Through the therapeutic process, people's lives can change completely, they may have to give up the old self and that may make it hard to tolerate old friends.'

Jane is in her second year of private therapy, and has spent a great deal of time talking about her difficult relationship with her mother. 'In some ways I feel worse now because it's highlighted the fact that I'll probably never be able to talk to my mother or the rest of my family. They always make me feel so bad, the inferior person.'

She also said that 'at times I feel denuded, stripped, of the devices I use to defend myself against pain. I know part of therapy has to be breaking down those defences, but that is, in itself, very painful. My therapist can also be uncannily right about things I have chosen to forget. One day she asked me if I had ever been beaten as a child. I then remembered I had been and was in some ways surprised at the memory, I so disapprove of beating children. She said she had asked me because of the physical postures I take up, I'm often physically defending myself.'

For many people, ending therapy appears as a terrible trauma. Sheila, for example, was so worried at the thought of ending that she herself brought up the subject: 'I couldn't cope with the idea of managing without therapy, I was so dependent. It felt like I would be losing my father all over again. But we talked and talked about that, and I became more ready to face it. A few months later she said she would have to talk seriously about finishing therapy because her NHS contract might not be renewed. So she set a date because she knew I would never say I wanted to finish, because I wouldn't want her to feel rejected. Looking back to the start, I think one mistake she made was to tell me that I would be there in therapy for as long as it took. That signified a lifetime for me, of being protected and nurtured. It might have been easier if I had known there would be some sort of limit on it.

'We finished on a very positive note. Everything seemed wonderful, I was on cloud nine. I had also a very good relationship with a man whom I married some months later. I felt like I had been reborn. A few weeks later, I was down again because it was so traumatic having no one to depend on in the same way, no one to talk to. I went through a period of feeling insane anger at my therapist for dumping me. I went back to ask her advice about some sexual problems, but that was horrible, she talked in a much more superficial way. It was an anti-climax, like talking to an ex-lover. She understood and told me she had had to return a few times to her therapist before she could let go and I was to feel the same.'

It is now over a year since Sheila finished her therapy and she is more objective, more balanced as she looks back at it. 'For me, with this type of in-depth analytical psychotherapy, three and a half years was not enough. I don't blame the therapist, it was the system, the NHS, that stopped it. Therapy in itself creates such a need, it creates such a dependent relationship that there has to be the time allowed to work through that until you don't need such a relationship. You see, my therapist was my mother, my father, all sorts of important people to me, and I had to break off all those "relationships" at once.'

Other people find they want to end their therapy, because, like John, they feel it 'is time I should try it on my own'. He believes that it would have ended earlier, but for the fact that he is male and therefore so emotionally illiterate and unable to talk to other men about his feelings and the reasons for therapy. 'Men are so absurdly macho, and will never admit to each other when things are difficult. I'm watching three male colleagues go through breakdowns or marriage breakups at the moment and it's so much worse because they won't admit to their feelings.'

How does psychodynamic therapy help?

It is hard to measure the effectiveness of any therapy, as I explain in Chapter 2. But the majority of the people who had undergone therapy, interviewed for this book, did believe they had been helped.

Sheila, for instance, said: 'If I hadn't had therapy, I might have become more physically ill (she had cystitis) or just drifted around in a sort of haze, unsatisfied with life but not knowing what to do about it. At worst, I might have killed myself. I certainly thought about it many times.'

People frequently said that their psychotherapist had saved their life. Maria has been seeing her psychotherapist, a social worker, privately for over three years. 'I don't think I'd be alive today without my therapist. She is the best friend I have, she listens, that is very important. She is understanding. She is very wise. But she is not a surrogate mother. And I wouldn't like her to fuss over me or pamper me.'

'Support' is a word Maria used to describe one of the most important aspects of her therapy. Although support and advice-giving are not specific aims of psychodynamic therapy, they are highly rated by patients. Shirley started seeing her psychotherapist after her marriage broke up. 'On a practical level, my therapist can act as a sounding board. If something is worrying me, I store it up and tell her about it, what happened, how I reacted. It's a bit like talking to mother, though I never had that sort of relationship with my mother.'

Psychotherapists always place the gaining of insight high on their list of goals and, though clients may rate it lower than reassurance or support, they do believe that understanding gained through therapy is a vital adjunct to learning to cope better and to change.

Shirley recalled: 'By talking about my family relationships, past and present, I began to understand why I reacted in certain ways. As a child, I was always the pretty one, but that also meant I was treated as silly, my intelligence was undervalued. I now realize that my husband also had completely wrecked my self-confidence by the time we split up. He told me I was ugly so often that I ended up believing him.

'Mind you, through talking to my therapist, I have also

become aware of how intimidating I can be, outspoken, saying just how I feel. I suspect I may have emasculated my husband in some ways too. I'm learning to temper myself, to behave more appropriately towards other people. I hope I am becoming less hard and aggressive, generally more sympathetic.'

Another woman who had therapy after her divorce felt similarly: 'Therapy has helped me work out what is going on between me and other people. It's meant I've been able to have a decent relationship again and feel confident it may last.'

When asked what therapy has given them, people constantly answer 'it has improved my self-confidence, my self-esteem.' A woman who had therapy because of her back problems: 'I had no self-esteem when I first went into therapy. My mother didn't have any either and she gave me and my sister the idea that we were all victims, that everyone was superior to us, that men could tramp all over us.

'I have discovered, quite painfully, what a weird and unhealthy support system existed in my family. I've learned not to respond to my mother's emotional blackmail any more, I'm still not very happy about our relationship, but I may have to accept it will never be very good. For the first time in my life, I feel responsible for myself, I'm no longer looking for a crutch.'

'I think therapy helps because you can be so honest,' said a man who had been deeply depressed and isolated for several years. 'You can talk about the most personal things, your fantasies about sex, for instance, and you know you won't be judged. You don't risk ridicule or being hurt when you talk to a therapist, so you can take more risks with them.'

Shirley mentioned honesty, but also said, 'It isn't always that easy to be honest with yourself, even in therapy. I find it very painful to talk about present relationships. I am still very insecure and have to work through that before any relationship with my present boyfriend can be totally successful. My therapist is very warm and loving. I couldn't take a colder one like some of my friends have. Mind you, she doesn't wave any magic wand, I have to do the work. Some sessions I try very hard to avoid the pain.'

Therapy also provides people with the opportunity, often denied in our society, to vent emotions. Carol, in therapy because of her anorexia, said: 'She helped me confront one problem in my life at a time. She would suggest that I let go, learn to express my feeling more. Sometimes I would walk in and she would say "you haven't had a particularly good week". I would soon be in floods of tears, the release was tremendous. I then began to enjoy things for themselves, to be spontaneous. And my self-confidence increased enormously.'

Louisa has a very responsible job as an advertising executive and felt she could never afford to show the depression she was going through. 'I remember driving to my therapist one night, crying and sobbing all the way there and for half the session. I could show my feelings to my friends, but not endlessly in the way my therapist could take it. When I was at my most depressed, I'm not sure how I got through the two days before my therapy without boring everyone.'

Psychotherapy often changes people in very subtle ways. It obviously cannot change impossible circumstances, such as unemployment or a chronic disease, but it can provide people with the inner resources to cope much better than previously. 'Of course you don't change totally,' commented Sheila, 'and my therapist pointed that out from the beginning, nor does therapy stop depression ever returning. But now I see it as quite creative, it forces me to look inside myself and now, after three years of therapy, I am able to make more sense of what is happening to me and why I am feeling as I am. I have learned to recognize myself.'

Sheila has found she is much better able to cope with the

pressure of her job as a teacher in an inner-city comprehensive. 'Now I can say no when the pressure is too great. I'm generally more assertive. This has helped me in my relationships too, with my mother, now I say if she is putting too much pressure on me, and with men. I've even managed to marry, I see men as real human beings now.

'I suppose the main change is that I can let go with people, I can cry, I don't suffer so much from guilt and I will show anger, which I never used to.'

James said he has changed completely through therapy: 'I'm not the person I was, by a million miles. But I can't describe the process, how it has happened. She has helped me find reasons for my depression, for my anger and vengefulness. I had an inkling of some of this, but what I had not realized was the total demoralization of my parents, they had such an awful psychic life and they passed it on to me.'

His parents were working class and very radical. 'The house was always full of left-wing books, but they were really quite reactionary. We were so *nice*. We didn't have bodies, and we didn't have feelings either. I don't like my parents any more but I now have some understanding. They are stoics, but they are also sad and lonely. My mother never breastfed me, and neither she nor my father ever played with me. I didn't know childish games until I had my first child and watched someone play with him.

'It's helped me to deal with my own children differently. I think parents have such heavy responsibilities in this society, within the nuclear family.'

'There is no point in going into therapy if you are not prepared to change yourself,' advised Shirley. 'The exercise is to face up to yourself and try to improve what you see. It is not always a very pleasant task.'

Some people learn to change their lives, if not themselves, quite radically. Bill is a fairly successful businessman in his fifties. He was having regular panic attacks which he interpreted as heart attacks. His GP referred him to a psychotherapist because there were no physical problems, but Bill had got to the point where he just felt life was not worth living. Through therapy he learned to live, to enjoy holidays, sunsets, have fun. 'I realized there was so much more to life than work, and got married for the first time, after many terrible relationships with women.'

The spectrum of problems helped by psychotherapy is enormous; at one end, there is a large group of people who, for various reasons, feel depressed, anxious, above all, lonely and isolated. Therapy will not find them a partner or soulmate, if that is what they are looking for, but it can help them gain the peace of mind, the inner strength, to cope with being alone, with the pressures of modern society. Jeremy is a teacher who had group and individual therapy. He found both helpful, but preferred individual therapy for an obvious reason: 'It's nice to have somebody to yourself, you feel less vulnerable than in a group. My therapist was not a detached automaton, she made me feel we had a good personal relationship. Living in today's world is a fairly lonely business for many people, and that feeling is magnified when you have a breakdown as I did. You really need support then.'

At the other end of the spectrum are those people who are suffering from very serious mental illnesses or conditions like manic depression. Psychotherapy can help them too, though it probably cannot cure the symptoms. Rebecca has suffered from manic depression for many years. After years of being treated with drugs, when months of illness alternated with long periods of being reasonably fit, she was admitted to a teaching hospital where she was offered psychotherapy. Over two years of therapy later, she believes that everyone with her condition should be offered therapy. 'It can't cure me completely, but it has strengthened the well bit of me and given me a much clearer understanding of the sick part of me. I used to see my illness as uncontrollable, beyond my understanding, something which descended on me from time to time. Through psychotherapy, I now see my illness as explicable, something that comes from within me, related to the way I was brought up and the way I live my life. It's not exactly controllable but I can take some responsibility for it. I know, for instance, that drugs won't cure me, but I should take them carefully because they at least help a little bit of me.'

Why is understanding so important? 'Madness is a loss of understanding, you don't understand yourself or your environment. If you're left high and dry with no attempt to help you understand that loss of understanding, then you are even more crippled for the rest of your life. Psychiatrists had previously divided me into the sick Rebecca and the well one. Now I understand that they are just different aspects of myself.

'It is also important that the therapy has strengthened the well bit of me so that when my illness recurs, I can cope with it better. There's no doubt that my therapy has healed a lot of the pain and anger in me, and though I know I will get other bouts of mania and depression, I do feel a better person.'

Sarah is a social worker, specializing in working with mentally ill people. She had psychotherapy with an NHS therapist: 'When I now work with clients who have been mentally ill and in hospital, I feel very sad that they were not caught in time. Now I know that I and everyone else out there has the potential to be ill. I think I did some of my best work, like counselling clients, when I was in therapy and in touch with the sickest parts of myself. I just wish more people could have therapy. For most, no one has ever taken the time to understand them.'

Feminist therapy

Feminist therapy – or rather feminist approaches to therapy, as there is no single unifying school – has developed over the past ten years or so. Since the early days of psychoanalysis, many feminists had strongly repudiated much of orthodox analytic theory and practice, especially Freud's, because of sexist attitudes to women and to homosexuality. But a feminist approach to therapy is positive, and not merely a rejection of traditional therapy. Some feminist therapists operate within the growth movement, using techniques such as Gestalt, but the most coherent strand is probably the psychoanalytic, as most famously practised through the Women's Therapy Centre in London. This was started in 1976 by two American feminists and psychotherapists, Susie Orbach and Luise Eichenbaum, in the basement of a north London house. It continues to thrive almost ten years later and similar centres have begun to develop in other parts of the country (see resource guide).

Whatever the techniques used, a feminist therapist approaches her clients with a clear view about women and their position in society, and the effects of this on their internal emotional life. Sheila Ernst and Lucy Goodison, both therapists involved in the Women's Therapy Centre, have explained in their book *In Our Own Hands* that: 'The assumption which is shared by all feminists involved in therapy . . . is that as women we are brought up to be second-class citizens in a male-defined world, and that this deeply affects our emotional lives. It follows that the role of a feminist therapist, or a feminist self-help therapy group, is not to *adjust* us to being second-class citizens but to help us to explore how this experience has affected us, what a struggle it is to have our ways of seeing the world validated, and how we can make ourselves stronger.'[2] So feminist therapists view eating disorders, such as anorexia, as closely linked to a woman's poor self-image. They do not see lesbianism as an illness, and they would understand that a woman who apparently has no sexual desires may be responding unconsciously the only way she can in the power struggle of an unequal marriage.

'Being a feminist therapist means that you have a particular attitude to women,' explained therapist Sally Berry who was involved from the early days of the Women's Therapy Centre. 'I am concerned about the use of certain words in traditional therapy which are often used to describe women, such as hysterical or manipulative. And what I feel is most important in the way my colleagues and I approach clients is an awareness of women's particular experience of upbringing, including parental attitudes, which so affect the way they live and feel in later life.'

It was a very deliberate decision to call the centre the Women's Therapy Centre rather than the Feminist Therapy Centre. 'We do not want to alienate those women who were nervous of feminism or felt threatened by it,' explained Sally Berry. 'We wanted to encourage all women to come for help and didn't want anyone to feel we might try to change them into a feminist. We did hope they might learn to think about themselves as women in a different way.'

'We do not throw feminism at people,' stressed Marie-Laure Davenport, a therapist and staff member at the centre. 'This is a centre for women of all kinds and all views. That is where feminism starts from.'

Feminist therapists aim to break down some of the traditional barriers between professional and client. Places like the Women's Therapy Centre have often been a last resort for women who have been through the 'psychiatric mill', spending years on tranquillizers, moving in and out of mental institutions.

This was the experience of a former client of Sally Berry's, a woman who had spent several years in a mental hospital and who had been given a set of labels, including 'hysterical', by male professionals. 'She was desperately crying out for some kind of contact, for nurturing after a very deprived childhood. But she never got that, nor any attempt to find an explanation for her depression and her suicide attempts. By the time I saw her, she was labelled as a very difficult person and I had to listen to her, to find out why she was so angry and why she had got herself into such a mess.'

Although feminist therapists who work psycho-dynamically adhere to the belief that clients should not know much about them and their personal lives, a major difference is, obviously, that the client does know the therapist has certain values and beliefs about women through the very fact that she is a feminist. This means many women can feel safer and more secure in therapy which in itself is usually a frightening prospect. Furthermore, explain Ernst and Goodison, 'Feminist therapists should have a commitment to recognizing and dealing with the power relationship between therapist and client.'[3] So the therapist recognizes the contradictory nature of the relationship, the risk of a power imbalance, and trys to be very nurturing to their clients, to provide another experience of mothering. They would not deny that other therapists, men as well as women, also work in this way. Equally, it must be stressed that one should not assume that a woman therapist will automatically be a feminist. Many adhere more closely to the theories of earlier analysts.

Theory

In their books, Luise Eichenbaum and Susie Orbach have developed a feminist theory of a woman's psychology and her emotional development. Some of this is based on the object-relations school, with its view that from very early childhood, there is a drive and a vital need to make rela-tionships with other human beings. But the key points of their theory about women in our society are that women are expected to be emotionally dependent on others but, instead, provide for other people's needs and dependency. They argue that women are not brought up to be autonomous beings, acting in their own right, but are expected always to defer to other people – that is, men. 'In essence, she is not to be the main actor in her own life,' write Eichenbaum and Orbach.

They stress the vital importance to every woman of her relationship with her mother. Mothers want to nurture their daughters but, recognizing that they will have to learn to put their own needs second, according to the expectation of society, they cannot allow themselves to meet all their daughters' needs. So, argue Eichenbaum and Orbach, inside every woman is a little girl whose need for nurturing was never met. One of the inevitable results is a lack of self-esteem and a poor self-image, those very attributes which have been shown to provide the foundation for good mental health and well being. Time and time again, women I have interviewed for this book referred to their lack of self-confidence and poor self-esteem. Some women retreat into depression, perhaps because other relationships have also failed to provide the caring they need. Others may develop eating disorders like anorexia or bingeing.

Feminist therapists explain that the way women react to therapy and their therapists reveals their low self-image and their unease about dependency. 'When women call the centre,' said Sally Berry, 'so often they will say they shouldn't be calling, shouldn't be bothering us. They are concerned about making such demands on other people.'

Women are reluctant to allow themselves to become dependent within therapy and regularly show concern for their therapist, that they might be making too many demands on her. Therapists like Sally Berry stress that the need to be cared for emotionally is there in every client they see. Their aim in feminist psychotherapy is to contact the hungry, needy little girl inside every woman, to help them acknowledge the validity of their own needs and their right to have them met, to nurture them whilst in therapy and eventually to help them leave, less needy, stronger, with much greater self-esteem. They will also have learnt that they cannot have all their needs met in therapy, any more than in life outside.

Feminist therapists, like those working from the Women's Therapy Centre, deal with a wide range of women and their difficulties. Therapists like Marie-Laure Davenport see many very severely distressed women who have a long history of mental illness and periods spent in mental hospitals; others feel less equipped to deal with such cases. 'We see all kinds of general difficulties associated with the quality of their life, love, jobs,' said Marie-Laure, 'but they are always to do with the way they were brought up, and their relationships within the family. In our groups, clients very quickly recreate their family situation.'

Jeanette had been unhappily married for eight or nine years when she decided to contact the Women's Therapy Centre. 'We had sexual problems we just couldn't work out, plus he wanted kids and I didn't. We had tried marriage guidance but it seemed very middle class, rather superficial with no real appreciation of my problems. Then a fellow teacher suggested therapy and both my husband and I went to a psychotherapist locally. The first one was male and just didn't suit me, so then I tried a woman. But I just knew she wasn't a feminist and didn't really understand the problems of women in our society. Luckily another colleague then suggested the WTC and they put me in touch with a therapist whom I saw for about five years.'

Why was having a feminist therapist so important to Jeanette? 'I didn't have to explain where I came from, or the way I felt about sexual harassment or about a relationship with a man like my husband who wouldn't take responsibility for anything. She knew that doing a bit of housework on a Saturday morning is *not* sharing. I just felt comfortable talking to her, even when I was going through traumatic episodes like the final break-up of my marriage.'

Feminist therapists who work psychodynamically use the same techniques as other therapists. Jeanette continued: 'I used to talk over all the problems I had, delving into the core of myself, advancing and retreating. After several months, I felt that I was about fifteen years old again, then after a few more, I was twenty. I changed so much during those five years, it was sometimes quite terrifying especially when it led to the end of my marriage. But it had to end because I was so different. I was no longer the dependent little woman my husband had married and still wanted. I had always been so frightened of being grown up, I had been crushed by my family as a child and had gone into marriage feeling very dependent.'

Chris also saw a feminist therapist after a relationship ended. She did not specifically choose the therapist because she was a feminist but her therapist was enormously helpful and sympathetic. 'She was very keen on pointing out when she thought a difficulty I was facing might be a consequence of the outside world, rather than my personal pathology. She also helped me to sort out the relationship with my mother. I no longer blame her for shortcomings but see her as just another woman. She would also often go back to talking about a baby's total dependence on its mother. I interpreted this as a mother being essential for a baby's survival, but once you're adult, no one is so essential and it isn't a role you can expect anyone to play in your life.'

Both Chris and Jeanette felt their therapy helped them. Chris said: 'I would certainly recommend it. I no longer see myself as a victim and I accept that my family is peculiar and scapegoats me as the odd one out. I have much more confidence in myself, I feel far less isolated. I have stronger friendships with other women and have, since ending my therapy, learned to organize my world so that the people within it support me when I need them to, as well as me helping them. I wouldn't pretend life isn't very difficult at times, but I'm not overwhelmed by it any more.'

Jeanette explained: 'The whole of my life has completely changed. I just wish I had seen my therapist years ago. Before, I was extremely nervous, dependent, totally discontented with my life, with no aims. I frequently had physical problems too. Now I'm so much more confident, independent, adult. Therapy gave me the confidence to live on my own after my marriage, though I can remember feeling very angry when the marriage first broke up as I felt it was my therapist's fault and that she had removed all my security. Now I know I was just terrified at the prospect of such a major change in my life.'

The Women's Therapy Centre and feminist therapists elsewhere have, to a considerable extent, led the way in working psychotherapeutically with eating disorders, namely, compulsive eating, anorexia and bulimia. These disorders affect large numbers of women and are apparently on the increase. Compulsive eating is estimated to have affected in some way and at some time 60 per cent of women between the ages of fifteen and forty-five. About one in a hundred schoolgirls between the ages of sixteen and eighteen become anorexic and this condition persists for several years. Bulimia, which is commonly known as bingeing and is a vicious cycle of bingeing and then vomiting or purging through laxatives, is also increasing and may follow an episode of anorexia.

Psychotherapy with women suffering from these disorders tries to help each woman look at why she is eating in such an unnatural way, what food means to her and the social pressures on all women to be thin, the supposedly perfect shape. The majority of women, but especially those who suffer from eating disorders, have at some time in their lives an abnormal attitude to food and hunger. More often than not, eating is not done to meet their appetite for food but for other needs, such as caring and comfort, love and security. Many women overeat to comfort themselves when they are depressed, and then a vicious cycle of depression and compulsive eating can develop.

Groups and workshops for eating disorders have proved to be very successful, not least because women suddenly discover that they are not isolated freaks in their strange eating habits. At the Women's Therapy Centre, for example, a group meets two or three times with a leader or facilitator, and then develops into a self-help group.

Chloe had been through several years of individual psychotherapy for her depression, but this did not affect her compulsive eating. She then went to a group at the WTC, and read Susie Orbach's seminal book *Fat is a Feminist Issue*. 'It all made so much sense,' she explained. 'After a couple of meetings, I began to think about food quite differently. I got into the habit of asking myself how I felt every time I planned to eat, and whether I was truly hungry or eating for some other reason. The groups are so useful because they encourage you to confront your emotions rather than allow you to suppress them through overeating. It was also a great relief to share such a shameful problem with other women.'[5]

6 Therapy in groups

'Yes; in the sea of life enisled,
With echoing straits between us thrown,
Dotting the shoreless watery wild,
We mortal millions live alone.'

Matthew Arnold, 'To Marguerite'

Apart from a very few totally isolated human beings, all of us belong to a number of groups: families, friends, work colleagues, societies, sport, church, school.

Increasingly over the past seventy years or so, doctors and psychologists have emphasized the importance of conflicts within relationships, as well as those within the individual's psyche, in the development of symptoms like depression. In recent years, there has been a tremendous growth in treating these problems by working in groups. It is one of the most commonly used psychological treatments, especially in the National Health Service.

The reasons for this may be glaringly obvious. One therapist can deal with far more patients in a group, so it is a much cheaper form of therapy. Group therapy often only lasts eighteen months to two years, which also makes it relatively economical. But whatever the financial benefits, it should not be assumed that group therapy is always, or ever, inferior to individual psychotherapy. Dr Malcolm Pines, who works with groups at London's Group-Analytic Practice, explained that at the stage of initial assessment, he and his colleagues do not necessarily think of individual psychotherapy as the treatment of choice. Group therapy may be more suitable for some people and some problems.

'Human nature is the same, though everyone brings different problems to the group,' said Dr Robin Skynner, a leading group analyst at the Group-Analytic Practice. 'Suddenly you come to bedrock and a common theme develops. For example, one day everyone talks about their mother, or about rivalries at work. Once the therapist sees this, it should be possible for him to find a comment which is meaningful to everyone there. Groups can be very powerful. Everyone is making lots of connections; a group member hears someone else talking about tensions with his wife, or trouble with work colleagues, and he connects it with events in his own life. That person may then see a pattern in his life, perhaps to do with jealousy, that had not been perceived before.'

An American chest physician, Joseph Pratt, is usually recognized as the father of group therapy. At the turn of the century he organized poor tuberculosis patients into groups in Boston with the aim of instructing them about diet, exercise and suchlike. The weekly meetings led to great improvements in morale and physical health. Pratt came to realize that the most value lay in the resource of the group itself rather than in what he taught them – that is, in mutual support, shared experience, the beneficial effect of the improvement of one member on the others. It was this work which led to the group therapy which is so often practised in psychiatric hospitals and clinics (though some groups are little more than ward meetings, not very well run).

Almost every school of individual therapy has developed its parallel group work, but there are at least two distinct strands in the development of group therapy; the humanistic, encompassing therapies such as encounter groups, Gestalt, and psychodrama; and the psychoanalytic. The actual terms 'group therapy' and 'encounter' were coined by a Rumanian, Jacob Moreno, who emigrated to the USA in 1925 and who invented psychodrama.

In psychodrama, an individual acts out problems or conflicts in their lives, supported by other 'performers', in an unscripted drama which is led by the therapist. The techniques of psychodrama, especially role-playing, are used in many kinds of therapies.

Moreno's ideas inspired a psychologist (also in the United States) Kurt Lewin who developed T-groups, or sensitivity training groups. In these groups, which were set up in industry, schools and similar organizations, people became more aware of group-functioning (through their experience of the group as well by studying it) and of interpersonal dynamics. Group methods are still used in industry, education, training for interpersonal skills. These T-groups eventually spawned the encounter group movement and the 'growth centres', such as Esalen in Northern California. The goals became greater self-awareness and personal growth, rather than dealing with particular problems. Groups based on these ideas still spring up, develop, die down and reappear though the encounter movement itself is much weaker than in its heyday of the sixties. There are different vogues at different times for the alternative or humanistic therapies. But many incorporate groupwork.

Freud himself never worked with groups but from his writing, he was clearly aware of the importance of the individual's dynamics within a group. Jung, on the other hand, was biased against group therapy because he believed that psychological illness was always an individual epxerience and therefore needed individual analysis and treatment.

Both here and in the United States, psychoanalysts have developed ways of working with groups, using analytic theory and modified practice. The aims are very similar to most of individual analysis: to help the individual to resolve conflicts and to gain a greater understanding of him- or herself and others, along with better adjustment to relationships with others. In the United States the emphasis tends to be on treating the individual *within* the group; the therapist concentrates on each individual in turn and the group is the audience. This makes very little use of group dynamics and tends to be seen there as a cheaper, second-rate substitute for individual therapy.

But the most widely used form of analytic group therapy in Britain today is analysis *through* the group. This was developed by an analyst called S. H. Foulkes, who founded the Group-Analytic Society and was one of the founders of the Institute of Group Analysis which runs a large number of training courses, so broadcasting its theories and practices beyond the esoteric realms of Hampstead (including many professionals using therapy in the NHS). The group itself is regarded as the therapeutic medium, and it is the therapist's job to nurture and facilitate the group's potential to help each member develop.

Foulkes himself wrote that group-analytic psychotherapy is 'psychotherapy by the group, of the group, including the conductor (that is, therapist) . . . the individual is being treated in the context of the group with the active participation of the group.'

'As the conductor of the group,' explained Dr Jenny Duckham, chairman of the Institute of Group Analysis, 'you do not set yourself up as a person in authority. You do not do all the interpretations. It's rather like in a family, where a brother and sister can help each other, at times, more than their parents can. Often someone in the group can help another member more than the therapist. On the other hand, I often have to be one step ahead of the group, looking out for problems, trying to draw in those people who do not take much part.'

Group therapists working in the National Health Service use different approaches, depending on their original professional training (doctor or psychologist, for example) and any further training, such as a course at the Institute of Group Analysis. Many of them are fairly eclectic in their work, often mixing psychoanalytic insights with humanistic techniques. Others are more strictly psychoanalytic.

Groups vary in their composition. In some, there is a mix of people with a variety of problems. 'Everyone was unhappy, but for different reasons,' explained one woman who attended group therapy in a psychiatric unit's department of psychotherapy. 'Some members had difficult marriages, others were trying to live with chronic physical disability or with psychomatic problems. Some were more desperate than others, but everyone's difficulty seemed to centre on insecurity and anxiety about their own personal worth.'

Other groups comprise people with the same specific problem, alcohol abuse, shoplifting or extreme shyness.

Why do people choose group therapy?

'I wanted to know what effect I had on people.' Joanna has been going to a weekly psychoanalytic group for two years. She decided to try group therapy some years after her divorce and a year of individual psychotherapy, which she had found helpful. 'But I was still having tremendous difficulties making relationships with men. I'd just had years of brief affairs which left me feeling very bad and angry inside. I had got the strong impression from some men that I didn't bring the best out in them, that I made them feel inadequate. I knew group therapy might help me understand why this happened. I felt I needed a safe place to sort it all out, and feedback from people I didn't know. It's too painful from people you know.'

Lillian has been in individual therapy for over three years, but she is still seriously depressed and very worried about her great dependence on her therapist. So she decided to go into group therapy (at a centre which integrates the ideas of psychoanalysis with humanistic psychology) 'as a desperate measure to get out of the transference with my psychotherapist.'

Jane has recently been promoted to head of department in a secondary school and was having problems in coping with this new role. 'I found it difficult to use my authority, what I had of it. I wanted to be democratic and everyone to like me. I wanted to give my staff everything they asked for, I was finding it impossible to set limits. One of my main problems is needing to please. I was working so hard because of all this, I was nearly killing myself.' Two of her friends had just had useful experiences in group therapy and she had previously been in a staff group, where she had found the discovery that other people had problems too 'very liberating'.

'Though work was my main problem, I also felt I wanted to understand more about my relationships with men (she is divorced). My father had died when I was very young, so I came as close as you can to growing up not having a relationship with a significant male. I knew there would be men in a group and that I would learn from my feelings about them and vice versa.' She has been attending an analytic group twice a week for four or five months.

Gaynor, who has been a member of an analytic group for over a year, has a background very similar to Jane's, and this contributed to her choosing group, rather than individual, therapy. 'I was an only child, brought up by my mother and with no other close family. So my feedback systems were in that sense very limited. I had not grown up having to relate closely to lots of different people.

'My marriage had hit a difficult patch, which brought up many earlier pains or difficulties in my life. I began again to be aware of certain patterns of behaviour in myself and in my relationships. With men, especially, I tended never to demand for myself, but to give everything. Then, later, I would ask. I felt that in some ways I was misleading them. I don't mean I was being victimized, but I was always trying to do everything and it's a mistake to be supermother. I now felt I wanted to change in some ways.'

Overtly, Charles's reason for having group therapy was that a psychologist friend of his had started running a group, based on the principles of humanistic psychology, and was looking for members. 'Like lots of people, I didn't feel I needed any help. But it wasn't long before I had some of my problems highlighted during the sessions.' He went once a week for about nine months.

Some people do not choose groups directly, but seek help, either through the NHS (perhaps encountering a psychology department which runs groups) or a psychotherapy centre. During the assessment, group therapy may be recommended or they themselves may prefer it, not least because it is often a saving in time and money. Or they might have a particular problem and become involved in group therapy through a treatment facility, such as ACCEPT for those suffering from alcohol abuse.

Jonathan went to ACCEPT two years ago, when his serious drinking problem was getting him into all sorts of trouble with the police. 'I was behaving in an antisocial way and regularly appearing in court on drunk and disorderly charges. I found it impossible to stop drinking on my own, and Alcoholics Anonymous didn't help because they don't help you to make sense of your problem. I wanted to know why I did it. At ACCEPT, in the various groups I attend, I've learned that my drinking was just a symptom of other problems.'

Mavis is in her early thirties and has been 'drinking steadily for over eight years'. She was working as a warden in a residential home for old people, but her drinking had become obvious to everyone and, after several warnings, she was asked to resign. She eventually went into a hospital detoxification unit to dry out, but remained in absolute despair because she still had the same problems to deal with and the desire to blot them out with drink. A psychiatrist recommended ACCEPT.

These types of organizations are increasingly being asked to help people who have become addicted to minor tranquillizers, such as Valium or Ativan. Jill came to ACCEPT after taking Ativan for eight years and finding she was unable to stop without suffering major withdrawal symptoms. 'When I moved to London a year ago, I asked my new GP for help to come off the tranquillizers. He didn't ask me why I'd been put on them in the first place and, far from encouraging me to stop, suggested increasing the dosage, saying I shouldn't feel guilty about them. He clearly saw me as yet another neurotic housewife and that upset me more than anything. I cried most about that. He just didn't want to listen to me.'

She now attends various groups at ACCEPT, including a twice-weekly pill reduction group where, among other things, they examine the reasons for taking tranquillizers in the first place.

If you are selected for NHS psychotherapy, it may be a matter of chance whether you are offered individual or group therapy; it may depend on the assessor's particular bias. However, because individual therapy is so much more labour intensive, it is more frequently offered to those patients with very serious problems. In most psychiatric departments, group therapy is the order of the day for most patients. Dr Pamela Ashurst is the consultant psychotherapist for Southampton. She explained that group therapy is one of the best ways to offer psychotherapy within the constrained resources of the NHS and that she believed it to be a very effective treatment. Some departments have a waiting list for groups as well as individual therapy, and they may offer an open group for those on the waiting list.

Janice wanted some sort of 'talking treatment' and was quite happy to be offered group therapy. 'I knew I needed some help to work things out. Since I was very little, I had suffered from various aches and pains, I don't come from a very settled background. My mother left when I was three, and my father was an alcoholic. He looked after us, with the help of my gran who really spoilt us. Then when I was eleven, we went back to my mum and it was terrible. She's the sort of person who puts you down all the time and she made me think I was a real problem.'

She married when she was only nineteen years old and soon after, though the marriage is a very happy one, the aches and pains returned and Janice spent three months in bed with severe back pain. Physiotherapy did not have any effect. 'I sat and thought one day, it's all something to do with my seeking attention. You see, when I was little and ill, I got made a fuss of. So I thought I should try to sort it out by talking to someone. I knew a bit about therapy because I had once thought of being a social worker. I went to see my GP and he thought it was a marvellous idea and referred me to a psychiatrist.' Like many NHS therapy patients, Janice is from a very working-class background, and though intelligent, did not have much education.

Antonia, on the other hand, felt considerable resentment when she was offered group therapy. 'My husband had a massive nervous breakdown after my son was born, and started having individual therapy on the NHS. One day I just exploded, said I was tired of being so supportive, so loving and who was going to support me? I went to see his psychiatrist and explained all this, and the fact that I wasn't happy with several aspects of my life, not just my depressed husband. She offered me group therapy. I was told there was no alternative and it took me a couple of months to decide to do it. I felt she was saying my problems weren't that serious, and I thought I'd get all those other people's problems as well. I've always been a member of a group, my family, boarding school, my marriage. It would have been nice to have had individual treatment.'

Some people have group therapy after individual therapy. Dr Robin Skynner and his colleagues at the Group-Analytic Practice see many people 'who have had analysis and are still looking for something'. Dr Malcolm Pines said that he sees the failures of individual therapy. On the other hand, said Dr Ashurst, some people go on to individual work after gaining self-knowledge in a group.

The symptoms group members present are wide-ranging: depression, anxiety, sexual and relationship problems, psychosomatic disorders. Asked what types of problems can be treated, various group therapy centres listed: neurosis, obsessions, anxiety, depression, family and marital conflicts. Loneliness, bereavement, compulsive eating, general problems of living. Low self-esteem, lack of purpose and direction. Work problems. Inability to express emotions.

Who is suitable for group therapy?

People especially helped by group therapy are:

> the socially isolated
> people who were single children with limited experience of close, nurturing relationships
> people from very powerful, overwhelming families, often ones with strong political or religious ideologies. The individual feels isolated, but also moulded by that sort of family, and wants to break free
> people who have problems with authority
> people who lack social skills and the ability to relate well with other people

Some people do not want the intensity of individual psychotherapy. 'We see many people who are not psychologically minded,' said Dr Malcolm Pines, 'they are not looking for a deep exploration of themselves, but they are aware of some disturbance in their relationships and want to do something about that. Their relationships may always be shallow or unsatisfactory, or there is some aspect of their personality they are dissatisfied with. Those who are very wary of therapy generally, but know they need some help, often find the idea of a group much more acceptable.'

People from all sorts of jobs, family backgrounds and classes go into group therapy. As with individual therapy, high intelligence or educational levels offer no guarantee of 'being good at', or effective in, therapy. People from a wide range of backgrounds can be, and are, very successfully included in the same group. The following list of groups' members, in no particular order, gives some idea of the range: shop assistant, nun, secretary, civil servant, health visitor, teacher, bank manager, businessman, grocer, computer operator, social worker, advertising executive, clerical officer, marketing manager, housewife.

'One of the useful things about the very varied mix of my group,' said one client, 'is that it makes you realize that, at the most basic levels, the similarities between us are greater than the differences.'

Who is unsuitable for group therapy?

Some people are too depressed, withdrawn or hopeless even to begin taking part in a group. Such people, often very fragile and vulnerable, need the closer, perhaps more nurturing, relationship with an individual therapist.

Someone with a very paranoid personality can quickly become alienated from a group because he is so suspicious and untrusting of other people. Or there is the 'hypochondriacal type', who continues to focus on his physical symptoms and bores and frustrates the rest of the group; or 'the narcissist', who is completely insensitive to other people, claims attention exclusively for himself and just cannot learn to interact with the other patients; or the reserved, detached, introverted individual who cannot survive in a group striving for open communication and intimacy.

Most group therapists, unless they are working in the secure confines of a mental hospital, will not take people who are suffering acutely from schizophrenia or manic depression, who are still out of touch with reality, their perceptions of the world and themselves very disturbed, regularly hallucinating and hearing voices. Clearly they need individual treatment, for their own sakes and other group members'. But, as Malcolm Pines and others said, once someone is over the really psychotic stage of such an illness, they may benefit greatly from group therapy and it may prevent a relapse back into psychosis.

At the Group-Analytic Practice (on whose work many group therapists base their own practice), there is a wide range of different types of groups, as well as people within them. Some forty to fifty groups run every week, meeting once or twice a week. 'Each group takes on its own culture,' Dr Malcolm Pines said. 'Some are slow, some fast. One of my groups is very psychologically minded, very keen to make use of the therapy situation, they work very quickly. They would not tolerate someone who is working and changing at a slower pace. Some groups are much stronger than others and therefore more able to include, and contain, someone who is depressed.'

When someone applies for group therapy, a very full individual assessment is made and people are carefully matched with groups (groups can be 'closed', which means they start and end at a fixed point and once started, are not open to others joining. Some are 'open' and members leave and join throughout the unspecified life of the group).

'It very much depends on intuition,' said Dr Robin Skynner, 'matching people with groups. It's a bit like selecting ingredients for a recipe. Generally speaking, I like to have a group where the personalities are reasonably assorted and they do not all have the same problem. So I mix introvert with extrovert, inhibited with uninhibited. There is never so much diversity that people will feel isolated or misunderstood. I would therefore prefer to have two gay people in a group, otherwise one may feel very much on their own.

'One has to strike a balance between having enough diversity so that they act as useful models for each other, but enough in common so they feel understood. I would tend not to place someone who is very sick mentally with those who are much healthier. It's better to have a group of people at a similar level of functioning then, if they are all mentally ill, for example, they move slowly but tend to get better at the same rate. Some groups are strong enough to take one person who is very disturbed, as long as they are not too boring or too diverting.'

Clinical psychologist Inge Hudson is in charge of a department in a large hospital which runs several groups; she herself runs one which is analytically orientated and another which is supportive. How does she decide who is suitable for which? 'I expect members of the analytic group to commit themselves for a longer period of time. I expect them to have some capacity for reflection and the ability to tolerate the psychological pain involved. The members of the support group tend to be those who genuinely need a place where they know people care about them, where they can share things week to week, what so many of us take for granted in our daily lives. They look forward to sharing their feelings and what has happened to them. They talk about the feeling that, when something happens to them, the group is behind them.

There happens at the moment to be a lot in this group with drinking problems which, of course, may tie up with their low ability to tolerate pain. But if resources were greater, there are definitely some members who could "graduate" from the support to the analytic group.'

The advantages of group over individual therapy

Clearly group therapy gives you the chance to communicate with more than one other person about your problems. Everyone has something to contribute and may give added insights. It is very supportive to be in a group where people have similar pains and difficulties, even if the problems or symptoms vary. 'Being in a group made me feel much less alone,' said Sally, who suffered from depression and compulsive eating for many years. 'I knew I wasn't a freak, other people had similar problems. Once you've shared something with a group – in my case, the guilty admission that I was a compulsive eater – then you feel more accepted, less ashamed and guilty. It begins to matter less and less that other people know your guilty secret.'

The group provides the opportunity to explore one's feelings about the other people there in a *safe* setting, and then to connect these feelings with one's reactions to people outside the group: spouses, work colleagues, friends. 'Sometimes I went along very reluctantly,' said Fred, a lecturer, 'but even if I didn't say anything, I would find what others said very useful. It is amazing how comments would trigger off something in my mind, help me to make a connection with something in my life. I've been able to suss things out about how people react to and see me, it is a very rich experience. It's given me the opportunity to work through the relationships within my own family. It's very helpful to learn about how to relate to other people and how you might modify some of your behaviour.'

Even analytic groups tend to concentrate on the present, the here and now, which means you can begin to 'practise' your newly thought out behaviour. Jim commented: 'In the group, I began to realize how I could rub people up the wrong way with my strange mixture of aggression and timidity. I began to change this in the group first.'

Dr Robin Skynner explained that in a group, there are more people to defend yourself against, and thus more dynamite to blow up your defences. 'In analysis you can keep your back to the wall for years.'

People began to experiment in different ways with themselves, explained a group therapist. One woman, for example, changed from being rather dowdy and withdrawn; she gradually began to use some makeup, dress more smartly, be more assertive. Group therapy is potentially less dangerous, explained Robin Skynner. There are more people to deal with the therapist who therefore cannot easily visit his or her own pathology on the patients. Charles Vetter, director of ACCEPT, where both individual and group therapy is practised, said that for some people it is better to offer groups because they may become overdependent on an individual therapist. Another aspect of the group support is that they, as a group, or individually, can always challenge the therapist.

The two practical advantages of groups is that this type of therapy is much less expensive and that group therapy is more available, especially on the NHS.

The major disadvantage is that the individual does not receive so much individual attention from the therapist. It may be useful to have some individual therapy for some of the reaons given above about suitability/unsuitability. Many therapists have stressed to me that people need different types of help at different stages in their lives, and this is nothing to be ashamed about. 'When I first went into therapy, I didn't want to know about anyone else's problems,' explained Joanna, now nearing the end of both individual and group therapy. 'In fact, I'm more consistent about regularly going to the group. I don't want to let the other people down.'

George had some individual therapy after a year in a group. 'The group was very valuable, but you can feel quite vulnerable in a group and it is nice to have somebody to yourself.'

How often and how long?

Analytic groups meet once or twice a week, other groups once a week. Sessions usually last one and a half hours, although some of the more humanistic therapies, Gestalt or encounter groups, may be open-ended. As with individual psychotherapy, group therapy often has strict rules about timing, not meeting members outside the group, taking holidays at the same time, treating everything spoken about in the group as confidential, notifying members of unexpected absences and giving at least one month's notice of leaving. And in most groups, there is a general rule about not meeting each other outside the group. Malcolm Pines explained that 'friendships alter the freedom people have in the group to explore things. These are not friendship groups.'

'We were encouraged not to meet outside,' said Antonia, who had NHS group therapy.

'It's a good rule, though it was sometimes broken, because it frees you to talk about anything and everything. If you start making relationships, it confuses things.'

What happens?

'At our first meeting, every single person said they didn't want to do group therapy,' recalled Antonia. 'It must have been very tough for the two therapists to conduct the group, with all that anger focussed on them. I suppose it was a way for all of us to deflect what was going on inside us.

'The time it took for people to trust the group varied. I and some others talked a lot from the start, and from the first meeting I found it gave me enormous support. I was *allowed* to talk about myself and my feelings.

'The tensions and the attractions between us also started immediately. One woman I liked a great deal, but there was also some tension, she was like a mother figure, and she recognized that when she said, "I've been a mother, I don't want that any more". One of the men immediately put up a wall in front of himself, and only after a year did it begin to come down. The group got very angry and frustrated with him. Another person just didn't seem to understand what was being said about emotions, but by the end of the eighteen months, he did.'

The initial sessions are bound to be painful; it is not easy to open up to strangers at the best of times, let alone when one is depressed and despairing.

'I was really worried about appearing silly,' recalled Mark, who attended a group because of his drinking problem. 'I wondered if they would all gossip about me behind my back. Socially I had never been good at letting people get close to me so the group was right for me. But after the first session, it took a lot of willpower to return the next week.'

'Once I got over my initial nerves, I found I could express myself,' explained Mavis, who attends various groups at ACCEPT. 'I needed to build up empathy and affinity with the other people. Otherwise I just retreated into my shell again.'

Jeremy wrote about his group, which he attended after suffering a nervous breakdown, in MIND's magazine, *MIND OUT*, December 1981: 'Their experiences are wide-ranging but we have one thing in common: we need help and support to cope with relationships. The group sits in a small conference room in armchairs for one and a half hours. Before the session and for the week after it, each member lives his own life and agonies. All is focused on that weekly session.'[2]

He makes an analogy with billiards: 'The group is a closed one so there is a feeling of confidence and security, but this feeling is tinged with doubt. The billiard table has a cracked wall so the security is not complete and confidence fluctuates. Each member is a ball and all the balls are on the table. The billiard cue symbolizes those forces within the group that led to actions, speeches and reactions within the group. During the session those balls crash, knock, glance off each other. That is to say, what is said, or not said, and how it is said, and the reactions of those who keep silent, are determined by the way the members react to each other at that moment.'

On one occasion, a member talked about the loss of his mother; and this led to others talking more generally about the subjects of loss, pain and bereavement.

'The more members or the more balls on the table, the greater the likelihood of something someone else says releasing some long-suppressed emotion.'

Joanna attends an open analytic group. 'It's a changing scene. There are eight of us, one or two have been in the group for years and years. One has returned after a four-year break. One man is very odd and I don't like him. One person came when she was taking great doses of tranquillizers and now she no longer takes so many. Another comes and goes without ever being really involved in the group.

'You do feel rather tentative to start with. There is sometimes silence for the first few minutes, or sometimes one member starts with some social chit-chat about their holiday, for example. Then the process becomes more therapeutic as, perhaps, someone talks about their unhappiness, or the therapist begins to draw someone out. There used to be one man who was gay, he said very little, made no impact on the group. You could almost visualize the huge barrier he had erected in front of himself, and that was his problem in the real world outside. We did try to draw him out but he just couldn't talk about personal things.

'The therapist tries to make connections, draws together common strands, parallels with each other's situation. He might link what I said today with what someone else said five weeks ago. Sometimes the analogy is rather tortuous and then we do say, "What the hell are you talking about. It doesn't make sense."

'There is a man in the group who I don't get on with, he keeps asking me about my childhood and his questions always seem very loaded. They make me very defensive. Then I realized he makes me feel like I used to with my brother. It can be a very draining process, a lot of feelings echoing around. Maybe, now, we can work towards a better relationship. It's amazing how safe it can feel, sitting there in a circle. I never feel ashamed of anything I say there, I trust the group.'

Several people mentioned the fear that in group sessions, they took up too much time by talking about themselves. Mavis said: 'I thought I was being selfish wanting something, some time, just for me. I felt I shouldn't take up other people's time. Then I finally realized that I wasn't there to get other people's approval. If they didn't approve, tough, and when I said that to the group, it was quite an achievement. I couldn't believe it was me who was saying it.'

'I really learned a lesson from expressing the feeling that I was hogging the limelight, talking too much,' said Antonia. 'And we all said it, men as well as women. It taught me that I am allowed attention, including my own. I've often used that lesson in my life since.'

She found the sessions highly structured, although the therapist did not direct in any obvious sense. 'They would never start the conversation, which meant there were often long silences, in the early days especially. But we never remained in silence the whole time. In fact, the better we got at dealing with silences, the less we needed them. I used to find them very unnerving, I would sit there thinking, "Someone's got to stop the silence, it had better be me." It's what I've done all my life, assume personal responsibility for everyone's well-being. I came to understand that it was a fundamental problem I had to deal with. I've conducted my whole married life, especially, on the false assumption that I must make other people feel good. I failed to recognize that other people, like my husband, are adults and autonomous.'

Sometimes sessions are very emotional, with at least one member spending the whole time in floods of tears. 'I got very upset about my husband on several occasions,' recalled Antonia, 'and just cried and cried.' Other people find it less easy to reveal their emotions to the group. 'I can talk about things on the surface,' said Janice, 'but it's harder to say what I really think and feel. Some people cried but I never could, it took me a long time to trust them. It often made me feel I'd missed out on a lot. Nearly all of us felt we hadn't lived up to the expectations of our parents, and two people had very similar family backgrounds to mine. And they also suffered from nervous aches and lack of confidence.'

'We were very orderly and well behaved, none of this confrontational encounter stuff,' said Martin, a civil servant who also attended a NHS group. 'People occasionally cried, got upset, but nothing freaky. I talk easily and tended to be pushy and rather angry about those members who remained silent most of the time. I used to feel I was doing all the work. I think it didn't suit two or three members who seemed quite incapable of talking about what was going on inside them. I think you have to be fairly together to take group therapy.'

The greater one's participation in the group, the more one will get out of it. So it is better to be as open as possible about emotions, for example, and also to be responsive to other people's feelings. The therapist (or therapists, as some groups are led by two people) play an important role in leading or conducting the proceedings, some in a more clearcut way than others. They help to create an atmosphere in which people can be open and communicative with each other, a truly therapeutic environment.

Marian, who is in an analytic group of nine members and the leader, said: 'What tends to happen is that people remain in silence at the beginning, then the leader breaks the silence. One of his jobs is to get things unstuck, as well as offering interpretations and insights. Sometimes one member will take up the whole session, and others will contribute their comments about that person's experiences or feelings. In one session recently, I spent most of the time talking about the fact that I had been attacked by someone the previous day. Inevitably it involved the whole group. The way the others related to the attack, their interest in what it felt like, the person's motives, their similar experiences, all helped me to work through my feelings and to feel stronger.

'Another session recently I related a dream I had had. The male leader, with whom I have problems, attempted to offer me his ideas about the dream. I rejected these ideas and explained my own ideas. He pointed out that my rejection of him seemed to be linked generally with my difficulty with men in some position of authority. It's too early to say whether that problem is being helped by group therapy.'

As in individual therapy, group therapy involves the powerful transference of emotion on to the therapist. 'I loathed the male therapist for months,' recalled Antonia, 'because, I realize now, he represented to me the figure of authority. In the end, I got to like him a great deal.'

'We had two therapists,' explained Janice, 'one was rather passive, the other more outgoing. I suppose that was deliberate. I didn't like the more extrovert one, I was really wary of her because she might have been my mother. I always got on better when she wasn't there.'

A group leader in Southampton stressed how powerful transference in the group could be. On one occasion, he had been ten minutes late, 'the first time in nine or ten months. One of the women screamed at me, said how could I leave them (her father was dying). But she was also speaking for the whole group. The group leader inevitably, at times, represents a parent to every group member.'

As well as focusing on individuals, the group leader, especially in an analytic group, talks about what is happening to the group as a whole, namely, the group process. He or she might comment on the fact that the group appears to be behaving very nicely in order to avoid being angry with someone. Inge Hudson, clinical psychologist, said: 'In the analytic group I lead, a particular theme builds up, perhaps on whether or not one should ever hurt other people. The group may reach the solution that it is never okay to do this, which I interpret as their meaning that we always have to be kind to each other in the group, individually and as a whole. I would explain this sounds like a very restrictive solution, without a lot of honesty, and that if enough trust is built up between people, then they can take the necessary hurt involved in the group process.'

'Our therapists certainly didn't intrude their personalities,' said Antonia, 'but they would confront us. If one or all of us were avoiding an issue, talking about something less difficult, they would point out what we were doing. They would often act as a focus for our hostility.'

James, a young businessman, went to a group led by a therapist trained in humanistic techniques and the growth movement (see Glossary). 'It was very informal, a case of lick it and see in the beginning. There was no great marketing of theories or any great expectations encouraged. It was the same core group for about eighteen months. Between eight and ten of us met once a week in the leader's flat for about three hours. We sat in a circle on the floor and usually the leader would go round everyone in the group, asking them how they were. Eventually, the focus would be on one or two people's problems. There was no obligation to talk unless one wanted to. He was very quick at spotting something indicative of a greater problem, like an argument between two members.

'After that "round", when one or two people might be feeling upset, he would usually give us some relaxation exercises. Or he might put some music on and we would dance a bit. We might discuss a common theme suggested by the leader – he might say, "Think about the last time you felt envious or jealous, ten years ago, or as a five-year-old child." We might split into smaller groups to have this discussion and to share those feelings. Or we might have some communication exercises, where you discuss with another person your reaction to what they said, and they then say what they think you really meant. The leader would also often say to us, "Okay, you have said what you think but what do you feel?"'

James admitted he had 'a real culture shock when I first went along. I didn't expect anything so involving or so dramatic. I had initially expected something like an analyst's couch. In fact, the group was very supportive and the process never felt glib.

'Early on, I liked to play out the role of the objective, detached observer. But after a time I couldn't help but become involved, however much resistance I put up. I found the psychodrama we sometimes did very effective. For instance, I once acted the role of someone's father to that person as a five-year-old child. For him, it stirred up some very distressing memories. Another time, I had had a very troublesome weekend at home with my parents, so we recreated it. It taught me a lot about the way I dealt with my parents, and brought out some of the unresolved problems since my childhood. But I also learnt, listening to others in the group talking about their parents, how close and supportive my family still was: I was really shocked at how bitter some people felt about their parents. Parents dominated the therapy every week. Over 90 per cent of people's problems seemed to be traced back to their parents and their childhood. There is a real continuation of passed-on hang-ups. My relationship with my father markedly improved in that eighteen months of therapy.'

Anthony went to a similar group; like James, he was not a hardened member of the growth movement. 'But I found I quickly acquired the ability to release feelings, it was a great way of unwinding at the end of a week's work. Most of us soon found it quite easy to cry or laugh loudly. Twice I think I opened up a great deal, feeling emotions very deeply. But I have such a sophisticated set of defences that I felt the emotions inside them, but couldn't let them out.

'In general, the men in the group were more reticent. Obviously, it's less common in our society for men to cry and they are less willing to touch. But the leader was a very good generator of emotion. He was also good at not getting too involved and, at the same time, not being authoritarian. He would sometimes talk about his own feelings.'

How group therapy helps

Anthony commented: 'I am definitely much more in touch with my feelings now, much more aware of how I usually react. If I get depressed I can look inside myself and admit I'm depressed, and try to work out why. I cope with stress better. I think that good therapy teaches you that life is a continuation, that most people are too involved in their feelings now, at the moment. They don't see today's depression as a stage to get through. It also taught me to accept the negative side of me, that it is sometimes all right to be angry or depressed. Therapy has taught me to recognize how I function emotionally, in the face of certain problems. But it has not taught me to overcome those problems. If I'm truthful, I think I got the most out of watching other people work and helping them. On some occasions people showed their emotions at their rawest. It was rather like a baptism of fire for me.

'I now understand that if someone has an over-the-top reaction, it may be nothing to do with you, but triggered off by an experience or emotion from the past.'

Asked to compare group therapy to his fairly limited experience of individual therapy, Anthony settled firmly for the former. 'I felt much more comfortable in the group. It obviously depends on the person concerned, but I found I could never open up when I had individual therapy. I'm still not brilliant at showing deep emotions, but the group helped me on the way. A group is also safer, you can hide up to a point. It was strange revealing things to them you'd never revealed to anyone before. I liked the informality and the friendliness. Groups also prevent you developing any narrow transference with the therapist.'

'I like groups, I feel much more comfortable than in one-to-one therapy,' said Marian. 'I feel much safer. There is too much intimacy in individual therapy. The same old painful problems come up, but I prefer dealing with them in a group. Groups build up great trust and confidentiality. People do learn to trust each other quite a lot.'

Inge Hudson agreed: 'I feel groups are very potent, at least as powerful as one-to-one therapy, if not more so. I think, also, that if you are interested in politics and in society's role in helping to create symptoms like depression, then groups are good. In my groups, I like people to make links between their individual problems and social issues. At least it can help shift the blame and the stigma from the individual. Generally, groups help with that feeling of alienation, members feel less alone. I think that some people are happier because there is less stigma, apparently, in going to a group, rather than having an individual therapist where they are the "well" one and you are the "ill" one. And, certainly, groups are a way of helping more people.

'Everyone brings their own ideas, their religious or spiritual beliefs to a group. You have to find a way of communicating with, and relating to, each other, it's like a microcosm of society. Groups can be very useful for learning about difficult subjects – sex, for example. In another group I was in, there was a very uninhibited woman who didn't mind in the least talking about her difficulty in having an orgasm. She modelled to the rest of us a way of talking frankly which permitted everyone else to talk like that.'

'What helped me most,' said Janice, 'was to realize that other people had problems, too, often a lot worse than me. I'm one of life's worriers but it's now under control.' She attended a group for nine months which may have been too short a time. 'I was only just beginning to open up when it ended. At first I admitted some of the emotions to myself, things I'd bottled up, but that made me worse.'

Therapy gave Janice much more self-confidence, which has been noted and rewarded with promotion at work. 'I've done so much better at work, I could never have managed so well before. I used to be very frightened going into a crowded room with lots of people, but I don't feel that any more. Even if the backache returns, I know it's tension and cope with it.

'It has made me much more aware of what I'm doing, I seem to change my pattern of thinking without clearly realizing I'm doing it. It's made me feel more of a person, I used to worry that my husband would leave me, not for any good reason, but just because I thought I wasn't good enough. I now know I'm not as bad as I thought I was.'

A considerable body of research work has been done into the effectiveness and benefits of group therapy. The therapists themselves are, perhaps not surprisingly, fairly optimistic. Robin Skynner remarked: 'I just know group therapy is effective. It's like asking me to prove that strawberries taste good. I see so much change in people. I often can't believe it's the same person at the end.' Malcolm Pines agreed: 'We're fairly happy about groups. A lot of people improve, though most people stay in the group with a lot of grumbling about how long it takes. People begin to "internalize" the group, they carry it around with them, hopefully making them more commonsensical and balanced.'

Dr Pamela Ashurst surveyed a sample of patients who attended group therapy in her department. She found that 90 per cent of them said the most helpful aspect was 'being able to say what was bothering me instead of holding it in' – unbottling. Three-quarters also rated highly their acceptance by other group members, the universality of early experience which was revealed in the group, learning from other group members and identification with others in the group. Most of them also welcomed the consistency of time and place, the regularity of the meetings, and their trust in the group conductors not to exploit them. Dr Ashurst explained that group confidentiality, trust and sharing may well represent an aspect of interpersonal relating that has been deficient, or totally absent, in their lives. And that rules about time and so forth 'are an unequivocal demand for personal responsibility, for oneself and towards others in the group'.

She also found that most of the people responding to her survey did not value advice or interpretation on the whole, 'but they greatly valued the exploration of relationships and the experience of personal interaction within the safe confines of a cohesive group.'

Inevitably, there were criticisms, mainly of inactive group conductors, the destructive and threatening aspects of unresolved group feelings, isolation felt by those people who could not disclose their real problems in the group, and the loss of other group members. Antonia recalled that two people in her group left and 'that was quite difficult for all of us to cope with, it was as if we had been rejected by them.'

The ending of group therapy was also very traumatic. 'I became extremely depressed in the three months leading up to the end, I was both angry and sad about it. I still haven't completely sorted out my feelings about that and now, having benefited so much from the group, I want to have some individual therapy. I'm constantly seeing changes in myself. Over the eighteen months I lost one and a half stone in weight and on the last day I had my hair permed and decided, right, this is the new me. I'm now going to control my life.'

Another member stressed the difficulty of coming out 'into real life' after the session. 'So many beliefs and emotions have been stirred up. You leave with so much going through your head. I'd often prefer to go straight home on my own, but it's hard to explain that to my boyfriend, who is rather jealous, anyway, of the group.

'He and others do not seem to realize that you're not in group therapy to make up funny stories and entertain people, but because you are having painful experiences and need to deal with them.'

Jeremy said: 'Group psychotherapy can provide a safe structure within which trust can develop the intensive relationships which a group engenders, can offer an "intensive course" on using one's own insight. Observing the reactions of others has helped me to learn to live with myself and others.'

Marian has also experienced encounter groups, which she found enormously helpful. 'I learned something about my being worthwhile. There was a lot of affirmation. It was very powerful to be told by the group that I was nice and loveable.'

Jill is a member of an analytic group: 'The safe therapeutic setting, which is so essential, allows you to express yourself with great honesty. You're given a great deal of support, but people are also very honest and questioning back to you. That is a part of the value of group therapy. Someone might say, "The problem is, you mentioned that last week and you're reacting in the same way this week." That can obviously be quite painful too. I have developed more tolerance for other people, I know myself and my reactions better, and that is helping me in new relationships. I am less easily hurt now by the fact that people may not agree with me, or are very different in outlook. I find it easier to express myself emotionally, I am suppressing less, though I hope not in any insensitive or brutal fashion.'

Joanna said: 'For me, group therapy has been a very intense experience, and very helpful. I have been able to understand better how people see me. It's given me the opportunity to work through my relationship within my family, to understand them better. It's certainly influenced the way I relate to other people.'

Melanie was in group therapy in a therapeutic community after several years of mental illness. 'Our group of five or six people met every afternoon. At first, I found it very strange and said nothing. I felt I was in a theatre, especially in the larger group I also attended. I enjoyed it until I had to become involved. Sometimes I would walk out, it just became too much. Gradually I found it useful. I realized I was not the only person in the world with problems, and the others accepted me for what I was. It seems to have given me some sort of hidden strength to cope better, for example, with my mother's death. Group therapy does bring out all sorts of feelings within you, including those you didn't want to come out. But the most painful are often the most helpful in the long run. I was pressurized into talking, I wasn't allowed just to be an observer.'

7 Counselling

'The light that a man receiveth by counsel from another is drier and purer than that which cometh from his own understanding and judgement, which is ever infused and drenched in his affections and customs.'

Francis Bacon, *Of Friendship*

Counselling is far more available nationally than psychotherapy. But, unfortunately, counselling has become a catch-word, used and misused in all walks of life. It has become a grand way of describing 'advice-giving': so the woman who sells makeup is a beauty counsellor, the person who advises on matching curtains and wallpaper calls herself a colour counsellor. Professionals, like some doctors and clergymen, offer themselves as counsellors often without any clear idea of what that means, and certainly without any professional training.

Counselling is commonly defined as advice-giving or guidance, (which is also the dictionary definition) and put forward as a more practical form of help than psychotherapy. But the majority of counsellors in the area of personal difficulties constantly stress the fact that they rarely, if ever, give advice, that they are non-directive.

The British Association for Counselling, a coordinating body which represents many counselling organizations at national level, defines the counselling task which is 'to give the client an opportunity to explore, discover and clarify ways of living more resourcefully and towards greater well-being.' The essence of all approaches to counselling, stresses the BAC, is skilled listening, without advice. Counsellors should be warm, genuine, concerned people, who never allow their personal troubles or feelings to intrude into the professional relationship (like all therapists, counsellors are encouraged to train and have some personal experience of therapy to enable them to do this). They should be non-judgmental. They are more than befrienders or emergency help-lines. Indeed it is questionable whether anything more than superficial counselling, in order to tide someone over an immediate crisis, can be done by telephone.

'My counsellor acts like a mirror, reflecting back the real me, and all the distortions which are causing me such distress,' said one client in her second year of counselling. 'She has a calm constancy and never feeds her own problems. It gives me a chance just to be me. I have begun to notice patterns of behaviour and habits, and begun to discard the ones I don't like.'

Done well, counselling is a very powerful form of therapy, and has been shown that it can be just as effective in helping people as psychotherapy.

Renata Olins, Director of the London Marriage Guidance Council, defines counselling as 'short- to medium-term psychotherapy, usually focused on one particular aspect of a person's or couple's life'. Counselling is about confronting issues which are often painful and difficult for the client to face, but which are at the root of their present difficulties. Counselling is not just reassurance, not comforting, not just a shoulder to cry on. Of course, when you are with a counsellor it is safe and acceptable to cry, but the counsellor may well ask you why you always cry at this particular point, when this particular topic is mentioned.

Marian said that she found her counsellor's concern 'very real, but importantly that concern and caring is matched with great professionalism. Having that space of fifty minutes to myself every week is wonderful. It's as if she had said to me, "for that period of time I am totally yours and whatever you say I will not judge".'

Benita Kyle of the Westminster Pastoral Foundation, an ecumenical organization founded by her late husband, defines counselling as 'the art of helping a person to develop his or her full potential'.

Rosemary Payne is a counsellor in Cardiff, working at a Well Woman Clinic and an alternative health and therapy centre as well as from home. 'I always tell my clients that counselling is to give them confidence. I think it's usually what they want. I never offer a cure, I don't give advice, I offer myself as a sounding board. I might try to help extend a client's range of options in life, but it is up to her to make the decision.'

Counsellors work in a wide range of settings: in the health service, social services, voluntary agencies, private practice. An increasing number of GPs and health centres offer sessions with counsellors; over 100 marriage guidance counsellors are working part-time in health centres.

Probably every higher education establishment in the country has its own counselling service for students and staff. Several counselling services have been established by churches or priests; the best known is London's Westminster Pastoral Foundation mentioned above, which has twenty affiliates throughout the country. One of the divisions of the British Association for Counselling is the Association of Pastoral Care and Counselling.

There is a growing recognition that stress in the workplace can be lessened and dealt with by counsellors, and commercial companies may have their own staff counsellor or use outside counsellors as consultants.

The largest network of voluntary counsellors is the 160 Marriage Guidance Councils. Most of the counsellors are

unpaid, but they have all undergone rigorous selection procedures and training courses. There are also the Catholic
Marriage Advisory Council and the Jewish Marriage Council
(I deal in more detail with marriage guidance counselling in
the next chapter).

It should, therefore, be relatively easy to find a counsellor,
wherever you live, and the fees charged may be considerably
lower than those charged by a psychotherapist. But
counselling is too often seen as the poor relation of other
therapies. Is it just a cheapskate form of psychotherapy?

Not at all. In fact, it is very hard to make a clear distinction
between the two; every time it seems the boundaries have
been defined, someone comes along to push them out of
shape again, to blur the edges. Like psychotherapy,
counselling's main tool is talking, and the relationship between two human beings. It involves gaining insight and
exploring meanings for feelings and events. There can be
more major differences of duration, training and techniques,
but there are also marked similarities.

Take time, for example. Counsellors rarely see their clients
more than once a week, but some do. Most sessions last the
classic fifty-minute hour. Probably the majority of clients
only see their counsellor for between six and eight sessions,
partly because of limited resources. Most centres and organizations have waiting lists.

But some clients are given, and gladly take, the opportunity
of much longer-term help, perhaps three, four, even five
years. Anne has been seeing her counsellor at the
Westminster Pastoral Foundation once a week for five years,
and 'occasionally twice at times of great distress'. She explained: 'The anguish lies buried so deep in me, it takes so
long to reach it and then to develop and change. There are
sometimes months on a sort of plateau, when you think
nothing is happening and nothing will ever change.'

Bill, on the other hand, went to a student counsellor for six sessions, after 'going through a difficult patch with two girlfriends.' He found the experience to be 'very good first-aid'.

Obviously, short-term, or crisis, counselling is a very different experience from anything long-term. In short-term work, counsellors have to be less concerned with finding out *why* someone feels as they do or what lies buried in the past that makes a person act in a particular way. There is less emphasis on (although not necessarily less awareness of) unconscious processes, such as denial, or resistance, or the Oedipus complex. It can be a much briefer journey.

Some counsellors have a very short training and have little experience of therapy, or anything to do with their own personal development. Training courses are usually part-time, lasting only a year. But other practitioners are fully trained psychotherapists, with a lengthy education in psychodynamic theory and practice. The Westminster Pastoral Foundation runs its own training courses, ranging from weekend workshops to a three-year diploma course accredited by the University of Surrey.

Brian Thorne, Director of Student Counselling at the University of East Anglia, and a partner in the Norwich Centre for Personal and Professional Development, a counselling and training centre, said: 'I believe it is essential that a therapist or counsellor undergoes some profound personal development whether that be analysis, psychotherapy or some other form of therapy training. He or she must always be extending the limits of their self-awareness.'

So counsellors may be as well trained and as skilled as any psychotherapist. Many have experience working in the 'helping' professions, for instance the social services or the church. The Isis Centre in Oxford includes in its counselling team psychologists, trainee psychiatrists, social workers, a clergyman, and counsellors with experience of educational and marital work. A very similar range of professionals work in the Westminster Pastoral Foundation and similar organizations, although in pastoral counselling services the practitioners usually include volunteers who may or may not have such a background, but who will have had some part-time training. Centres and organizations that offer counselling insist on strict standards of practice and ensure that all counsellors, whether professional or voluntary, are carefully and regularly supervised. These days, counsellors are rarely just enthusiastic amateurs or 'ladies bountiful'.

There is certainly less mystique surrounding counselling, it seems a more ordinary activity than psychotherapy. So it may also appear less threatening or disturbing to someone with a problem, but who is wary of seeking help. Helen Crisp, an American counsellor working in South Wales, said it was easier to call herself a counsellor than a psychotherapist in that area. 'It is a more acceptable form of help.'

Counselling is often removed from the medical model which many therapists retain. For example, asked what types of people they treat, analysts and psychotherapists sometimes reel off lists of diagnostic labels, go into details about psychopathology, borderline psychotic and so forth. Counsellors, on the other hand, talk more simply about people with problems in living or in relationships. The nearest they might get to a diagnosis is to use the word 'disturbed'.

Brian Thorne believes that counselling is a more 'open world' than psychoanalysis, more accessible to the client. 'Power is a crucial issue in analysis,' he explained. 'In counselling we hope we are enabling people to get in touch with their own power. The relationship between counsellor and client is, I believe, more equal.'

Such ideas of equality are at the heart of the therapy or counselling originated by American psychologist Carl Rogers (who then went on to devise encounter groups). It is called *client-centred* counselling, which tells it all. The client is supposed to be in control.

There are a growing number of people like Brian Thorne, who define themselves as client-centred counsellors. The largest group is probably to be found in the educational sector. The Norwich Centre is the only counselling centre which works solely on Rogerian lines, but it is practised and taught in many other centres and organizations. Rogers's ideas have permeated counselling generally: counsellors often use his terms and the National Marriage Guidance Council training has incorporated many of his ideas.

Carl Rogers trained as a psychologist in the 1920s, and his early clinical experience was very much rooted in the analytic tradition. But he soon rejected the use of diagnosis and interpretation.

The essence of Rogerian counselling is that while the counsellor goes *with* the client, it is the client's journey. Rogers himself has written that: '. . . it is the client who knows what hurts, what direction to go, what problems are crucial, what experiences have been deeply buried'[1] whereas, the analytic, psychodynamic view is that the client is in such pain because he does not know necessarily what hurts, what experiences and feelings have been deeply buried. Rogers has an essentially optimistic and positive view of human nature, a complete contrast to Freud's. In this and other aspects, any link with the analytic tradition is with Jung.

In his book *On Becoming a Person*, Rogers writes: 'One of the most revolutionary concepts to grow out of our clinical experience is the growing recognition that the innermost core of a man's nature, the deepest layers of his personality, the base of his 'animal nature' is positive in nature – is basically socialized, forward-moving, rational and realistic.'[2] Thus Rogerian counselling, in its theory and practice, is very much part of the humanistic tradition which underlies Gestalt and other growth therapies.

Rogers and his followers see every human being as unique, trustworthy and capable of completely fulfilling their potential. This tendency in us all to move towards fulfilment – a move too often thwarted and thus the need for therapy – is called the 'self-actualizing tendency'. Rogers does not totally deny any negative forces in human beings, but argues that with people, as with the whole universe, there is a constant move towards creation as well as deterioration.

Central to Rogerian theory is the idea of the 'self concept', that is, the self-image which, in so many people, does not correspond with the true self. This self concept is heavily dependent on other people's attitudes, especially those of parents, through everyone's natural desire for approval. As those in therapy constantly demonstrate, many people are brought up in an atmosphere of disapproval, rejection and censure. Inevitably, such an individual's self-image is affected and may, to the outsider, appear very different from that person's real self. A literal analogy is that of the person suffering from anorexia: asked to draw an outline of her body, she will always produce a shape which is vastly larger than her real shrunken body. Time and again, one meets people whose lack of self-worth and self-confidence supports Rogers's view. Nor is this concept in any way at conflict with what psychodynamic psychotherapists (especially those who base their views on Bowlby and Winnicott) see as a common cause of psychological disturbance – loss and rejection in early childhood.

According to Rogers, explains psychologist Keith Oatley, people develop of their own accord. 'They have their own sources of growth and rightness . . . What goes wrong for people is in the way that they are socialized. Parents know what is best for children, and will give or withhold love or approval according to whether the child does as they think best.' So children frequently stop acting as they really want to, and act according to the way they think will win approval from their parents (and in adult life, they react in the same way towards other figures of authority). 'Conflict, or as Rogers calls it incongruence, between what a person actually is feeling but hides, and what she thinks she ought to do, causes the trouble . . . Incongruence is anxiety, self-doubt and despair.'[3] So the Rogerian counsellor lays stress on entering the client's own world, with unconditional acceptance of that world, in the hope of helping the client move towards their real self, away from the false and troubling self concept, and towards self-actualization – that is, to go much further, and more comfortably, towards fulfilling his or her potential.

'Our approach is enormously concerned with a client's subjective reality,' explained Brian Thorne. 'That is what we value and completely accept. So often, it is the way someone feels about themselves, that they are completely worthless, for example, which makes their life so unbearable. We stress the need for the counsellor to be empathic and genuine. Can I really understand this client? How can I convey that understanding?

'Therefore, the expertise I hope I can offer a client is my ability to relate to someone and to help them understand themselves better. I am offering a particular type of relationship which should give them the chance of facing themselves in a different way.'

In *Individual Therapy in Britain*, Brian Thorne reiterates how important it is for the therapist to relate closely to his client: '. . . unless the person-centred therapist can relate in such a way that his client perceives him as trustworthy and dependable *as a person*, therapy cannot take place. The person-centred therapist can have no recourse to diagnostic labelling nor can he find security in a complex and detailed theory of personality, which will allow him to foster "insight" in his client through interpretation, however gently offered. In brief, he cannot win his client's confidence by demonstrating his psychological expertise, for to do so would be to place yet another obstacle in the way of the client's movement towards trusting his own inner resources.'[4]

In order to establish an equally balanced relationship, it invariably means that Rogerian counsellors never work with transference, though obviously they accept that it occurs. Brian Thorne explained: 'I'm clear in counselling that people are projecting all sorts of feelings and reactions on to me which do not belong to me. I would *talk about* that projection, and why it happened, but I would never *work with* the transference. That would be quite contrary to the trusting and egalitarian relationship I am trying to establish with a client. Transference would stand in the way of that.' A client said: 'There is no projection in counselling for me. My counsellor is fatherly, but never is my father.'

Similarly, Brian Thorne and his colleagues would see any dependence on a great body of theory as 'getting in the way' of the counselling relationship. 'I am not frequently thinking of the theoretical underpinnings of phenomena,' he explained. 'It would be like wearing a white coat, as some form of protection. Ours is a lighter garment, and intentionally so, though critics often accuse counsellors like myself of being superficial and facile.' Like many in this field, he finds analytic insights very 'precious and helpful' (he has studied analytical psychology and experienced personal therapy) but believes that if such insights are treated as if they are the bible of the human psyche, and therefore infallible, that can undermine a person's move towards self-actualization and be slightly demeaning to the client, 'however intellectually stimulating for the therapist'.

The goal of Rogerian counselling is that the client becomes a fully functioning person, that is, moving towards fulfilling their potential, their talents and abilities and towards greater knowledge of themselves. They will be in touch with their deeper feelings without having to censure them or being disturbed by that censure. Such a person would feel responsible for themselves and what happened to them, would value themselves and would become their own counsellor, having developed the ability to listen to their own feelings.

Megan went to a Rogerian counsellor feeling 'very inadequate' about every aspect of her life and herself. She was working part-time, looking after small children and trying to cope with a husband who was very depressed. The marriage had not been very successful for some years. 'I felt I was to blame for all this. But gradually, each week, I began to understand where so much of this feeling came from. My parents had never thought I was bright enough, however well I did at school. I would take home a string of 0 level successes, all grade 'A' but one, and they concentrated on wondering about why that hadn't been an 'A' too. They were never satisfied. Over the years I had come to feel I was never good enough for anyone, my husband, the children, friends. During the counselling, I worried a lot about whether I was a good enough client, taking up too much time.

'My counsellor has helped me to feel worthwhile, to accept my capabilities and to trust where I am. I feel responsible for my own life now.'

Who goes to counsellors and why?

Counsellors' clients are not very different in type, or in their problems, to psychotherapists' patients. They probably come from a wider class range because counselling is often free or very cheap, and more available. But the middle classes still predominate.

Helen Crisp works as a counsellor in Cardiff, Carmarthen and Swansea (until recently a therapeutic wasteland). 'Most of my clients are middle class but a few are working class. One man was pushed into seeing me by his girlfriend and, despite his resistance (he was truly averse to opening up about his problems), he did surprisingly well.'

At the Isis Centre in Oxford clients come from all age groups, although there is a concentration of those in their twenties and thirties, and a cross-section of classes. Its great strength is that it is an NHS resource with an open-door policy: no one needs a referral from a doctor or any other professional, and it is not attached to a health service facility like a mental hospital.

In the Norwich Centre's Annual Report for 1983, is the comment: 'In background, age and work situation . . . clients constituted as heterogenous a cross-section of the local population as could be imagined. They ranged from the professionally successful and affluent to the unemployed, from old-age pensioners to children, from graduates to those without any educational qualifications.'

The National Marriage Guidance Council carried out a survey in 1982 of 'the marriage guidance council client'. They found that clients were drawn from all social classes and all age groups. Class was assessed from occupation (present or former) so, not surprisingly, social class 3i (skilled, non-manual, such as secretarial work) predominated among women clients (25 per cent) and social class 2 (such as junior management) predominated among the men. When a marriage guidance council service was established in Salford, an area of Manchester with considerable social and economic deprivation, it was used by a good cross-section of Salford's residents. In a sample of clients, 10 per cent were found to be unemployed and a higher percentage of clients came from semi-skilled and unskilled classes than those using all marriage guidance services nationally.

It is hard enough for anyone to seek help through counselling; it can easily, though quite wrongly, appear as an admission of failure. But if someone is also poor, unemployed or generally feels inferior in class and education, then they are even less likely to go for help. But surveys like the NMGC one, stress the fact that counselling services can be used by, and benefit, anyone.

Unfortunately, like so many similar organizations relying on government and local authority grants, marriage guidance councils are feeling the pinch economically and often suffer from a shortage of counsellors; at the same time, economic hardship and unemployment are producing more and more potential clients. Also, in areas where local authorities refuse to finance them, marriage guidance councils may not be set up.

What are the problems people bring to counsellors?

A major reason people go to counsellors is that they are experiencing some difficulties with relationships, usually personal but sometimes at work. In her study of clients attending the Isis Centre, Susan Oldfield found relationship problems include problems with parents (for example, dependence on parents in adult life, or worries about an elderly parent becoming dependent on a daughter); marital difficulties (the most common relationship problem) and sometimes after a marriage breakup; difficulties with girl- and boyfriends, either a relationship ending or a need to assess and make decisions about continuing relationships; anxieties about adolescent or grownup children. A group of clients were concerned about relationships in general. One said: 'I have difficulty in forming a relationship with anybody.' Oldfield writes: 'For a variety of reasons, from self-consciousness and anxiety to irritability or excessive dependence, they all had difficulty in "getting on with people"; "forming relationships"; "establishing and maintaining personal relationships".'[5]

Janice, who is in her early thirties, went to the Isis Centre after her divorce and after another relationship with a man had ended. 'I was so desperate, very depressed and very miserable. I felt my friends were fed up with me. It was marvellous that the Isis Centre was there, free of charge and not needing any referral.' After several months, she felt much better and stopped, knowing that she could always return. She did, when she started another relationship which became very serious. 'I felt very scared this one wouldn't work either, so I went back to the counsellor because I didn't want to screw up this relationship. I had to sort out some of the mess in my head, the tremendous uncertainty and insecurity. My ex-husband was a very critical and domineering personality and he had almost destroyed my self-confidence.'

Helen Crisp listed the most common sort of relationship difficulties she sees: 'They have always wanted a lasting relationship and it never worked. The woman who is chronically attracted to the wrong sort of man. The woman in an old-fashioned marriage who becomes more feminist and is feeling stuck and downtrodden. Gay people experiencing similar difficulties or fears of admitting they are gay.'

Obviously, a major counselling resource for relationship problems is marriage guidance. Clients do not have to be married; they include gay people, single people, people who may feel depressed and isolated because they do not have a relationship.

Loss is a common reason for seeking help, loss of a spouse or close relative, or loss of a job. Similar emotions are aroused by the birth of a handicapped child or the development of a chronic illness, such as multiple sclerosis or diabetes, or the loss of part of one's body, for example, after breast cancer. Some people never allow themselves to grieve properly and it may be years before they realize they need help.

Mike lost his mother ten years ago. He had been desperately upset then, but had to return to work quickly and get 'back to normal'. Some years later, he suffered from regular bouts of depression and started talking a lot about his mother, and bursting into tears uncontrollably. He went to a local pastoral counselling service, on the recommendation of his priest.

Gillian had her breast removed two years ago and since then has made a complete recovery. But she cannot accept the loss of her breast and worries constantly that her husband will reject her, find her ugly, misshapen, have affairs with other women. A friend realized something was wrong when Gillian told her of her suspicions (quite unfounded) and appeared to be totally obsessed and jealous of a younger woman neighbour. The friend recommended a private counsellor.

At the Well Woman Clinic in Cardiff where Rosemary Payne works, she sees women whose concerns may be with physical problems, but the anxiety may be overwhelming and affect their emotional health. Along with the normal run of relationship difficulties, she talks to people with phobias, obsessions, depression, unworked grief, isolation. One client was recently widowed. He had moved house so his isolation was doubled, now that he no longer lived amongst familiar faces and streets. He was smoking heavily, drinking a little, and complained of tension headaches and a bad back. Older women who are depressed at the time of menopause also visit the clinic.

In her survey, Susan Oldfield found another group of clients' problems at the Isis Centre related to physical problems or particular symptoms. People commented: 'My physical health has cracked', or complained of being very tense, often using a lot of tranquillizers without much effect. Difficulties included anxiety attacks, phobias, nervous tension, and a number of people were seen with problems relating to work or study. Clients were anxious or depressed about not succeeding, their inability to concentrate, pressure of work, lack of self-confidence in work, a job they hated, inability to cope day to day.

As with all talking cures, counselling attracts clients who may have ill-defined, but very strong, feelings that all is not well with their world. They may have symptoms like depression, or anxiety, or they may just feel 'not right', unsure which direction to take in life. 'My clients often come feeling very boxed in,' said one counsellor. 'I felt as if I had to find the life flow again, it had been dammed up,' said a client. A forty-year-old man quoted in Susan Oldfield's study said: 'I felt a sort of general disorientation really. I didn't quite know why I was behaving as I was; a sort of general collapse of self-confidence. I was looking in myself for something to cling to, and finding nothing at all. A great, gaping well.'

Brian Thorne described some of the emotions felt by clients at the Norwich Centre. 'People come who feel they have never really had the chance to discover who they are, to take stock of their lives. I call it the "conveyor belt mentality", the sense of having got on, and you're now unable to get off, to change anything. People may feel they have a chance to change, and so come to us, at certain stages in their life, on retirement for example.

'People who have a desperate need for faith in things beyond themselves, but traditional religions don't offer what they want. They are searching for some spiritual meaning in their life.'

Jane is an artist, who started counselling with a counsellor at the Westminster Pastoral Foundation four years ago. She had become very depressed and tense, and found work pressures quite overwhelming. 'I was frightened of everything, and it was seriously affecting my painting. I was so much in distress when I went that I didn't care who I saw, what their theoretical orientation was. But now I am so glad I am seeing someone who takes into account my spiritual side, the "Other". She happens to be a Jungian. I find her approach especially helpful as I was so adrift. All I wanted in the beginning was support, but now I know and appreciate I have received so much more.'

What happens?

Some centres and organizations stress the importance of a thorough assessment before someone is assigned to a particular counsellor; in others, there is such a long waiting list that individuals are often allocated to the counsellor with the next available session.

'A client's journey begins with the intake session,' explained Benita Kyle at the Westminster Pastoral Foundation. 'That meeting should be therapeutic in itself, not just a history-taking. Right from the beginning, clients need to be received, heard, valued, enhanced by that experience. They discuss why they are seeking help at this particular time, then one asks them to tell the story of their life. It's a very powerful thing, to tell one's story. They may begin to see some connection with what is happening now. Throughout this hour or hour and a half, one is assessing what is the need, what can we offer, and has this person the potential for making use of this model of help. Someone may seem severely mentally ill, and we might ask him or her to see our psychiatrist. We consider and discuss whether this person, given the degree of damage or pain, is likely to benefit from counselling and from what type.'

Parry Oakden is a counsellor at the Isis Centre. 'In the first interview, the client will work out what they want. There is a range of possibilities. For instance, they may come with a very particular, very difficult problem. That is what they want to talk about and we may decide it needs only two or three sessions. They need reassurance *and* information, mainly. Other people want to know more about themselves, to probe and to explore their feelings. They ask, "Why am I like this?" Even if this is only short-term, say ten to fifteen sessions, it is more like psychotherapy.' In that first session, it might be decided mutually that some other agency may be more appropriate.

'The issue at stake in deciding what can be done,' explained Brian Thorne, 'is the counsellor's personal limits. If someone wants to change their behaviour in a very radical way – for example, to overcome shyness or a phobia – we may be able to help, but a more behaviourist approach might be more suitable and quicker.'

Similarly, if someone wants advice, does not want to take responsibility for themselves, prefers to be told what to do, is not capable of the reflective talking counselling entails, then some other form of help may be suggested.

Counselling is frequently short-term, partly because of the nature of the work, and partly because of the nature of clients' problems. It is therefore often more focused, takes a more problem-solving approach, than psychotherapy. 'We are a small resource and always have a waiting list,' stressed Parry Oakden, 'so there must always be an emphasis on finding a focus for the work.'

Jacky is a college lecturer in her late twenties. She moved jobs and towns two years ago, very depressed after the break-up of a long relationship with a man. Desperate to talk to someone, with very few friends nearby, she first went to her GP. 'I was very put off by his suggestion – the outpatients department of the local mental hospital. I also felt very angry. What did he think was wrong with me? Was he suggesting I was mentally ill? He seemed very unsympathetic. Luckily I persisted, and went to the student counselling service. But I could have been so put off that I might have given up the search for help and become even more depressed.'

She saw her counsellor for six weeks, once a week. 'Because it was crisis rather than long-term counselling, she was not so interested in finding out a great deal about me, or probing into my past. But she got me to talk about my immediate situation, how I felt about it, she rather discouraged me from talking about my childhood or my parents. The focus was very much on me and my relationship with men.' Counsellors will obviously deal with clients' past experiences if that seems appropriate and, as Brian Thorne stressed, if the client wants to go that way. 'The emphasis in counselling is to stay and go with the client, and to shine a light in the direction they are going.'

Counsellors tend to be more concerned with the 'here and now' than the past, though inevitably relationships, say, with parents, arise as a subject of discussion. 'I found the focus on me and mainly on the present very helpful,' said Jacky. 'My counsellor helped me to recognize the ambivalence I felt about the break-up of my relationship. I began to understand there was some good in it, too. She helped me split the guilt I was feeling from the grief.'

Because of this focused approach, the counsellor and client may in the first one or two sessions decide what the main subjects for discussion will be. Some counsellors will guide the talk more than others, but this may depend on how much the client wants or needs some guidance.

An Isis Centre client quoted in Susan Oldfield's study explained: 'We worked out what would be brought. At first, it was not quite clear. I got much more decisive as to what I would talk about . . . Very often it was to do with reassessing something. I would feel burdened down by a thought or a feeling. She would highlight different aspects of it . . . The counsellor suggested a different perspective, alternative views of myself, revaluing . . . We mainly concentrated on current affairs but with reference to childhood.'

John had counselling for about ten sessions after his divorce. 'It helped enormously. It was much more than talking to a friend. Every week we would go over and over again how I was feeling, my reactions to events. A lot of the time the counsellor didn't say very much but she would ask clarifying questions which would also clarify things for me.'

'The power of the attention he gave me was amazing,' recalled Sarah, who saw a person-centred counsellor for ten months. 'He focused so much energy on me. I had been receiving so little in my other relationships, I needed some nourishing for myself rather than giving it to other people.' Sarah originally went into counselling because she had problems in her marriage and with her mother. Quite soon, she realized that she wanted the counselling for herself, that she had 'lost her way' and wanted help in finding it. 'We worked on how I had got where I was, emotionally as much as literally, and who I was.'

As I have explained, person-centred counselling is exactly that, going *with* the client. A primary goal for this type of counsellor is to see, feel and experience the world as the client sees, feels and experiences it. This also means, as Brian Thorne writes, that 'there are no techniques which are integral to the person-centred approach. Person-centred therapy is essentially based on the experiencing and communication of attitudes, and these attitudes cannot be packaged up in techniques.'[6]

As with all psychological treatments, it is hard to describe how a counsellor talks to a client. Keith Oatley explains that the Rogerian therapist listens attentively, 'and takes part with the client in his self-exploration, which in turn reveals series of experiences and feelings that he had, as it were, lost touch with.'[7] Rogerians talk about 'reflecting back' what the client says, but it is rather more subtle than it implies. Oatley quotes an interchange between Rogers and a male client, transcribed from a tape recording of their forty-eight sessions together:

CLIENT: I certainly have felt recently that I have more respect for, more objectivity towards my physical make-up . . . It feels to me in the past I used to fight a certain tiredness I felt after supper. Well now I feel pretty sure that I really *am tired* – that I am not just making myself tired – that I am just physiologically lower. It seemed I was just constantly criticizing my tiredness.

ROGERS: So you can let yourself *be* tired, instead of feeling along with it a kind of criticism of it.

CLIENT: Yes, that I shouldn't be tired or something. And it seems in a way to be pretty profound, that I can just not fight this tiredness and along with it goes a real feeling of I've got to slow down, too, so that being tired isn't such an awful thing.

Some counsellors unfortunately seem to practise very simplistically and the 'structure' of their work creaks. Godfrey saw such a one, after his wife had died very suddenly. 'It was quite useful to air my grief, but she seemed to be working in a very clichéd way, saying, for instance, "I understand what you're saying, but I can't get at the feeling behind." She seemed to be stuck with what I said, and unable to get at any underlying assumptions or experiences. Sometimes her interpretations were helpful.'

Sarah found that she and her counsellor met on several levels, that the counsellor could support her, at times, unbearable pain and help her both to contain it and to learn to understand it, to cope better with her difficulties. She never felt she was reduced merely to being a client, as she saw it, as sessions were sometimes invigorating intellectual discussions, as well as emotional outpourings from her.

'I found his ability to articulate and clarify my thoughts and feelings enormously helpful and stimulating. I sometimes felt I was groping my way through an enormous fog, and he was illuminating the way. The work was usually very intense but then I am an intense person. He also seemed able to bear any level of pain. Sometimes I did very little but cry the whole session, or remain silent throughout. There was never any pressure to say anything.'

Counsellors work with present feelings and, if appropriate, link them to past feelings or experiences. Sarah, for example, was always talking to her counsellor about her feelings of inadequacy, her lack of self-esteem.

'Some of this became reflected in my relationship with the counsellor. About halfway through, I started worrying about whether I was a good client. I felt I was taking up too much of his time. It was how I had often felt in other relationships. But he reassured me and said it didn't matter how long it took. He always seemed to ensure that by the end of the session I would feel okay about leaving. We also discussed the end of the counselling and he said I would know when that time came. He was right.'

The counsellor also reassured Sarah that she did not 'have to go anywhere' in the counselling, that she did not have to change if she didn't want to. 'He said I was okay, it was very self-validating.' Counsellors hope that by accepting the client as she is, she may then have the courage to move on.

Sarah had always felt that she was not 'good enough'. Through counselling, she came to understand that this was linked to her feelings of 'black despair' and to work on the sources of these strong emotions. 'I often arrived at the session full of blackness, feeling self-destructive. Sometimes it felt like black slime oozing out of me.'

One day her counsellor suggested he should regress her back to the experience of her birth. 'It was the one and only time that I felt he was using a particular technique. Part of me felt a bit silly. I had to lie down on a mattress and he sat beside me. Usually we sat facing each other on chairs. Then it started to feel quite real. I became very upset and my breathing changed. He asked me to imagine what it was like for my mother when I was born.'

It may have helped that Sarah had once overheard her

mother talking about her terrible labour with Sarah, the pain over the two days that it lasted. 'I did get into her feelings, her fears, her resentment about the pain, her feelings of not being able to cope, that she didn't really want me anway. I had learned to look at the origin of these black feelings and though they did sometimes return after that, they were easier to cope with because they weren't nameless, not so frightening. I had pinned them down in some way.'

Some clients find that a very straightforward outpouring of emotion – fear, anger, jealousy, or whatever – is enormously helpful, to someone who is, as a counsellor described herself, emotionally neutral, but at the same time warm and empathetic. George went to see a counsellor because he had developed uncontrollable, and unfounded, feelings of jealousy about his girlfriend. 'The relationship was fairly new and going well, and I was terrified that my jealousy and my insecurity would ruin yet another relationship. The counsellor helped me to contain those feelings, to understand that my constant jealousy was a symptom of my insecurity which was something we would have to deal with. He also helped me to look realistically at what I could and couldn't expect of quite a new girlfriend.'

Counsellors certainly acknowledge the unconscious and its processes, though they do not work with them in the same depth as many psychotherapists. Discussion of dreams was mentioned by most counsellors I met; all agreed they would work with dreams if the client brought such material into the sessions. Similarly, some clients mentioned dreams. 'I sometimes brought dreams to my counsellor because they were so violent and so disturbing,' explained George. 'Then we talked about what that meant for me, but he always took the cue from me.'

Techniques from other therapies are sometimes used by counsellors. Rosemary Payne may use guided fantasy: 'I might ask someone about their daydreams or their nightmares. I might then get them into a state of deep relaxation and then "take them" into that situation they feel threatening, or I might talk to them in a positive way about what they fear. Perhaps they always feel palpitations when the boss comes near them. In deep relaxation, I will "bring the boss" into the room and their fears will begin to lessen.'

She believes it is very important to help people learn alternative and healthier ways of coping with stress or anxiety, so relaxation techniques form part of her armoury.

'So many of my clients lack self-esteem, so I use different techniques to build that up. I might teach them some assertiveness skills. I might ask them to write an account of themselves as if by their best friend. They're often surprised by what they find themselves writing.'

In discussing a particular difficulty, Rosemary Payne will move from focusing on it closely to distancing herself and her client. She might ask the client how they would feel about such a problem if someone else owned it. People are often able to cope better by distancing themselves.

Support is a vital element in counselling. As one client said, 'The whole process was like being supported while I learned to walk.' Dependence is not enouraged and, in a sense, support is only given on the understanding that the client will learn to walk on their own two feet, however falteringly and however long it takes to learn.

'I give far more support in the first few sessions and towards the end of counselling I work in a much more challenging way,' explained Rosemary Payne.

'I found the support very valuable at the beginning,' explained Marjorie who went to see a counsellor working in a health centre after her marriage ended. 'My counsellor was a middle-aged man, he was very gentle, a real kind of father figure. You could say he was like a very gentle, approving father. I was so ashamed when I went because I was in such an emotional mess and feeling so depressed. But he let me know I had every right to be miserable, that I shouldn't worry about being in such a state and reassured me that we could work towards my feeling better.'

Towards the end of the counselling, Marjorie felt her counsellor was almost over-supportive, too nice about her. 'I suppose it means I hadn't overcome all my feelings of inadequacy but as I felt stronger, I would have liked him to have been more confrontational.'

Lesley had a much longer, five-year analytically orientated counselling. She found the support essential, especially as she uncovered and confronted the sources of her pain. 'It never increased my pain. I would certainly have left my counsellor if I had felt unsupported. It was wonderful knowing that at least one person was on my side.'

Her counsellor was attached to a pastoral counselling service, which recognizes the spiritual aspect of human beings without in any way trying to convert or preach at clients. At the Westminster Pastoral Foundation, counsellors come from a range of differing religious backgrounds, Christian, Buddhist, even agnostic, but clients do not have to be attached to any religious sect or creed. 'Our model is strongly influenced by Jungian concepts,' explained Benita Kyle. 'We believe there is in all human beings a built-in drive towards wholeness and the ultimate truths. We work towards personal growth. The counsellor is a facilitator and works with the client on their journey.'

'One of the beautiful things about my counsellor was that she took into account the Other, the spirit, not just the material world. I found that very useful when I was so adrift,' said Lesley.

The Norwich Centre counsellors also place an equal emphasis on the spiritual, without being remotely dogmatic or evangelical (again the religious beliefs vary considerably). Janet was a client there and found this aspect tremendously helpful and fulfilling. 'The counsellor opened up spiritual experiences and interests I had when I was much younger. It gave an added dimension to my life, as well as another way of coping. He has also opened my eyes to spiritual experiences which are different from the Anglican traditions I was brought up with. I now practise meditation, for example, and am open to psychic phenomena and experiences. I used to be very rational and scientific, very closed and over-intellectual. If something couldn't be proved, it didn't exist. I have learned about things which I would have dismissed with scorn five years ago. It has opened my life up into very fruitful and creative areas, like music. I have started playing the piano and singing.'

How does counselling help?

'My work is much better,' said Jane, an artist. 'It is freer, more real, less what I thought the world wanted it to be or what I felt it should be. I used to think that if I lost all my tensions, and complications – that is, my ups and downs – I would never be so creative. But it's the opposite that has happened, my creativity has been unblocked.

'And,' added Jane, 'I have learned that it's not so terrible to be ordinary or mediocre at some things. Whereas at school I had been told if I wasn't good at something, it wasn't worth doing at all. It's quite valuable just to be ordinary at something. As to some of the symptoms I took to my counsellor, I've lost most of the paralysing fear and anxiety.'

Those clients who went in a crisis, in a sea of desperate emotions, like Mary after her husband walked out, stress the wonderful support of the feeling of being 'stabilized', that they had been helped to find the strength to go on with life.

Mary welcomed the fact that her counsellor happened to share her feminist views. 'It was more important that she shared my feelings about women than that she belonged to any theoretical school. I had thought I wanted to talk to her about specific circumstances, the end of a relationship, but it was more focused on me as a person, my feelings. It was good to have that time for myself and it certainly helped me to cope with my emotions and to feel life was worth living.'

Shirley went to a Rogerian counsellor for almost two years. 'It helped me to find my way, to work out who I was. The changes therefore were internal rather than external. But as a spin-off if you like, it has enabled me to cope much better with my crumbling marriage, which I'm not prepared to leave yet, and my not very good relationship with my parents. It's made me more understanding and accepting of them. At least I know I'm okay now. Friends have commented how different I am, that I behave differently, even look different, apparently. I've coped with considerable practical upheavals, and financial problems, in a way I would never have done two years ago. And I'm really enjoying my life, I take whatever turns up, I would say I have a much richer life and that I am very happy.'

As Susan Oldfield discovered in her study of the Isis Centre, some people are very disappointed that counselling is non-directive, that they are not told what to do. They want specific advice and guidance. However, many clients appreciated that their counsellor was warm, but also calm and objective, 'not imposing on the client, but quite open, and willing to contribute thoughts and ideas, prepared to be honest and to be quite active if necessary'.

Clients found that being given the opportunity to talk, being given a 'safe place', being allowed to drop the 'coping front', all very helpful. They commented that the counsellor could act as a useful catalyst, who triggered off thoughts and ideas.

'She noticed things that I didn't – that was most important.'

'The counsellor asked some very acute and penetrating questions. This was marvellous – like flashes of light.'

Isis Centre clients also valued being enabled to see their problems in a new light; being helped to 'create order'; making links in their life; being given positive feedback about oneself; being encouraged to become independent of the counsellor.

Some found their problems less overwhelming but no less comprehensive. Others objected to interpretations made by their counsellor, or the feeling that a certain theoretical framework was being forced onto them. Susan Oldfield suggests that some of their dissatisfactions might have been avoided if counsellors had been more willing to explain their thinking and the psychodynamic processes behind it, 'and to accompany their clients more closely in applying these thoughts to their lives'.

How to find a counsellor

In the Resource Guide, I list the major organizations and centres nationally which offer counselling. Information may be also available from a local health centre, so ask your GP. There are specific services oriented towards specific problems: bereavement, abortion, rape victims, battered wives, addicts, gay people, young people and career difficulties.

The British Association for Counselling (BAC) can put people in touch with their local branches throughout the country, and have information about specific areas of counselling, such as pastoral care or education.

Once again, I would stress with the BAC, that it is wiser to find a counsellor through an organization or centre, as it usually guarantees certain standards of practice and safeguards clients against exploitation. It also means counsellors, however experienced, are supervised in their work, or at least have access to other professionals to discuss work. Members of the BAC have to agree to a code of ethics, but many counsellors are not BAC members. It is probably better to avoid individuals advertising their services in newspapers or shop windows.

The BAC does have an accreditation scheme which counsellors may choose to do. Brian Thorne is a member of the accreditation committee: 'We hope it will generally raise the standards of counselling,' he explained, 'but it is not compulsory.' He understands that some counsellors object to such a scheme because it may seem to reinforce their *differentness* from clients, following the medical model, adding to the mystique. On the other hand, it can be reassuring for someone to choose a counsellor who is accredited as it ensures a certain standard. To be accredited, the committee has to agree that one's training (length of time, subjects covered, clinical supervision) is sufficient and that in practice, one is receiving sufficient clinical supervision or has access to consultative advice. The counsellor also has to demonstrate that he or she are continuing to pursue their own professional and personal development. Accreditation only lasts for five years, and then the whole process is repeated.

What advice would Brian Thorne give? 'Find a counsellor who is accredited to BAC. Get the opinions of other people, particularly those who've had experience of counselling. Try to find someone with some sort of institutional support, through an organization or centre. It is always useful to be given the opportunity of an exploratory session first before making any final decision about having counselling.'

'It is very important to find someone you like and feel right with,' added a client. 'The first counsellor I saw insisted on telling me in my first session what was wrong with me, my childhood, tearing it all to pieces. I didn't go back.'

8 Therapy for relationships

'Talking in bed ought to be easiest,
Lying together there goes back so far,
An emblem of two people being honest.

. . . Nothing shows why
At this unique distance from isolation
It becomes still more difficult to find
Words at once true and kind,
Or not untrue and not unkind.'

Philip Larkin, 'Talking in Bed'

'I find marriage a very strange institution. The facade we put up, individually and as a couple, disguises totally what the real relationship is like. You can never tell what even your closest friend's marriage is like.' (Simon, who had marital therapy with his wife after many years of marriage.)

An awful lot of people do not seem to be very good at close personal relationships like marriage. Britta Harding, a London social worker and sex therapist, believes there are very many people who must be living a 'twilight life' within marriage, often very depressed. Over a third of marriages end in divorce and many others continue in a rather unhappy condition. So it is hardly surprising that time and time again, relationship problems are given as the reason for seeking help from a therapist or counsellor. Sometimes people are depressed because they do not have a close personal relationship with another human being; they feel isolated, unloved. Many men and women are miserable and anxious because having 'achieved' such a relationship, it is not working well.

Individual or group therapy may help, if only giving you the opportunity to let off steam and discover that other people are equally miserable in their marriages. But if the main cause of your depression, or insomnia, seems to be something about your marriage (I include live-in or long-term relationships, but will call them all 'marriage' for simplicity's sake), then it may be more effective to see a therapist who specializes in relationship problems, and to focus on those.

This is perhaps especially true in cases where both partners would like the relationship to continue. If a woman's depression is treated by an individual therapist in isolation, and the major cause is her marriage, it may be like taking an aspirin for a headache caused by a brain tumour – the person, the relationship, will almost certainly die in the end. And if a marital or sex therapist feels, after the initial assessment, that the individual needs one-to-one therapy because his or her depression is as much to do with personal problems as with relationship problems, then they will suggest that.

Janet had been suffering from depression and anxiety for several years, since before her daughter was born. Her GP first prescribed anti-depressants, but she felt that drugs were not enough so she asked to be referred to a psychiatrist. 'He gave me yet more drugs but he also suggested that a psychiatric social worker should visit me regularly. She was more help than any of the pills because she got me talking about what was wrong and why I felt like I did. It soon became pretty obvious that my husband entered into the question. Over the years, there had been so many pressures, often caused by him. We'd moved home several times as he changed jobs; he was a real workaholic, very insecure about work. By this time he was running his own business which meant I only saw him late at night. The social worker suggested we try marriage guidance. Three years later, our marriage is much better and I am no longer depressed. We still have many of the same problems but we talk about them now and cope better.'

So many people do not ask for counselling early enough. Either they continue to receive pills for their depression (or some vague backache or insomnia) from a GP who never questions why they should have such feelings, or they act out their unhappiness by having affairs or drinking too much. Then divorce seems inevitable and the solicitor's office is the first port of call. Counselling may be considered at this point but very much as a last resort.

'Perhaps we might have been able to work something out if we had been helped earlier,' said one woman, 'but I couldn't bear to hear my husband complaining about me, saying how wonderful and sexy his mistress was, how he had never really been happy with me. However skilled the counsellor, there seemed no point by then in bothering, so we separated in anger and despair.'

Not that a counsellor would ever claim to have the power to heal truly broken relationships, but they can make the break-up less bitter, which is especially important when children are involved. But there is still a great reluctance to admit there are problems in your marriage, and to ask for help.

'There is so much stigma attached to saying you can't cope with your husband's infidelity or your wife's lack of communication,' said marriage guidance counsellor Frances Campbell. 'There is still so much shame felt about coming to marriage guidance.'

'I really was at the end of my tether, and our marriage was on the rocks, when we finally decided to try marriage guidance,' said Mary, who is now divorced. 'It really felt like an admission of failure. You know, you can't work out your problems for yourself, you are having to go and ask somebody, a complete stranger, to sort things out for you.'

'Any close relationship like marriage involves the very deepest parts of ourselves,' said Frances Campbell, 'and to feel that you've failed in a relationship means that you are bound to feel you've failed as a person in some way, so shame and fear are very common experiences for anyone whose relationship is going through distress.'

Most couples go through difficult patches in their relationship, so when is it time to consider outside help? Frances Campbell suggested: 'I think quite a good indication of when it might be good to talk to someone about your relationship is when you can't actually think what to do next, and when you need help to understand more about what's going on.'

During and after separation, people may find counselling or therapy very helpful because separation, whether it involves divorce or not, is like bereavement. Loss is a great source of stress and depression, and working it through with a counsellor may prevent more pain and more problems later. Zelda West-Meads of the National Marriage Guidance Council explained: 'After divorce, people may feel great stress. There is not very much social support for divorced people. They often find themselves acutely lonely and living in poverty, with the children acting out their distress.'

Marriage guidance

Marriage guidance councils are the major source of specialist therapy for relationship problems (*not* just marriage); there are 160 councils throughout the UK, with about 1850 counsellors. There are two much smaller marriage guidance councils for Catholics and Jews (see Resource Guide) and there is the Institute of Marital Studies, now a branch of the Tavistock Institute of Human Relations, which takes a very psychodynamic approach to marital problems. Outside London, there are some therapists who have trained at IMS.

Marriage guidance is an unfortunate term which leads to a number of misconceptions about the help you might receive. People assume counsellors will only see married couples; in fact, clients include people who are divorced, people who have never married, and homosexuals. If you go for help with an existing relationship, the counsellor will probably suggest they see both partners but for various reasons, practical or otherwise, they accept you may have to be seen separately.

A frequent misconception is that you will be counselled to save your marriage at all costs. 'I don't see it as any part of my job to save anybody's marriage,' stressed Frances Campbell. 'I think that would be an impertinence on my part. I'm not here to give tips to people on how to be happily married. If anybody's got some, I'd like to hear them.

'Counselling is to understand what's going on in the relationship, for both people; to find out what they want from it, what they hope for, what they fear is happening in the relationship.'

Gillian and her husband went to a counsellor after months of rows and miserable silences. 'It wasn't what I expected. I thought somebody would leap in and rescue me, sort all my problems out for me, sort of list them for me and say "look, look, this is your trouble. If you do this it will sort it out." It's not like that at all. It's more a case of, well, recognize it for yourself, see what your problems are. You can only sort it out, no one else can do it for you, but at least the counsellor can help you see it from different angles.'

Renata Olins, Director of the London Marriage Guidance Council, said: 'A man may say you're no use if you don't help me get my wife back. But if you can get him to turn it round and look at what has been going on in the marriage, and how things went wrong, he may learn a lot and may have acquired a lot of inner strength and confidence. That will help him through the divorce and in any future relationships.

'If someone tells me she has found counselling useful, that's good enough for me. We can't perform miracles, despite what people expect. Sometimes it seems as if people have substituted expectations of counselling for love potions.'

Marriage guidance counsellors do not (or certainly should not) tell clients what to do. They should be non-judgmental, accepting; they do not express opinions based on their own feelings.

'I am not here to give advice,' explained Renata Olins. 'I can enable you to understand why things went wrong and work towards making things better, whether that means staying together or separating.'

The point of such counselling is to help clients understand their difficulties and for them to make choices based on this understanding.

Frances Campbell said: 'A number of my clients have told me they were very surprised when they first came that they weren't actually told what to do – they half expected that I would listen to both sides of the story and then say well, now you can do this, this or this . . . carry on. In fact, it's very different . . . we all of us explore the situation together.

'Clients come expecting me to be moralistic, condemning, judgmental,' said Anne Green, a counsellor in South Wales. 'Some expected they would have to put their case to a panel of counsellors who would then take a vote. They wrongly assume we're going to apportion blame to one or both partners.'

Several clients expressed surprise about the type of people who were counselling. 'My counsellor wasn't much older than me,' said one woman from the Midlands. 'Like most people, I had thought she would be fifty or more, very middle class and smug with a happy little marriage. I eventually discovered she was divorced.'

'It really helped that our counsellor was in our age group,' said a couple from Berkshire, 'not a wise old owl like our parents. She had the same views on life as us and we found it much easier to talk about intimate things to her.'

With a few exceptions, all counsellors are unpaid volunteers, but the selection procedures are quite rigorous (over 50 per cent of applicants are rejected) and all training is quite lengthy and professionally organized. 'I was amazed when I realized they were trained,' said a woman who had, before reading about the training, turned down the idea of going to a counsellor. 'I decided to go then because they weren't the amateurish, do-gooding busybodies I had assumed they were.'

Joan Sullivan, who until recently was Head of Counselling and responsible for the training of counsellors, explained: 'We are looking for counsellors who can relate to others in an enabling way. If someone says they have had no problems in their life, there's a big query. What has happened to their interactions with other people if things have gone so smoothly through life? If they really have had few difficulties and therefore no opportunity to resolve them, then it will be very difficult for them to help others come to some resolution. On the other hand, if someone is very emotionally damaged, perhaps they are still going through their own divorce, they may need too much support because the work will cause even more stress.'

She explained that they are looking for people who come over as 'a real person – whatever that means', who may be struggling with some problems in their own lives but who have sufficient inner strength to cope with that. Academic ability is 'by the way, but they need sufficient intelligence to read and articulate, to feedback to clients. Warmth and empathy are important qualities.'

By and large, they select people between the ages of thirty and fifty, although there are exceptions. Marriage Guidance Councils are keen to encourage men to become counsellors, but it has always attracted more women. Men who counsel tend to be clergymen, teachers and social workers, who see counselling as part of their job, or who have jobs with flexible hours, for example college lecturers. Obviously, counsellors have to be motivated; nobody would consider doing it if they just wanted something nice to fill up a few spare moments between coffee mornings and afternoon teas. The training includes six residential weekends in Rugby, the national headquarters, regional training events, individual supervision tutorials with an experienced counsellor and discussion groups with other counsellors.

The training course focuses on theory and practice. Trainees learn some psychological theory and are trained in counselling skills. As well as learning to deal with relationship problems, they are shown ways of guiding their clients towards personal growth and self-understanding. During the training they are expected to read widely around the subject, to observe experienced colleagues at work and then, under supervision, to work with clients. Assessment is a continuous process over the two-year training period, involving individual supervision training reports from the residential course tutors and face-to-face evaluation with the personal tutor on progress throughout training.

An internal accreditation certificate is awarded when the basic training has been successfully completed and after three years' practice as a counsellor.

Even then, counsellors do not work in isolation; in most areas, there are regular (usually fortnightly) case discussion groups with other counsellors and three times a year, personal supervision from a tutor.

The NMGC stresses that it is an independent body, not attached to any sectarian, denominational or cultural institution. 'Its members are not required to assent to any dogma or beliefs, and in practice are drawn from all creeds and none . . . most, if not all, members would accept that it is based on belief in the autonomy of the individual, an awareness of people's needs for interdependence since "no man is an island" and on concern about human suffering.'

So the approach is client-centred, on the lines of Carl Rogers's work, and the theory is often based on psychodynamic principles and insights. The extent to which an individual counsellor works psychodynamically, or perhaps behaviourally, depends a great deal on their personal orientation. Some counsellors, for instance, choose to have their own psychotherapy as extra training, but others frown on this.

Clients

The NMGC did a survey of their clients in 1982 which showed that clients do come from all social classes, generally reflecting the population curve percentage breakdown with the largest number from social class 3, that is, 'skilled non-manual'.

Anne Green works in Cardiff where she sees clients both from the city and from the nearby mining valleys. 'On the whole, they are a very different type of client. Not surprisingly, city clients are more cosmopolitan; in the valleys they tend to have a very traditional view of marriage and they also have very close-knit families.'

A counsellor in North East England spoke of a working-class couple who first saw him three years ago, and then returned after a two-year break. 'They are both very violent, they both come here and talk about killing each other. I hope I've helped to contain this violence a little bit. He has spoken of his childhood, how he was illegitimate and pushed around by his family. That's no foundation for a happy marriage.

She had married previously when she became pregnant at the age of fifteen, and she married this husband just to get a father for her children. They are both totally uneducated and he's really rough, and I like them both very much. They can talk about their emotions and they recognize the repeated patterns from their own childhoods. He also understands the problems of being a stepfather, he always hated his own stepfather. Very educated clients are often more defended against revealing too much emotionally. They know the words to defend themselves with.'

The complexity of this case is typical of the problems brought to counsellors; when a relationship starts to founder, there are usually many gales which have blown it towards the rocks. Infidelity on the part of one partner is a common problem (a factor at least in a quarter of cases, the NMGC survey discovered), although that is often not the sole reason for difficulties in the relationship. Infidelity may well be a result, not the cause, of them.

Alison was married to James for fifteen years (they live in the Midlands). He was a skilled carpenter and she, after years of clerical jobs and bringing up their three children, was revelling in her newfound academic abilities. She had gained an Open University degree and was now pursuing a second degree at the local university. 'Then, quite out of the blue one day, I discovered that he was having an affair with one of my closest friends. I was devastated, it felt as if my whole world was falling in. He didn't want to talk to me about it, suddenly he seemed like a stranger. I didn't understand the way he felt, I thought we'd been very close, that we'd got on well and sympathized with each other very deeply, and suddenly I found that I didn't understand him at all and he didn't understand me. I felt absolute despair.' After several months of misery, with no communication between them, they went to marriage guidance.

Their case is unusual in that more commonly it is the man

who is surging ahead in his career, often leaving the woman feeling inadequate and unsatisfied. They may find their interests have diverged, apart from the children, and either or both may have an affair. 'In the first few years of marriage,' explained Zelda West-Meads, 'the man is more often extending himself more than his wife. It may well need painful adjustments later if they are to stay together. We often find that we need to work hard to restore a woman's confidence before she can extend that into the relationship.'

Inevitably if people marry fairly young, they change and develop a great deal and such changes may be painful. 'One would hope that some changes would take place in the personalities involved,' said Frances Campbell, 'and that may well involve, and rightly so, separation. We do have high expectations of developing ourselves and our personalities.'

She explained that people often come for help when a problem arises at a 'change point' in the relationship or a major event in life, such as the birth of a first child. Is the wife going to stay at home and be a full-time mother and wife? 'What happens when she gets a job? That's often a very difficult time for a couple. What happens if the husband becomes unemployed and stays at home all day, which is a problem that we're increasingly seeing. Or one of the issues that comes up again and again is that of being dependent and being independent.'

Quite often, it is the woman who is feeling trapped in the relationship and wants more independence. 'It's surprising how often it's the man who wants to keep the relationship going,' said Frances Campbell, 'and it's the woman who wants to leave. I certainly think marriage is just as important for men as it is for women.'

Although marriage guidance counselling is not applying Band-aid to wounded relationships, some couples contact them when break-up is imminent, if not a certainty. The outcome varies.

By the time Rosemary and Bob contacted their local marriage guidance counsellor (on the recommendation of their GP, at whose health centre the counsellor did sessions), she had left him because she could no longer cope with his severe depression and apathy. He had been made redundant once again and was staying at home with their child while she went out to work. 'The complete reversal of roles was very problematic. We each resented the other's situation. So I just walked out, I felt there was no point in going on.' They started with separate sessions, then went as a couple for about a year. They have remained together. 'Now we're really talking to each other again. We should have gone to her years ago.'

Gillian was pretty sure her marriage was over when she went for counselling. 'I needed confirmation of this and I also needed some support and help to sort myself out. I had huge problems with the break-up, and there were times I thought I must be going mad. I saw marriage guidance as a sort of lifeline.' Her marriage did end and she has since returned for more counselling. 'I had started another relationship and I was suffering from quite uncontrollable, and unjustified, jealousy as far as this new boyfriend was concerned. I needed to talk to someone who was an outsider, not a friend or a relative. I feel I could take any personal problem to my counsellor.'

Increasingly, counsellors are seeing people who are not in the traditional heterosexual partnership, or are not in any partnership at all. Some people want to talk about the fact that they cannot form any good relationship. One counsellor regularly saw a single young woman for several months, who thought she might be lesbian. 'In the end,' explained the counsellor, 'we decided, so what – it didn't matter as long as she could now cope with the possibility.' This same counsellor had a female client who was living with a bisexual man, and who was very anxious about his fears of commitment. Inevitably, the problems taken to marriage guidance counsellors do, to a considerable extent, reflect changing social patterns.

'We went through a phase when everyone seemed to be coming in with sexual problems,' said Anne Green. 'However complex the problem, clients always have to have some introductory difficulty. The complexities and nuances appear later.' When the problem is specifically sexual – for example, impotence or vaginismus – then the client will usually be referred to a counsellor who has been especially trained in sex therapy.

Is anyone unsuitable for counselling? Renata Olins explained that 'very disturbed people – and I would stress we are all slightly disturbed at times – cannot usually use what we have to offer. They usually need more support than a counselling session once a week. But it generally takes at least one interview to assess if someone is suitable for counselling.'

What happens?

'It was very hard at first,' said Jan, who had counselling with her boyfriend two years ago in Oxford. 'It wasn't the counsellor's fault, she's very easy to talk to, but we were both so distressed, especially me, I was on the verge of tears for the first few interviews, very near collapse. I think we went several times before it got to be a comfortable easy discussion. We had those awful long silences when you weren't quite sure whose turn it was to speak, and what you would say if it was your turn.' The man she lived with did not find it any easier as time went on, and eventually they separated and saw the counsellor separately. 'He's very shy about things like that anyway, he finds it difficult to talk about his feelings to someone close. The idea of talking about them to a stranger I think he found almost obscene.

'I find it's quite a comfortable atmosphere once you get

used to the idea. They even occasionally bring you a cup of coffee.'

'At the beginning I expected a miracle cure,' said Rosemary, 'but of course it wasn't like that. We would often leave her on a Thursday feeling much happier but by the following Tuesday, I could have walked out on him again and it was terrible to wait for the next session. My husband just couldn't express himself at all and I could no longer encourage him. But the counsellor knew how to ask the right questions.'

There is often instant relief when counselling begins because there is, at last, an objective outsider who is interested and concerned, and the opportunity to express freely strong emotions. Explained Frances Campbell: 'One of the things a counsellor can do is accept that there is a lot of pain and a lot of distress, and accept very unhappy, strong feelings and not be frightened of them, not want to change the subject, like friends or relative, might do. I think the accepting in the first place is calming for anybody and then, after that, you can begin to look underneath at what is really going on.'

That is where there can be much more pain, as feelings and situations are explored, and hard lessons learned. 'Counselling is about confronting issues,' said Renata Olins. 'Issues which are often painful and difficult for the client, and are at the root of their present problems. We are not here to offer reassurance, we are not a comforting shoulder to cry on. Of course a counsellor may offer reassurance and comfort at times, but it is not enough to do only that. We have to try to help people understand themselves better, to be aware of the psychodynamics in their life and their relationships.'

'It can be quite indescribably awful to confront certain aspects of yourself, that you either didn't want to know or weren't aware of,' recalled Jan, 'and to have to take more responsibility for what's happening. It's terrible to realize you haven't been straight with yourself, you've not been honest about your own feelings. I had an image of myself which I projected on to other people, and which I believed to be true of me, and in counselling I came to see that part of that was an illusion, and I had other feelings, quite shocking ones, I hadn't wanted to recognize.

'I had thought I was a very good, kind, helpful person. I never harboured nasty thoughts about people, I thought I always considered other people and saw things from their point of view. In fact, as far as my relationship was concerned, I had been pretending everything was okay and happy, that I was being my kind, concerned self, and what I was really doing was ignoring the problems of people close to me, especially the man I live with. To face them would have meant admitting that things weren't as happy as I wanted them to be.'

She explained that counselling was often 'very repetitive', going over the same ground but considering things from different perspectives. 'For a long time we were skirting round less distressing areas like talking about our childhoods and trying to understand ourselves from that point of view, what makes you feel the way you feel now, what's happened to you before to make you feel like that. Gradually, and chronologically, we got into the more distressing areas, the more recent past, the present misery.'

Some clients find talking about their childhoods equally distressing, but it is often essential to discuss past experiences to understand present difficulties. In this and other ways, marriage guidance counselling verges on psychotherapy. It varies from case to case. 'There was some delving into the past,' said one woman, 'but it was more about the here and now. However, I realized that a lot of my feelings now went back to when I first got married, and we needed to look at that.'

When Gillian went a second time, after her marriage had broken up, in order to try to control her feelings of jealousy, 'we went right back to my childhood, and my counsellor then said, "no wonder you feel like that". It was a great relief to begin to make sense of it.

'I liked the fact that she seemed to have no preconceived notions, ideas or set answers, but waited for me, focused on what I said and asked the right questions, gave pointers in the direction I should be looking. She might say "that doesn't sound very good, why are you in that situation?" She enabled me to make choices and decisions, and I left feeling much more confident, with greater self-esteem and ability to cope as a single parent.

'The focus was always on me, my counsellor was always very professional, I knew nothing about her life. But I felt very close to her and was very sad when the counselling ended.'

'Inevitably one encounters couples who have marriages very similar to one's own, and similar problems,' said Frances Campbell, 'and I have to keep clear what belongs to them and what belongs to me. Marriage guidance counsellors don't all have perfect struggle-free marriages.'

Bob and Rosemary wish they had tried marriage guidance years ago, they feel they learned so much about each other, their families, their relationships with other people. 'For me,' said Rosemary, 'it was like an analysis of me first, sorting me out, and only then the relationship. The counsellor was warm and concerned, but always very professional. I realized how influenced I had always been by my own family, far too much by my mother, and this had influenced my relationship with my husband. We talked a great deal about the differences between our families and the way we were brought up. In our family, we talk a great deal, but in his, they rarely express any emotions or talk about them. I know Bob felt disloyal talking with our counsellor about his mum and dad.'

Anne Green said: 'In counselling I try to help people

discover themselves, and in relation to other people. It's like helping them to put the bits of a jigsaw together so they can see the whole picture. Then they are in a position to make choices and decide to change if they wish. But I can't force anyone to change.'

Many clients said they saw their counselling as a great opportunity for learning, an educational as well as therapeutic experience. They felt they could take their newly gained knowledge about relationships into other areas, such as work.

Most people who remain in counselling feel they have benefited from it. 'It gave me so much confidence,' said one client, 'I left with more energy, the counsellor let me know I was strong enough to cope on my own.' A woman who finally separated from her husband said, 'I'd be in the same dreadful mess I was eighteen months ago if it weren't for my counsellor. She helped me see the problem from different angles, instead of the very narrow view that I had been seeing it from. And to see there were things I couldn't expect from somebody else. I couldn't expect my husband to change completely and he couldn't expect me to accept him as he was, continuing to be unfaithful.

'She gave me support and useful advice too. She laid down some pretty sensible rules for separating: don't see each other for a while because it's very difficult to remain on a casual friendship basis with someone you've lived with. She also suggested sorting out financial matters and sharing possessions, getting those things out of the way first, and not having stupid arguments about who owns the television set.'

The NMGC has carried out research into whether clients have found their counselling useful. In two-thirds of cases, counsellors were said to be some, or of considerable, help.

Although counsellors will see individuals without their partners, several counsellors and clients stressed that it is better for a couple to have counselling together. But this very much depends on motivation. 'I would be very careful about recommending counselling,' said one very satisfied ex-client. 'I think it is very important that both of you want to go and that no one feels pushed into it. I was very lucky that my wife also wanted the relationship to work. So it was a very valuable shared experience. We would talk about what happened in sessions during the week, it was really enlightening. We both valued the commitment the other made.'

In another case, where the couple did not stay together, the husband felt forced into it and continually resented the weekly sessions, often managing to claim some prior work engagement which meant he could not go. His heart was not in marriage guidance because it was engaged elsewhere with his new girlfriend. He was not even prepared to work at it in order to make the separation more painless.

However, there are inevitable criticisms. Some people want more directive help than the reflective, psychodynamic work most counsellors offer. Others found that counsellors, who naturally vary in expertise and personality, were too obviously using techniques or theories (one counsellor, a male, suggested to a woman client that the pencil she was playing with represented a penis, and she left, objecting to his unsophisticated and crude attempts at interpreting symbols). One male client found that, considering the state of collapse he was in, his counsellor was rather brisk and lacked warmth and concern. 'She immediately commented that this was the first time I'd had to cope on my own without a woman, suggesting, I thought rather harshly, that I was a wimp. She may have been right but I didn't think the first session was the right time to say that. I didn't go back.'

Similarly, a woman who went after her husband had walked out, was asked by her marriage guidance counsellor: Is being on your own so bad? 'It was a sort of pull yourself together message, which implied I was being feeble. I felt pretty feeble anyway. I went to another counselling centre where I received reassurance and the feeling that far from being feeble, asking for help was being quite brave.'

Obviously, like any group of therapists or helpers, marriage guidance counsellors vary, and there is always the risk of poor quality counselling (though all have the same basic training). In large cities and towns there is a wider choice of potential counsellors and professional advisers than elsewhere. As there is no matching of client and counsellor, inevitably some people just do not get on with each other. One major drawback is that most marriage guidance councils have a long waiting list, often five to six weeks, which is very hard for those people who feel despair and an inability to cope. A way of seeing a counsellor early on is to take a daytime appointment, which is always less popular than evenings.

In London, for example, there are about 400 people on the waiting list which can mean a wait of eight to nine weeks, but if someone is prepared to travel to the West End office, at any time, they may be able to see a counsellor within a week. Waiting lists can be even longer in other areas of the country.

Most marriage guidance counsellors work without pay, but because the organization is a charity (with some national and local authority funding), it asks clients to contribute what fees they can. The average number of sessions for most clients is nine or ten. However some will just have one or two (that does not always mean they are dissatisfied) and, far less frequently, some go for a year or more.

9 Sex therapy

'Sexual intercourse began
In nineteen sixty-three
(Which was rather late for me) –
Between the end of the Chatterley Ban
And the Beatles' first LP.

Up till then there'd only been
A sort of bargaining
A wrangle for a ring,
A shame that started at sixteen
And spread to everything.

Then all at once the quarrel sank;
Everyone felt the same,
And every life became
A brilliant breaking of the bank,
A quite unlosable game.

So life was never better than
In nineteen sixty-three
(Though just too late for me) –
Between the end of the Chatterley Ban
And the Beatles' first LP.'

Philip Larkin, 'Annus Mirabilis'

Never before, it seems, have men and women had such high
expectations of a good sex life. One survey shows that couples

marrying in 1970 had 50 per cent greater hopes of good sex than those marrying twenty years earlier.

Never before have men and women looked to sex as a provider of so many goodies – not just physical pleasure, but also as an expression and guarantee of long-lasting romantic love, and as a source of personal growth and fulfilment. Good sex will solve every problem and is the 'key to happiness', whatever that means.

However sophisticated we may be, we often think of good sex as, at the same time, natural and magical, and confront any difficulties in bed with despair, distaste or straightforward ignorance. 'In England,' said Quentin Crisp, 'incompetence is the same thing as sincerity.'

'Sex is perfectly natural but not naturally perfect,' explained Anita Blum, coordinator of London Marriage Guidance Council's sexual function clinic, a sex therapist and marriage guidance counsellor.

Counsellors and therapists are frequently confronted with couples who are very unhappy about their sex lives, either because of a particular difficulty (or dysfunction), such as impotence, or just general dissatisfaction. It is not always easy to disentangle the sexual and emotional elements of the problem: has the impotence, for example, led to the marriage foundering, or did problems in the marriage lead to sexual difficulties? Frances Campbell explained that: 'the sexual relationship is often the first to go when things are bad because it's very hard to make love to somebody you're extremely angry with. As sex flows out of a relationship, so sex is often only as good as the relationship at the time.'

In some cases, sex is only part of the overall problem and counselling or marital therapy may be the answer. If that helps the relationship – the lack of communication, the misunderstandings – then the sexual difficulties may sort themselves out too. If not, it may be useful to follow counselling with sex therapy, as Jacky and Mike did. They first went to marriage guidance because she was very depressed and he was working hard, which meant their marriage survived on a very slight foundation. 'The counsellor was marvellous,' recalled Jacky, 'and after a few months, things were a lot better. After six months, we had talked about almost everything with him: worries about money; time, which we'd never had enough of for ourselves as a couple; babies; work. Then he said was there anything else we would like to talk about, so I plucked up my courage and, turning beetroot, I said sex. So it was then decided that we would continue with him for another six months in sex therapy.'

Sex therapy as a specialist area of work has burgeoned over the past decade, ironically paralleling in its growth that of the 'permissive society'. Until the mid 1950s, the only form of help available was psychotherapy or psychoanalysis, with a tendency to see sexual difficulties as being primarily caused by psychological conflict between the will to enjoy sex and the unconscious fear of so doing. As such therapists only worked privately it was restricted to people with money or, if the problems were seen as deviant, to those receiving psychiatric treatment.

The psychotherapeutic approach is still used by some sex therapists, but is frequently combined with the behaviourist approach first devised by the pioneers of sex therapy, the Americans Dr William Masters and Virginia Johnson. In 1966, they published their book *Human Sexual Response* in which they reported on their research (the first of its kind) into the actual bodily changes which occur during human sexual response. They observed more than 10,000 acts of sexual intercourse between men and women, of all ages between eighteen and eighty-nine. They discovered that the male and female have a similar response and they divided this into four phases: excitement, when the penis becomes erect and the vagina enlarges and lubricates; plateau, when sexual excitement increases; orgasmic, when the man ejaculates and both man and woman have rhythmic muscular contractions; resolution, when the sexual organs return to their pre-excitement state.

Most importantly, they revealed the strength of female sexuality: that women, unlike men, are capable of multiple orgasms, and that, contrary to Freud's belief, women only have one kind of orgasm that is both vaginal and clitoral. This orgasm occurs whether the clitoris or vagina is stimulated, and through masturbating as well as intercourse. So much for the immature, inferior female orgasms. They also discovered that sexual functioning continues well into old age.

They followed up this research by devising a method of treatment for the most common sexual problems. This method aims to reduce anxiety, teach the couple new skills and attitudes to sex, and to improve general communication. It does not seek to dig deep for psychological causes, though the majority of British sex therapists do combine Masters and Johnson techniques with some form of counselling or psychotherapy; they treat the sexual problems within the context of the relationship and, depending on their theoretical standpoint, consider any psychological conflicts which may be involved. 'I would say that in almost all cases,' explained sex therapist Patricia Barnes 'there are invariably relationship problems, either as a cause or consequence of the sexual problem, and these come to light during treatment. Very few clients don't find repercussions within their relationship from the sexual problems.'

Like other natural functions, sex can be completely impaired by psychological processes, physical illness and social pressures. Problems with sex do not mean, as some people seem to believe, that the whole relationship is at fault. Couples can give up too soon, assuming they should part, suppressing their sexual feelings or diverting them elsewhere. They might blame each other – 'he doesn't give me an orgasm', 'she's frigid' – and refuse to take any responsibility themselves. They may sink into depression, regarding themselves as abnormal: 'Everyone else is coming seven times a night and we can't make it once.'

In fact, it's rare to find any man who hasn't been impotent at least once (just think of the effects of too much alcohol) or a woman who hasn't occasionally felt some pain during intercourse.

When might sex therapy help?

'Some therapists see specific sexual problems as just another symptom,' explained Roy Shuttleworth, director of the Family Institute in Cardiff where sex therapy is practised as well as family therapy. 'It's like the chicken and the egg, which comes first? If a relationship is working well at least on the sexual level, the emotional consequences may be good for the whole relationship.' But, as he explained, sexuality is often used as power within the relationship, both by men and women. A man, for example, may become impotent as an unconscious way of fending off his dominating wife.

When clients are referred to them, sex therapists will usually spend the bulk of the first session deciding whether the problem is primarily sexual and can be dealt with by Masters and Johnson techniques, or whether there are other, deeper underlying conflicts in the relationship. Occasionally, even serious mental problems might be detected at this stage. So often sex is used as a bargaining tool or a weapon, and may reflect other problems, such as lack of desire because another lover has come on the scene, or because a partner has been made redundant. If the relationship is rocky, and especially if people outside the relationship are involved, many sex therapists would be reluctant to offer sex therapy because the chances of it succeeding are immediately reduced in those circumstances. For example, when a woman is passionately in love with someone other than her husband, she does not really have any vested interest in the sex therapy succeeding. Counselling might then be recommended, if only to try to ensure as pain-free a break-up as possible. If they did then decide to stay together and still had sexual problems, sex therapy might be the answer.

Anita Blum stressed the importance of the initial assessment of the problem because success in sex therapy is very strongly linked to a correct assessment being made in the beginning of the balance between the 'psycho' and the 'sexual' components of the difficulties. If there are more psychological than sexual problems, sex therapy carries a much poorer prognosis.

A problem like lack of libido may well be hiding a more serious conflict. One counsellor saw a young woman who complained of this and asked for sex therapy. The initial interview showed that her real problem was her inability to resolve her very painful and guilty feelings about an abortion three years previously. A type of bereavement counselling was recommended; behaviourist techniques to improve her sexual performance would have been quite inappropriate.

Sex therapists stress the importance of finding help before the problem has become so intractable that it may have damaged the whole relationship. 'Unfortunately, I think Brits are less likely to define themselves as having a sex problem,' said Roy Shuttleworth, himself an Australian, 'or to seek help at a very early stage.'

'Don't wait until the sexual problem threatens your whole happiness,' advised psychologist Tony Lake. 'Seek help if sex is painful, or embarrassing or frightening, or has been unsatisfying for too long. If you can't talk about the problem with your partner, you need a third party to help you communicate.'

He stressed that the choice must always be up to the individual and if, for instance, a woman is perfectly happy with her relationship even though she does not have orgasms, she should resist the social pressures of being made to feel odd, if not pathological. 'I also warn people that they must be prepared when they start sex therapy, to discover that the underlying cause of the problem has nothing to do with sex, it's about their relationship.'

The stigma attached to not performing in an earth-moving fashion sexually can discourage people from seeking help when problems occur. Patricia Barnes ran groups at a London teaching hospital for non-orgasmic women. 'One of the strengths of the groups,' she recalled, 'was that the women no longer felt so abnormal. You know, people with sexual difficulties think they can be picked out in the street.'

In fact, as most general practitioners will tell you, psychosexual problems are very common. Masters and Johnson estimated that they occurred in 40 per cent of American marriages. An Edinburgh survey found that one in ten of women attending family planning clinics had sex problems.

Anita Blum said it was impossible to say how many people had such problems but that, in her experience of more than ten years as a counsellor, people are focusing their relationship problems more on sex. 'A woman used to complain that her husband didn't give her enough housekeeping money. Now she is far more likely to complain that he doesn't "give" her an orgasm.'

Clearly, the accent today on sexual performance throughout the media and society in general does not help to engender sexual confidence in many people – in fact, the exact opposite is often the case. Women may talk fairly openly about their sex lives to each other but in general men do not.

Who seeks help and why?

Some couples, or individuals, go to a sex therapist with a specific problem, possibly impotence or the inability to have an orgasm. By the time help is sought, the psychological consequences for the individual involved and the relationship may be considerable.

Mark met his future wife only a few weeks before having a circumcision operation (he was twenty-nine). They did not try to make love until some weeks after the operation because 'sex had always been painful for me,' explained Mark, 'which was why the doctors decided I should be circumcised at such a late age.' When they went away for their romantic weekend, sex was a devastating failure. Mark said: 'I was quite unable to have an erection and I can remember a feeling of suffocating panic, helplessness, then terrible frustration. Joan was torn between being sympathetic and feeling it was the aftermath of the operation, and wondering, she told me later, if I was gay.' His impotence continued for several months and he became more and more depressed. 'I went to my GP in the end but he just said "don't worry, it happens to me from time to time" and prescribed me some vitamin B tablets. They didn't have any effect and I was becoming quite desperate, especially as by that time we had decided to get married, when luckily a close friend recommended sex therapy.'

Mark was suffering from what is called secondary impotence, that is, he had functioned quite satisfactorily for some years before. Only a very small number of men have never been able to obtain or sustain an erection long enough for penetration. They account for the 10 to 20 per cent of cases of impotence which are caused by physical rather than emotional factors, and are very hard to treat.

Premature ejaculation, that is, 'coming too soon', is the most frequent male problem sex therapists have to deal with. If it is untreated, it may lead to impotence and inevitably the relationship suffers because the partner often is so dissatisfied that she 'turns off' completely.

Mary and Russell had a good marriage but from the

beginning, he had experienced premature ejaculation. One of the problems was that he suffered from arthritis and a very stiff back, so they always made love with him on top. They were unable to talk about her frustrations; he felt she only 'had sex for me' and she found herself tensing up every time and resenting his demands. Like so many couples, other problems arose, they were no longer communicating, he became very withdrawn and she, in desperation almost, had an affair. A relative suggested they saw a marriage guidance counsellor and eventually they decided to try, asking to see a counsellor who was also trained in sex therapy. 'It was a hard thing to admit we needed that sort of help,' said Mary. 'After fourteen years of marriage it's really galling to admit you can't make love properly.'

Gillian had never found sex with her husband very satisfactory. He was a 'premature ejaculator and quite unskilled'. She explained: 'I had never had an orgasm when we had intercourse, though I did when I masturbated.' She started having an affair with a man who 'paid me far more attention sexually and did all the things I asked him to do'. Her husband, in desperation, suggested they saw a sex therapist, but by this time the problems were far from straightforward, and they eventually separated.

Women who never experience an orgasm feel tremendous failure and it is the most common female problem taken to sex therapists. Some women have never had an orgasm, others occasionally experience one or only through masturbation or with manual stimulation, but never intercourse.

Over the past decade or more, it has become clear that there is nothing abnormal about women who only have orgasms when their clitoris is manually stimulated. An American researcher Sherry Hite discovered that only about a third of women could climax without such stimulation. But there are still women who, for various reasons, do not climax and therefore seek help. Or those who still believe, explained a sex therapist, the myth that 'fingers-only orgasms don't count'.

Some women may just need some basic teaching about their bodies and their sexual responses. 'It really is sometimes a matter of a lack of basic information about physiology,' said sex therapist Patricia Barnes. In her women's groups, she used a plastic model to explain this. 'People often have no idea about those parts of their bodies.' This ignorance may be linked to a feeling of inhibition and fear about sex; orgasms may be seen as 'letting go', an unseemly loss of control. And clearly a woman's ability to have orgasms is often bound up with the quality of the whole relationship, and the lover's sensitivity to her needs.

Two other common female difficulties are painful intercourse and vaginismus. Most women will have experienced painful sex at some time, but for others, it is always painful because they are not producing enough lubrication. There may be a physical reason, so, as with most of these problems, a physical examination may be recommended first.

Jack and Eileen came to a sex therapist because they had not had sex since they married, eighteen months previously. They had avoided full intercourse before the wedding for Eileen first found it very painful, and then impossible, as she had developed what the experts call vaginismus. This condition occurs when the pelvic muscles contract so much that intercourse is impossible. It may have a physical cause, but more often involves anxiety and fear about sex and penetration. Frequently the man becomes impotent as a result and some therapists would argue that such couples have deliberately chosen each other because they share the same fears and inhibitions about sex.

'I've gone off it.' One of the most common complaints sex therapists hear is the loss of sexual desire, or libido. Some people have never been interested, and their partner has become increasingly unhappy and frustrated with this situation; in other cases, the sexual relationship was fine and the loss of interest in sex by one or both partners is either part of a wider relationship problem or the result of a specific difficulty, such as painful intercourse.

If sex has never been very satisfying, one partner may have decided to 'give up on sex'. Just like our appetite for food, our appetite for sex is often highly sensitive to life's stresses and strains, anxiety about unemployment, for instance, or physical health problems, delinquent children or a burdensome overdraft. Every sex therapist has seen at least one couple whose relationship, usually marriage, has not been consummated; namely, the male has not fully penetrated the woman's vagina with his penis. Jean Glover, who practises as a psychosexual counsellor in a family planning clinic, believes it is often due to a phobic state, the fear of penetration. 'The woman just cannot bear the thought of something going into her, she may have conveniently developed vaginismus so that intercourse is physically impossible. It often centres around the fear of being split open and one's insides falling out.' Other people are afraid of pregnancy. There are also, even in the 1980s, those couples who do not know the basic 'facts of life' and who only discover they have never had intercourse when they cannot understand why the wife does not become pregnant.

'I sometimes wonder where have all the easy cases gone,' said Alison Clegg who runs the training course for marriage guidance counsellors in sexual dysfunction. 'Most people present with fairly complex problems.' However, many sex therapists find they have a high success rate with couples who seek help for the reasons outlined above.

'Getting people to admit to a sexual problem in the first place is a major task,' said sex therapist and psychologist Patricia Gillan. 'Once they have done that it's often plain sailing as far as treatment goes. I often see people who complain of phobias, but at the root of the phobia, like agoraphobia, is a sexual difficulty. GPs often find that complaints of low back pain, stress or anxiety are covers for poor sex.'

Sex therapists see people from a wide range of backgrounds, and all classes. Most therapists will treat individuals as well as couples, although if someone is in a fairly stable relationship, they would prefer to see them with their partner. 'I believe that there is only a very limited amount of work I can do if someone does not have a partner to go through therapy as well,' said Patricia Barnes, a sex therapist who has worked for several years in the NHS and now works privately. 'Partners are necessary to practise techniques and to give confidence. It's very hard to treat a man, for example, who is impotent if he does not have a partner on which to test out his new-found techniques and knowledge.'

Like all therapists, Patricia Barnes sees people whose partners (often the men) refuse to go to therapy. 'Again I am limited in what I can do, but perhaps I can help them sort things out in the relationship and help them give their partner ideas to try out in a non-threatening way.'

Jean Glover often does therapy with individuals, usually women, who feel very unconfident about their sexuality and perhaps have problems with orgasms. 'I help them to become more assertive, to be more responsible for their own sexual feelings, to help them grow up sexually. A classic case is the woman who feels like a mother rather than a woman, she has lost all self respect and self-confidence. If they can't learn to be women again, they can't be sexual beings.'

Like many sex therapists, Jean Glover feels that when a couple come for treatment they should have a commitment to the relationship working and to the sex therapy. 'They have to be motivated, though I always warn people that the treatment may not work and that they will at least know a lot better where they and the relationship stands. Sometimes it does turn out that I help them to split up. And sometimes, if I see them individually, one partner will admit to having an affair without the other's knowledge and then I have to say that I can't work with them under those circumstances.'

Misconceptions

People are often fearful of asking for help with sexual problems because they have strange ideas about what happens in sex therapy. The most common misconceptions, which every sex therapist I interviewed begged me to refute, are:
(1) You will have to perform sexually in front of the therapist and be judged. This never happens.
(2) You will have to appear in front of a lot of students throughout therapy. At a teaching hospital, you may be asked if one student could sit in as part of his or her training. It is *always* your right to refuse.
(3) You will be offered help through sex with a surrogate partner. There is one famous clinic in Birmingham which offers, though never imposes, such help. Otherwise there may be private therapists who would find a surrogate partner if necessary for those people with partners, but no one advertises such services. It is *not* part of mainstream sex therapy.
(4) You will have sex with the therapist. This *should never* happen.

An understandable barrier for older people is the possibility of being offered a therapist who is much younger. If you feel unhappy about this, or any other aspect of your therapist, then you may have to ask for a different person. As always, this will be more difficult to arrange if you are having treatment within the National Health Service.

What happens?

'As a sex therapist, my job is to improve a couple's sexual relationship – and there's a heck of a lot more to that than helping them put a penis into a vagina,' said Jean Glover.

If you go for sex therapy in Britain today, whether to a NHS clinic or privately, you are most likely to be offered a combination of Masters and Johnson behavioural treatment and, depending on your problem, psychotherapy or counselling. Some therapists concentrate more on psychotherapy, exploring people's feelings and anxieties about sex. Most sex therapists believe that they should aim to help people feel comfortable with their sexuality and improve the quality of their sexual relationships, as well as deal with specific sexual problems. Some may encourage sexual fantasies through studying erotic pictures and films, or imagination.

The National Marriage Guidance Council trains a number of counsellors (about 165 at present in 70 different places) to provide sex therapy, based on the techniques of Masters and Johnson. An important goal is to help a couple communicate with each other better, especially about their sexual feelings and needs. Anita Blum said that the sex therapist is primarily an educator, often giving out very basic information about physiology and a 'permission giver'. People might feel, for example, that sex is only right in the so-called missionary position, or that real sex only occurs with intercourse, that cuddling and touching always means they have to 'perform'. A man may secretly believe it is 'not nice' for a woman to enjoy sex.

Though the basic techniques are the same, every sex therapist aims to modify them to suit the couple's individual needs. Alison Clegg said: 'The skill of sex therapy lies in adapting a set Masters and Johnson programme to each couple.'

The first interview is of vital importance: each partner is interviewed separately for about an hour and a half, when a very detailed history is taken. They are asked about their family history and relationships, their childhood, their sexual experiences from earliest times (including sexually-linked games such as doctors and nurses) and parents' attitudes to sex, their present relationship, sexual preferences and feelings about their partners.

The therapist then has to assess whether the problem is primarily sexual or psychological; if it is the latter, then counselling first is advised in order to deal with the wider relationship or personal issues and conflicts involved. Some people have never experienced an intimate relationship, even with a mother, so they would never risk it, fearful that they would always be 'let down'. Counselling may help these people. If the problem is mainly sexual, the therapist and clients agree a contract about treatment.

'The beauty of this type of sex therapy, including the history-taking,' said Anita Blum, 'is that we don't pussyfoot around, we ask in some detail what works and what doesn't. Do you mind about that? What turns you on? Sometimes the woman will say for the first time, he never washes before going to bed or he doesn't clean his teeth. Or they worry that they're not having sex as much as the people they read about in magazines.'

Treatment always starts with Masters and Johnson sensate focus sessions. The couple are forbidden to have sexual intercourse, but told to concentrate on giving each other pleasure through touching and stroking each other (though avoiding the genital areas). 'No sexual intercourse doesn't mean no sex,' said Anita Blum, 'but it turns them into erotic beings, less goal-orientated. We take away the anxiety of having to achieve intercourse, and we get them talking to each other.' Another therapist said: 'It's like an ideal rerun of adolescence. We tell them sex is fun.'

'It was a great relief for us both when the therapist told us no intercourse,' said Marilyn, who went with her husband to a marriage guidance council trained sex therapist in the Midlands. Their sex life had become increasingly less satisfying, partly because Ron had always been a premature ejaculator, and they had become estranged from each other emotionally. She started having an affair and was then persuaded to try counselling.

Marilyn and Ron were told to set aside three evenings a week for their sessions. 'She told us that you have to give each other time for making love. She gave us sensible advice about the bedroom being warm and clean, and attractive, relaxing in a bath beforehand, locking the bedroom door so the children couldn't come in. The basic rules about touching made sense and got us talking to each other about how we felt and what made us feel good.'

They were told to ask each other for a session and were given permission to say no on the understanding that the asker should not feel rejected, but understand that each had a right to say no to sex. Marilyn felt this was the beginning of 'learning to have control of your own body and to have respect for each other's sexuality. It also meant we didn't take each other so much for granted.'

The rules were strict. 'If I had asked for a session,' explained Marilyn, 'I had to stroke and massage Ron for twenty minutes. He then did the same to me for another twenty minutes. It was a revelation to us both, learning to give and receive pleasure in this way.'

Ron said: 'At times I found it all a bit of a ritual, especially as any spontaneous sex was forbidden. I also felt we'd failed on the occasions we gave in and had intercourse.'

The ban on intercourse is partly to reinforce the importance of all that precedes it and also to take the pressure off having to 'perform'. Patricia Barnes explained that like many people, she uses 'the standard package of Masters and Johnson, plus some psychotherapy and a lot of common sense'. She stressed the importance of the sessions in therapy when the couple describe the sensate focus sessions, how they are communicating with each other, whether they have difficulty expressing their desires. 'It very much highlights what is going on between them. "Tasks" like sensate focus exercises can be diagnostic. For example, the therapist will ask *why* are the couple not massaging each other? Why does he refuse to masturbate? This then has to be discussed with the couple and worked through. They can learn so much more about themselves, before they put the pressure on to have full intercourse. It means they can develop a lot of sexual awareness, an understanding of arousal which is the most important. Intercourse, I always tell them, is "the cherry on the top".' She also said one of the biggest problems can be to sustain people's interest in just touching, and to encourage them to develop all their senses, through wine, music, lighting, perfume. Anita Blum commented: 'If people come back and say they didn't have the time to do the exercises, then we have to look at the unresolved anger or fear which is getting in the way.'

Gradually the couple are 'allowed' to stroke and massage the genital areas, perhaps masturbate, and specific techniques are taught for specific problems, such as premature ejaculation or the woman's difficulty in having orgasms. This may well include some basic sex education. Marilyn was shown slides of male and female bodies. 'We thought we knew it all, we were amazed at our ignorance. Why on earth don't they teach it at school properly? For instance, it helped so much to learn how a woman's body reacts to touch and changes during love-making. No one ever says the truth about bodies in novels, how women have a sort of erection on arousal. No wonder so many women don't have orgasms. We needed our therapist to tell us what to do, we knew we hadn't got our sex life right.'

In their particular case, Ron wanted to learn to control his ejaculation, so the therapist told Marilyn to sit on top of him (he also had back problems), but he was not allowed to ejaculate. That way he learned to control ejaculation and gradually learned to relax, instead of becoming anxious about his performance.

If the sensate focus sessions are not helping a couple, then the therapist may renegotiate the contract, Alison Clegg explained. There may be a switch for the therapist to a more full-time counselling role, in order to uncover any unresolved conflicts which first need dealing with. 'Behavioural techniques do have their limitations so we often combine counselling.'

Marilyn and Ron saw their therapist an hour a week for about six months. 'She often talked to us about our childhood experiences,' recalled Ron. 'Going back to our childhoods helped us to understand why we behaved as we do, or did, in every way including sexually. We gained a much better understanding of ourselves and our relationship, as well as a great improvement in sexual techniques.'

Anne and John had marriage guidance counselling first for several months, then decided they needed some help with sex. They had deliberately chosen a counsellor who was trained in sex therapy so he could continue working with them. 'He explained to us that he puts on a different hat. As a counsellor, he is a sort of chairman; as a sex therapist, he becomes very much more directional,' explained Anne. 'What was marvellous all the way through was his attitude, his kindness and the fact that he was a man, which was particularly important for John. It was vital that my very shy, retiring husband should get on with the therapist who, I suppose, was a sort of father figure to him.'

Anne said she had become very uninterested in sex. 'But I was also very unhappy. There was a building up of resentment and tiredness, after our first child was born, my lack of interest was a sort of paying him back. We could find no way through that sexual problem, though counselling had begun to help our relationship in other ways. We needed the discipline of an objective outsider telling us what to do.'

They also started with sensate focus sessions. 'In a way it was like going right back to the beginning of our relationship,' said Ann. 'I will never forget the first session, I can remember saying this is ridiculous, and being so embarrassed. Gradually we both realized it was rather nice. We also gradually found it easier to talk to each other about our sexual feelings and desires. We became so much less inhibited.

'One important lesson we had to learn was to be more balanced in our sexual relationship. I had always been the very passive partner and I had to change. I had always felt very inferior. It was also very important that we had to try to put those separate hours apart just for ourselves, and it wasn't always easy to find the time.'

They found that their therapist was enormously good at never making them feel guilty or a failure. 'It's so guilt-ridden a subject anyway.'

They stressed the importance for them of having the counselling first. 'The background to our sexual problems was so bound up with who we were, the pressures in our life, work and so on, I don't think sex therapy alone could have been so successful.'

Some sex therapists rarely use Masters and Johnson techniques but rely almost solely on psychotherapy. Madge and Jim were referred by their GP to a private therapist who works in this way, because Madge had no interest in sex. They had been married for two years and his main concern was not so much the lack of sex, but her depression. Both were seen individually and the therapist then discovered that Madge felt weighed down with guilt about an early sexual relationship. She was only fourteen years old when she had sex with an older man; she had enjoyed the experience but knew he didn't love her and so felt used by him. Then she discovered her mother was being unfaithful to her father and anything to do with sex seemed cheap and nasty. She married Jim because he loved her despite her lack of interest in sex. With the support of the therapist, and after some lengthy single sessions analysing these feelings, Madge was able to explain it all to Jim and they soon began to enjoy love-making. In such cases, a more psychotherapeutic approach is likely to have a more successful outcome.

However, some problems may be treated in a more straightforward manner; it often depends on the attitude and approach of the therapist you see. Jean Glover said: 'I use all sorts of techniques, I talk about my bag of tricks, because the problem is so often not purely sexual.' As a nurse, she stressed that her advantage is that she can examine patients. 'That is especially an advantage when a woman presents with vaginismus. I would recommend anyone with that problem to make sure their therapist can examine them.

'It is not just a clinical examination,' she emphasized, 'there is something about touch which is therapeutic. When I examine such a woman, I can put a finger in her vagina without hurting her, it's all very practical and down to earth, and perhaps I can then get her to put her own finger in. They're so thrilled when they feel able to do that, not so tense that it is impossible. You then build on that initial examination by sending her home with increasingly larger vaginal dilators. You also teach her control exercises, you encourage her, give her permission to enjoy it.'

Jean Glover said her approach tended to be very practical though 'the most important thing any therapist can do is listen. People tell you about their past, things they have been bitterly ashamed of, sexual abuse, it releases huge areas of themselves that have been so locked up. It can go a long way towards solving their problems.

'Premature ejaculation can be cured in about two visits. Those problems are the gems and for every one of those, you have a tangled relationship problem, lack of communication, unresolved anger, which is very difficult and painstaking to treat.

'I treat premature ejaculation in a behavioural way. It's rather like potty training. I think women have given men this problem. Male animals don't hang about, but women have discovered they enjoy sex and men have now to learn to control themselves and wait. I give men exercises to do, the squeeze technique (squeezing the penis in order to prevent ejaculation too soon) and these are done at home and usually very successful.'

Even when sex therapy successfully treats a specific problem, that does not mean the relationship is perfectly intact. Anxiety about the problem may have disguised more fundamental difficulties in the relationship.

Dave and Maria finally got referred to a NHS sex therapy clinic after months of anxiety and despair about his impotence. Eventually a social worker friend urged them to seek help as quickly as possible (Dave's GP had dismissed it as something every man suffers from time to time and refused to refer them to a therapist) and they rang round the various London teaching hospitals. Finally one clinic said they could go on their waiting list and would probably be seen in six months' time. 'Then someone cancelled and we were offered an appointment the next week. I immediately felt better, relieved,' said Dave, 'knowing that help was on offer.' They saw a male therapist, a psychiatrist, who used a mixture of Masters and Johnson and psychotherapy.

Dave said: 'It all seemed very pragmatic and practical, related to the specific problem. However, he made it clear that it was not just that I was impotent but that the two of us had to cooperate with each other. He reassured me that sex was not a matter of a good or bad performance, which is how I'd always seen it. There is no sexual standard to strive for, your body's your own to enjoy in your own way.

'After about two months of seeing him fortnightly and doing the Masters and Johnson exercises, things were pretty well in working order. But there was still a lot of insecurity in my mind – would it come back? – I still tended to be depressed about that, so we continued, at less frequent intervals, for another three or four months.'

Dave's impotence did not return, but the therapy had been quite traumatic for Maria. 'Once the impotence had gone, the spotlight was on me. I felt under tremendous pressure to be receptive to Dave, to involve myself in lots of sexual activity and I wasn't really enjoying sex at all.'

Maria explained that she 'found it very difficult to talk to two men in a room about my sexuality, about not being turned on. I felt very lonely in that room at times. I felt I'd done all the supporting, that I was like some sort of dummy being used to bring his sexuality back. I really liked our therapist, he was compassionate and understanding, but I felt there should have been a female cotherapist to help me. I do think men see sex very differently. On the other hand, it taught me a great deal about men and how they function.'

She was also reluctant to talk too much about her lack of orgasm in front of Dave in case it brought back his sexual insecurity. On balance, Maria feels the therapy was very good at dealing with Dave's impotence and that it has pointed the way in which they can go to improve their relationship and learn to communicate better.

'I think it's also a question of adjusting to marriage and being together all the time.' She has also decided to refer herself for individual therapy.

Groups

A few centres, like clinics in NHS hospitals, offer groups for people with sexual problems, but they are still fairly uncommon. The Women's Therapy Centre and similar organizations also offer groups or workshops on female sexuality. Groups are far more common in the USA and have been found to be very effective, especially for women who have difficulty in having orgasms, or have never done so. Anne Hooper has written a fascinating account of a workshop for pre-orgasmic women, *The Body Electric*, and advises on the setting up of self-help groups.

Patricia Barnes ran groups for women who had never, or rarely, experienced orgasms, when she worked at a London teaching hospital. 'Groups are very useful; they have educational value as women learn about their basic physiology. They help people to appreciate that they are not abnormal, many other women share their problems. They provide a splendid opportunity for changing attitudes and decoding myths.' For some women, it may be the first time they realize that clitoral stimulation is, for the majority of women, the only way to have an orgasm, or that it is not evil to masturbate. In these groups, women are encouraged to use masturbation in order to explore their sexuality, as well as have orgasms, and may be provided with vibrators.

Patricia Barnes explained that the women ranged in age and type, from the 'more traditional forty-five-year-old to the punky teenager. They gave each other tremendous support, especially if someone felt she wasn't doing very well.'

Along with Patricia Gillan and Susan Golombok, she did a study of the effectiveness of one of these groups and they discovered that 60 per cent of the women who had group sex therapy had 'increased orgasmic response', that is, they began to have orgasms when they hadn't before, or they had them far more frequently and with intercourse rather than just masturbation. These women also had more sex and their anxiety was greatly reduced. They also found that vibrators were 'a useful therapeutic device'.

Social skills groups can be very useful for single men who may be virgins or have never experienced satisfactory relationships with women. In such groups, members can practice difficult situations, such as asking a woman out, and learn to improve their behaviour. They may need some training in assertiveness and to generally increase their self-confidence.

How effective is sex therapy?

There is very little research into the effectiveness of this type of therapy, and therapists are on the whole fairly conservative in their estimates. Patricia Barnes reckoned that there are about 30 per cent of couples you would never cure, whatever method you used; 30 per cent you would cure whether you used sex therapy or a placebo like fennel tea; and about 40 per cent would do pretty well on the standard sex therapy package, once a week for about twelve to fourteen weeks.

'Obviously,' she said, 'the more carefully you select your clients, the more successful the results can be. They will not be so good if a couple has serious difficulties with the relationship or personality disorders.'

In a survey of 107 patients with sexual problems, Jean Glover found that factors such as the state of the couple's relationship and the presence of personal conflicts within one or both individuals, were more important than the presenting problem in determining the outcome of treatment. She found that there was improvement in 60 per cent of cases and the remainder were assessed as 'no change'.

She also pointed out that even when there was no change with the sexual problem, there was often a marked improvement in the couple's relationship. Other sex therapists have confirmed that an added advantage of treatment, whether or not the specific problem is dealt with, is often renewed closeness and better communication. On the other hand, if the couple were really bored and weary of each other, sex therapy wouldn't stand much of a chance.

Most of the people I interviewed felt their therapy had been enormously successful. Jonathan's impotence disappeared after two months of weekly sessions at a family planning clinic. 'I have extreme gratitude, my therapist probably saved my life, I felt such despair.' His girlfriend also said she would recommend the treatment and would encourage people to seek help as soon as possible, because 'sexual problems so quickly become entrenched and more difficult to treat'.

Kay saw a private sex therapist because her sexual relationship with her husband was so unsatisfactory; she never experienced orgasms with him, though she had with other men before they married. 'She was so reassuring that I was quite normal and that it wasn't wrong to want sexual satisfaction. So many women are sexually unsatisfied and feel unable to talk about it, especially with their husbands. Women don't stick up for themselves. It really helped that my therapist was a woman, I felt she could truly understand how I felt.'

Marilyn and Ron feel their relationship has been transformed. 'I don't know what sort of mess we would have been in without her,' said Marilyn. Ron commented: 'It's a shame that so many men must need this sort of help but are too proud or shy to find it. Our therapist was very unthreatening, we really felt she was our friend. She helped my wife to drop a lot of inhibitions and hang-ups. I used to think she just had sex for me, then I began to realize she enjoyed it too. She had feared I was too demanding, but therapy taught her that my having an erection didn't always mean I wanted intercourse. She learned that sex is okay and nothing is taboo.' Marilyn added: 'Sometimes we just go to bed early for a cuddle. Our "sessions" really helped us enjoy each other so much more, and it's still very romantic. Ron doesn't feel he always has to perform.'

Anne and John also found sex therapy helped their relationship considerably. 'I don't have the same hang-ups any more,' said Anne. 'I don't have the same negative feelings about sex, I want to have a go. I'm also much more loving to John and want to show that love sexually. I used to be so angry when he didn't respond to me. Now I understand better how he feels and he is more responsive to me. I think it helped him a great deal to have to talk about his emotions and to learn to express them more, as he comes from a family where emotions are never shown and never talked about. I wanted us to sort out our sex life because I realized that sex is a very good way of communicating emotionally without talking.'

She feels she would never become pregnant again if they had not had sex therapy, although they both accept its limitations and stress that 'we may always have to work at sex and we can always go back for more therapy, but certainly things have completely changed.'

For both of them it was very important that each was prepared to make such a major commitment to the relationship by going to a therapist. 'I feel it couldn't be the same if you didn't share it as a couple,' said Anne. 'If one of you didn't want to go, it could make things worse and provide another basis for resentment.'

Where to seek help

Many couples first consult their GP. Some doctors are very sympathetic to such problems and will usually refer them for more specialist help or, less frequently, offer help themselves. A number of health centres now have attached marriage guidance counsellors. A small number of GPs have done extra training in sex and marital therapy. But be warned: too many GPs still take the view that such couples are wasting their time. It's not so long ago that one of Anita Blum's clients was told to 'go and have a cold shower'.

'Remember that doctors are human too, and many of them have not resolved their own doubts and needs about sex,' said Tony Lake. 'Doctors are still too inclined to tell their patients what to do. Don't work on these problems with your GP if you don't like him or you don't always understand him, and he makes you feel inferior.'

On the other hand, a GP's advice may be sufficient if the problem is more to do with ignorance about basic anatomy. He may be able to usefully dispel some myths. In an article in *General Practitioner*, Dr David Delvin wrote: 'It is still true that large numbers of our patients think that any form of sexual foreplay is sinful – whilst others have never even heard of it. Not altogether surprisingly, a man who has such ideas may find it almost impossible to elicit any sexual response from his wife during intercourse, and so he may send her to the doctor with the complaint that she is "frigid".'

If you first approach your GP and he refers you to specialist services, he is most likely to refer you to one of the few NHS sex therapy clinics (growing in number, but still thin on the ground and most likely to be found in cities), or the clinics run by Marriage Guidance Councils or the Family Planning Association. Unfortunately all these may have a long waiting list.

All Marriage Guidance Councils will try to help with sexual difficulties but only about sixty now have specially trained staff. The London Marriage Guidance Council, for example, has between twelve and fourteen couples in treatment at any one time: it usually has a waiting list. Their sex therapists use modified Masters and Johnson techniques as well as counselling, if needed. You can refer yourself to these clinics, but you have to go as a couple, in a committed relationship (not necessarily marriage).

Brook Centres and other Youth Advisory Centres specialize in counselling young people, and there are several offering help with sexual difficulties.

There is also a wide, though patchy, network of private clinics and sex therapists, though there is no central register or directory, to provide addresses or, most importantly of all, supervise and check for cranks and charlatans. (The Association of Sexual and Marital Therapists has a register of centres and tries to uphold ethical standards.) Many private therapists are part of the wider 'growth' movement, including therapies such as encounter and Gestalt. The majority are sound and should help. Some will use behavioural techniques such as Masters and Johnson, other may include, or focus on, techniques from psychotherapy or one of the alternative therapies. If this approach appeals, or there is no other clinic in your area, you could ask your GP, the Family Planning Clinic or Marriage Guidance Council for contacts. The British Association for Counselling also publishes a directory of agencies offering help for psychosexual problems.

Do not be ashamed to ask for help and, if you do, be prepared to put work and effort into sorting out these problems. 'What other equally important activity,' asks Anita Blum, 'would you expect to do so well with as little time and energy as most couples married or living together, allow themselves for making love? I always ask couples how much time in the week they consciously timetable for each other, alone together. We make more effort for friends, even casual acquaintances, than we do for our partners.'

10 How to find a therapist

Having acknowledged that things are not right in their world, many people will first make an appointment with their doctor. What happens next depends to a considerable extent on the individual doctor's attitude to psychological problems. (Is he or she sensitive to picking up such difficulties, or does the doctor feel happier treating the most problematic physical condition rather than psychic pain?) GPs have become increasingly aware of their patients' psychological needs and now have at least a very basic training in this area. Some are skilled and interested enough to offer themselves as counsellor, either within the dreaded time limits of general practice or by offering extended appointments to such patients. Other family doctors prefer to use practitioners such as marriage guidance counsellors or psychotherapists.

But there is still, I regret to say, a distinct possibility that such a patient, depressed, anxious, not sleeping, will be offered medication – whether tranquillizers or anti-depressants – and little else. It takes very little time to write out a prescription, so these psychotropic drugs seem a boon to the GP with a packed waiting room. And many doctors do not feel equipped to help in any other way. One of the major criticisms of medical education, from within and outside the medical profession, is the fact that it hardly touches on human relationships, or psychological problems, or the apparently simple task of communicating with another human being.

Of those patients who have a psychological problem, only about 10 per cent are referred by the GP to the specialist psychiatric services. Once again, if you see a psychiatrist in an outpatients' clinic, you are far more likely to be prescribed drugs than psychotherapy. Drugs are the major tool of British psychiatrists, even though they deal only with the symptoms (and not always that effectively) and can never reach the root cause of someone's depression or anxiety. Mrs Jones was sent by her GP to a psychiatrist because she was was so depressed and exhausted – not surprisingly as she had four young children, a very low income, her husband was unemployed and beat her up. 'But the doctor never asked me about my life or my problems, he just upped my tranquillizers and gave me some other pills.'

Psychiatrists in Britain do *not* have to undergo any training in psychotherapy at all. They have a basic medical degree and usually a two-year postgraduate diploma in psychological medicine. The majority of British psychiatrists believe that mental illness is primarily organic, caused by some as yet unknown disorder of the brain's biochemistry. The minority put equal weight on psychosocial factors as the cause of mental distress, and practise various types of psychotherapy. This group includes the small number of consultant psychotherapists, psychiatrists appointed primarily to train other psychiatrists in psychotherapy and to administrate NHS psychotherapy facilities. But at present, there is only one such consultant per 870,000 of population.

Drugs

It is important to mention drugs because they are so commonly prescribed (one in five women and one in ten men will take a tranquillizer at some point during one year, and one adult in forty takes these drugs every day of the year) and because they work in completely the opposite way from psychotherapy.

Tranquillizers, such as Valium, are mainly given to treat anxiety, but they can be prescribed for depression, insomnia, impotence, worries about a driving test . . . they have been prescribed for every problem under the sun. They do not cure the symptoms, they simply alter the person's mood and relax them because they dampen down nervous activity in the brain. One woman described it as changing her world from colour to black and white (she had been on Valium for twelve years but that's another story . . .). They relax the muscles, so that you feel better but also less alert, not to say drowsy (some of the sleeping pills are in the same family of drugs as tranquillizers, they are just tranquillizers taken in larger doses). But they can also make you feel more depressed. Major tranquillizers tend to be prescribed for more serious mental conditions.

Antidepressants are also commonly prescribed, such as the tricyclics (the brand names include Tryptizol, Tofranil and Anafranil). These drugs appear to act on the biochemical pathways inside the brain to restore the person's mood to 'normal'. Like tranquillizers, they have side-effects (a dry mouth, blurred vision, constipation, nausea) and they can take much longer to have any effects on the person's depression, perhaps three to five weeks. Then they might have a dramatic effect in lifting someone out of a depression, but many doctors feel they are useless if the depression is a reaction to an event like someone's death.

What none of these drugs do, tranquillizers or antidepressants, is to help the person confront a strong emotion like grief, and to trace it back to its source. After a spouse has died, many a widow and widower is permanently prescribed tranquillizers or antidepressants; but they never deal with the grief, the sorrow, perhaps anger, they are feeling. Most psychotherapists prefer their patients to manage without such drugs so that they *can* confront the pain, work through it, and, one hopes, come to some resolution and thus remove the depression or anxiety.

Maria had been having regular panic attacks for some

months and her GP eventually referred her as an outpatient to a psychiatrist. Unlike many, he is also a psychotherapist and began exploring her background, her family, her marriage and home environment. He discovered that there were many problems in her life and she had 'chosen' to cope with them by developing panic attacks. In similar circumstances, other people become depressed or may develop agoraphobia. He is now seeing her for psychotherapy.

Depression or anxiety, insomnia or migraine, are signs, warnings if you like, that all is not right. The person suffering from depression may or may not know what is wrong. It will take some time for the psychotherapist to help Maria to understand what the true cause of her panic attacks is, and only then to help her to try to make some changes in her life. Some doctors might argue that pills put someone in the right mood to consider change, but even if that were possible (and is being drowsy and numb the right mood?), most doctors do not offer their patients the time to discuss what changes are necessary and to offer the support needed through that change.

Whether you are confronting a GP or a psychiatrist, if you want psychological therapy rather than chemotherapy, you must be very clear on this point and may have to be persistent (admittedly not easy if you are very distressed, in which case you could ask a relative or friend to accompany you and give you support). 'My advice always,' recommended clinical psychologist Inge Hudson, 'is that the more clearly you say what you want, the more likely you are to get it. So stress that you want to talk to someone about your feelings or your difficulties, that you want to try to understand yourself better. Spell out the fact that you don't just want drugs.'

What is available on the NHS?

Unfortunately, the National Health Service does not provide a uniform nationwide psychotherapy service. It is often a matter of luck, and where you live, whether you will be offered a pill or a 'talking cure'. At the level of general practice, a growing number of GPs are aware of the need for a more psychotherapeutic approach. A few progressive individuals or groups in health centres offer sessions with a visiting therapist, or will willingly refer patients for psychotherapy.

This will usually be provided through a psychiatric out-patients' department or a hospital psychology department. Referrals almost always have to be made through a GP, social worker or another health professional, and the waiting lists may be several months long. Nor will you have any choice about the psychotherapist offered you.

In London there are some specialist NHS psychotherapy centres, notably the Tavistock Clinic. (See Resource Guide.)

There are inevitably many criticisms from professional therapists about the NHS's patchy service. Ron Lacey, MIND's campaign director, explained that generally there is a qualitative difference between private and NHS psychotherapy. 'In some psychiatric hospitals, anything which is not specifically medicine or occupational therapy is called psychotherapy.'

'It is a lucky dip who you see in the NHS,' said Dr Robert Hinshelwood, a psychiatrist and one of a growing number of NHS consultant psychotherapists. 'The NHS is changing its attitude quite a lot towards therapy, and many professionals are claiming they offer psychotherapy. In one sense, resources are so limited that anything is better than nothing. But I believe there is so much bad psychotherapy by people who have no training in it and no understanding of the principles behind it.'

Like several people I spoke to, Dr Hinshelwood pointed with some frustration to many doctors and psychologists who state that they and their trainees are capable of doing psychotherapy just by virtue of the training; as has already been pointed out, neither group have to have any specific training in psychotherapy, although many do. The point seems to be that, especially within the NHS, professionals must recognize their limitations and must work within a framework of a team where supervision and training are important. Certainly the best centres will offer this.

Derek Russell Davis believes it is not essential to have undergone a personal analysis to practise psychotherapy (but then he does not claim to offer analytic psychotherapy). 'I know the argument that your own analysis makes you alert to your own prejudices, but I also believe it can make you very orthodox to your doctrines, rather than continuously sceptical, as therapists should be.

'Supervision is very important. Therapists should always have someone else to report to so that they can be alerted if something is wrong, and so that there is a constant process of critical evaluation.'

'One of the major pitfalls in therapists who are not trained,' explained consultant psychiatrist and analytic psychotherapist Dr David Sturgeon, 'is that they may be tempted to befriend patients. But this can be dealt with in supervision.'

Because of the limited resources and constant threat of cutback, formal psychotherapy on the NHS tends to be offered only to people with serious problems: people who may well see this as their last chance; who might have been refused psychotherapy elsewhere; people who regularly overdose; who appear to have a serious mental illness, perhaps bordering on psychosis.

'We see people who have often been through other agencies like marriage guidance,' said Dr David Sturgeon. 'They have very difficult problems, some quite deep-rooted personality problems, extreme neuroses, behaviour disorders, perversions. Many centres and individual therapists would not feel able to help them.'

Limited resources also result in long waiting lists. It can

take a long time in the NHS system before psychotherapy is recommended. Mary, who is now forty, a quiet, nervous librarian, became anorexic thirteen years ago. She was referred to a psychiatrist and admitted to a psychiatric hospital. She was given major tranquillizing drugs and electro-convulsive therapy; the only talking treatment was a ward group twice a week and she was too drugged to talk and join in. She left because she realized starting to eat would get her out, but soon after, she fell back into her old ways as she could not bear her new 'fat self'. After that, she suffered from migraine and other stranger physical symptoms, such as her body becoming swollen. Various hospital tests revealed nothing and she was then referred to a psychotherapist. But he left after a few weeks and she was again put on antidepressants. Her GP referred her to a hypnotherapist but she did not find it very useful. Eventually three years ago she was referred to a psychotherapist within the NHS. She had to wait a year for her first appointment.

Most psychotherapy departments do long, careful assessments of people referred for psychotherapy. This will involve a discussion of what the person wants, some explanation of the treatment and time involved. Individual psychotherapy might be ruled out in favour of, say, marital or family therapy. Group therapy may be recommended, partly because the waiting lists are not so long for them. At University College Hospital, London, there is even a group for those people waiting for group therapy, as a sort of holding operation. Therapists are well aware of the problems of asking patients to wait for so long.

This is one reason why many NHS therapists choose to practice brief psychotherapy. 'I believe you can do a lot of work in twelve to twenty sessions, an hour a week,' said Dr Andrew McCauley from St George's Hospital in south London. 'The important thing is to identify a specific aim, to have some idea of possible outcome and to work towards change. I also recognize I have a limited range of skills and must only take on those patients my skills can help.'

Derek Russell Davis said: 'You can do an amazing amount to help people in a few sessions. Giving someone the chance to talk makes an amazing difference sometimes. Perhaps asking them about whether they have suffered a recent, or not so recent loss, the death of someone close, for example, can open the floodgates. I worked with one couple for an hour, we talked about their child's death. Some time later, I saw them again and they told me, "We've been talking to each other since then in a way we've not talked in twenty years."'

What type of individual psychotherapy is offered on the NHS? This again varies according to the individual therapist. I think it can be safely described as 'eclectic'; many consultant psychotherapists are analytically trained but the majority of psychotherapists will have learned it 'on the job', often attending training courses and working under careful supervision. Some, especially social workers and psychologists, will have had personal or group therapy.

Choosing a psychotherapist in private practice

Anyone can advertise themselves as a psychotherapist; there is no register of therapists, no agreed training or code of practice. So it is important to be cautious about choosing a private therapist. The main routes seem to be word of mouth, through friends or colleagues (this obviously assumes an openness on your and their part about the need for therapy), and the medical route, through a GP or psychiatrist. The latter may have some names of reliable therapists or groups in private practice.

If you have no contact with anyone in therapy, you could call your local MIND association or their regional office; they will not make individual recommendations but they do have lists of centres and organizations. The local Community

Health Council or Marriage Guidance Council might also give advice.

Before making your final choice, it is important to consider exactly what you want help for, and about how much time (and money) you are prepared to commit to therapy. As I have explained, psychodynamic psychotherapy can be almost as lengthy as psychoanalysis. There are sound reasons for this but if you do not want to embark on such an exploration of your psyche, then you should consider more focused work. Many therapists, analytic or otherwise, nowadays practise what is called brief psychotherapy and this can have excellent results, especially with specific problems.

It is obviously much easier to find a psychotherapist in a large city, especially in London. Organizations such as the British Association of Psychotherapists have members outside London, but only a scattering. BAP offers a clinical assessment and referral service for *analytical* psychotherapy. The assessment is with a professional experienced psychotherapist who will explore with the patient whether psychotherapy is appropriate and feasible; if it does seem so, then a referral is made to another professionally qualified psychotherapist. A fee is charged for this assessment.

Centres like London's Lincoln Clinic also have similar diagnostic sessions. Although psychotherapists are by no means always medically qualified, some centres insist that all new referrals are first assessed by a therapist who is. It also gives the individual an excellent opportunity to ask for information about what psychotherapy entails. Or to ask about alternatives, such as counselling.

The BAP assessors try to make a careful match between patient and therapist, although they are often restricted by geography and the shortage of vacancies. An example I was given was of a forty-year-old man who had anxiety attacks. He was still living at home with his parents and had no girlfriends. It was considered very important at first to match him with a very gentle person, male or female. There was a lot of 'early stuff' to work through and he needed many months of metaphorically 'being held'. (Later a more 'masculine' approach might be suitable.)

Some people will shop around and talk to two or three psychotherapists before choosing. You certainly have every right to do this, although the costs might mount up. Just as in analysis, everyone I spoke to, therapists and patients alike, stressed that the key to good therapy was the relationship with the therapist, so the initial choice is important. On the other hand, I have to say that the majority of people I interviewed stayed with the first psychotherapist they saw and were reasonably content with that person.

Obviously you are often at your most vulnerable when you are at the stage of seeking therapeutic help, so you must be careful not to be exploited, either financially or sexually. It seems safer to avoid any individual psychotherapists who advertise, unless they have been recommended by others too. Most of the therapists I interviewed would never advertise (BAP members are forbidden to do so). Some of the complaints made to MIND about therapists have concerned individuals who advertised their wares in the personal columns of newspapers or magazines.

In the private sector both BUPA and Private Patients' Plan will now pay for psychotherapy if it is recommended by a doctor. Both organizations have lists of psychotherapists, though I was warned by a leading analytic psychotherapist that their vetting was 'pretty cursory'.

'I think you have to use your own instincts, your intuition, when deciding if a therapist is right for you,' said one psychotherapist. 'You should also check out what training they have done, what courses.'

There is no nationally agreed, or statutorily regulated, training in individual psychotherapy. Certainly, anyone who calls themselves an *analytical* psychotherapist should have undergone their own analysis for several years (the BAP demands a training analysis three times a week for five years, the Lincoln Clinic three times a week for at least four years). Psychotherapists who are psychodynamic may have undergone a variety of training courses, at the Tavistock Clinic, Westminster Pastoral Foundation, the Institute of Group Analysis (although that only qualifies someone to take group therapy).

Many psychotherapists are social workers, psychologists, nurses or doctors. This does not mean they have done any lengthy training in psychotherapy, and many will not have undergone their own analysis or therapy. But the fact that they belong to one of these professions means they have to adhere to an ethical code and are subject to some degree of regulation by their colleagues. (If someone is inexperienced in therapy, for example a newly qualified psychiatrist, they are likely to be working under the supervision of someone more expert.)

The fact that a therapist is a member of the BAP, or is attached to one of the Centres listed in the resource guide, is some guarantee of competence and minimises the risk of exploitation. Unfortunately, because psychotherapy is such an ill-defined art, some charlatan therapists can argue that almost any activity can be therapeutic. Never believe any psychotherapist who says that having sex with him, or her, is part of the psychotherapy.

Whatever excellent qualifications or recommendations, a therapist must feel right for *you*. First impressions are often crucial. Mary had been recommended two or three before she chose hers. 'I went to see him telling myself it was just an assessment interview – assessment of him by me. But I immediately knew he was right for me. He is extremely warm, a lot aren't, though in my view they ought to be.'

A man who is now himself an analyst said: 'It was by chance I met my analyst but as soon as I met him, I knew he was right because he exuded that trust and confidence I was looking for. I felt he could deal with me but I didn't feel he was looking down on me.'

This man's advice is: 'Trust your feelings. It is valid to ask whatever you feel like asking the analyst. It is important not to feel intimidated and important to feel that the analyst is sensitive to what your needs might be.'

'Use your intuition,' said Ron Lacey. 'It's the quality of the relationship that matters; there is not a lot of evidence that very lengthy training necessarily makes you a better therapist or analyst.' He also quoted Jung: 'I didn't go to my analyst for love but for understanding.'

A Jungian trainee added: 'It's a leap of faith, there's no doubt about that. If the analyst gives you good feelings, that's all you can hold on to.'

'Don't let anyone tell you any school of analysis is better than another,' advised Gerhard Adler. 'The qualities of a good analyst, or therapist, are honesty and humility . . . and humour. Jung told some marvellously funny stories and I often do the same with my patients.' And he added, 'In my experience, everyone finds the right analyst for him- or herself. It's like the old Chinese saying: when the time is right, the teacher will come. And so will the analyst.'

Some practical and very important advice from Kleinian analyst Dr Pat Gallwey is, 'you must be honest to the therapist about your life. External circumstances, such as having small children, do matter when you are making such a major commitment of time and money. It should all be discussed. Do be frank about your life circumstances. Can you really afford it? Who will look after the children every day? Or will you be able to leave work early?'

Psychotherapy is, by its very nature, an unpredictable business and no psychotherapist can, with certainty, promise great changes or complete removal of symptoms. The research on its effectiveness is still very patchy (see Chapter 2) as is the work on any harm therapy might cause. Certainly some research has shown that the personality, attitudes, and general social adjustment of the client make far more difference to the outcome of therapy than anything the therapist can do.

The potency of therapists should not be exaggerated, commented a leading psychotherapist; on the other hand, she added, some therapists are incompetent and potentially harmful. It is widely believed that clients do not do well with therapists who show them coldness or hostility, who tend to ridicule them when trying to be challenging and who use their relationships with patients to satisfy their own ends. If your therapist consistently shows such personal traits, then it is worth considering changing to another. Nor should therapists be totally inflexible in their techniques, *nor*, stressed this therapist, should they set goals for the client which are inappropriate, unrealistic or not shared by the client. You may well be aware of this danger. 'Therapists who really care about their clients, and who are prepared to use common sense and flexibility, are at least unlikely to make them worse. It is perhaps when they take themselves or their therapies too seriously that they risk doing harm.'

Not surprisingly, research has shown that experienced therapists produce more benefits for their clients. They tend to communicate better, show more empathy, genuineness and positive regard for the clients, to take the initiative in therapy to a greater extent and to be less distant and exploratory in their interventions. In sessions, clients of experienced therapists are more directly involved and express more feelings. These clients are also less likely to leave therapy prematurely. And the few studies available indicate that experienced therapists get better results. However, they may not always be available or may charge fees above your price range. There are advantages in seeing a trainee or newly qualified therapist; enthusiasm (which rates highly in research studies on the outcome of therapy), more careful supervision by seniors.

Theory

Whether theory matters or not depends a great deal on the individual client. People who are of a more spiritual inclination might tend to choose a Jungian therapist or a counsellor working in a religious setting. Someone who is homosexual might avoid a rigid Freudian, who might see that person's homosexuality as an arrested stage in his development. Feminists might seek out a therapist with a feminist perspective.

Jean is in her second year of analytic psychotherapy. She advised: 'It's relatively unimportant to know about theory, but you should have some idea of what you are buying. For example, if you have a Freudian analysis, the view is that the major source of conflict lies between the ages of three and six, and the Oedipus complex is very important. A Kleinian will take you right back to your first year of life. Behaviourists may show no interest whatever in childhood conflicts. Good therapists will certainly not bandy round phrases like Oedipus complex, or self-actualization, unless it seems appropriate. Nor should they stick so rigidly to theory that every patient has to be forced into their world view. Behaviourists are less coldly scientific than is generally believed, and may well mix in analytic insights and counselling.

'I went to see a Jungian but it really doesn't matter what school he is. He could have been a nasalist – one who follows his nose – the theory is purely a method by which he gets into my material, dreams and so on, as far as I'm concerned.'

James was in Freudian analysis for seven years: 'I didn't know much about the different schools, though I was aware of Jung's mysticism and that didn't appeal to me. I felt that the rigidity of a very traditional Freudian analysis might give me the stability I needed and I was right. I found a woman analyst, she sounded very Germanic, like a music hall take-off of an analyst, that seemed quite right.'

Caroline who had been in therapy in the USA before moving to England, said: 'My first two therapists were Freudians and doctors, and I disliked both of them intensely and felt neither of them had helped me. After four years with them – two years each – I was still very unhappy and depressed. So when I decided to go into analysis it was likely I would not choose a Freudian. As a child I had always loved mythology so Jung was very interesting from that point of view, even though he himself is very difficult and unclear to read. I also felt he had a more forward-looking and optimistic approach than Freud . . .'

Those people who have read some theory beforehand tend to feel an affinity with a particular approach, like one man training in Kleinian analysis: 'It just feels right, what Klein says about early childhood fits in with my memories and feelings about that time.'

It is also important to remember that the writings and official teachings of the leading schools of therapy usually turn out to be much purer than the way they are practised. Therapists and patients/clients alike, judging from the experience *and* research findings, stress the importance of the right therapist, rather than the right theoretical school. Some people had no idea what theoretical school their therapist belonged to. One eminent Jungian analyst said he would always prefer someone went to a good Freudian than a bad Jungian (substitute two opposed political parties and you will appreciate the enormity of what he was saying).

A woman who went to a Freudian said: 'What mattered was that I trusted him.' A woman who went to a Jungian said: 'Any good therapist will base the therapy on the relationship that is formed with the client, not on ideology.'

Hazards

The main hazards of choosing a psychotherapist who lacks skill or experience, or is not governed by an ethical code, are outlined in MIND's guide to the talking therapies (written by Professor Derek Russell Davis). 'Some of those who seek help are not ready to talk about painful experiences, or their adjustment is too precarious for them to do so safely at the time. Clients may become unduly dependent on the therapist, or adopt the therapist's views uncritically. Sexual feelings are occasionally aroused during the work with the therapist, who may then exploit them. The therapist may take advantage of clients' dependency and exploit them financially or emotionally. He may not be scrupulous in keeping confidential what clients reveal to him. He may encourage or allow clients to make unnecessary disclosures about others. Failing to recognize the nature of an illness, and the limits of his competence, he does not advise clients to seek elsewhere other forms of help.'

Derek Russell Davis recommends another safeguard: tell someone else, such as your GP or a close friend, about what is happening in the therapy sessions – especially if something worries you. Also, from the beginning of the therapy, a contract should be agreed about the fees, when they have to be paid, and what intervals, how many, and how long the sessions are to be. Usually a small number of sessions are agreed and then the contract is reviewed.

MIND would advise people to be very cautious about seeking treatment from individual therapists who advertise in personal columns. You should be very wary of people who offer short-term cures. No reputable psychotherapist can, or would, guarantee to cure a specific problem, such as smoking or overweight, no matter how well qualified.

Ron Lacey advised: 'Don't be scared of checking up on someone's credentials.' If someone says they are a member of a body like the British Association of Psychotherapists, it is not difficult to check out. MIND does have a list of psychotherapy centres but has *never* given any formal approval to individual psychotherapists or any private agencies.

An American book, *Ethical and Legal Issues in Counselling and Psychotherapy* by W. H. van Hoose and Jeffrey Kottler lists the sort of unethical behaviour unfortunately found among therapists. These include betraying patients' confidences; promoting a feeling of dependence in a patient; trying out a new technique at the client's possible expense; the therapist bringing around the conversation to his problems; imposing personal values and judgments on the patient; using a client to get other referrals; telling a client he can be helped, even if it is unlikely, just for the money; and what are euphemistically called 'beyond the couch' relationships.

'A therapeutic relationship may well evoke extreme dependence,' admitted one English male psychotherapist, 'and this may take the form of sexual desire. And if a patient thinks someone is wonderful, he or she may obviously be vulnerable to sexual or financial exploitation. In turn, if a patient thinks you are marvellous, it is obviously pleasing to accept this. It may be that someone who hasn't spent time in self-analysis, in understanding his own boundaries, may succumb to advances by patients. But if a person says they would be perfectly happy if you slept with them, and you look very hard at it, you will probably find that is the way they have related to all important men in their life. By getting involved in that sort of situation, you would reinforce the problem, not cure it.'[1]

Whether sexual or not, the dependency some patients develop on their therapists, or rather the transference, to use the analytical word, is sometimes quite overwhelming, bordering on the pathological. 'People must realize that when they go into individual psychotherapy, especially if it is analytically orientated,' said Ron Lacey, 'they are very likely to evolve a very heavy dependence on the therapist. It may take the form of tremendous hostility, or something resembling love.'

Mary had been seeing a psychotherapist for over three years. She was referred because of years of depression and inexplicable symptoms. Her therapist is a psychiatrist at a leading London hospital and has agreed to treat her, once a week, on the NHS. She had developed tremendous dependence on this man, who, in turn, seems to have treated her very shabbily.

'He is the only person in the world I can really talk to. My father died when I was six and I feel very deprived of a father figure. My therapist is in his late fifties and quite paternal in his attitude towards me. But in other ways he is like a husband and I regularly have sexual fantasies about him. My life centres around seeing him and hardly a minute of the day goes by without my thinking of him. I find it very difficult to discuss this dependence with him. I once tried and he said it was sad but wrong, and that I needed to feel it at the moment. One day I would feel it for my husband. It must be very tedious for him to hear how strongly I feel and I am scared of making him angry.'

Clearly one could say that this is a clear-cut case of transference taken to extremes and that Mary is reacting to this man as she reacts to all important men in her life (and possibly women as well). 'He is my lifeblood to me, I cannot imagine ever not needing him.'

But her therapist is behaving very unethically, and untherapeutically, by frequently cancelling sessions. 'From Wednesday onwards (she sees him on Fridays) I worry constantly if the session will be cancelled. It makes my life a misery.' He has very occasionally just not turned up. Such irregularity, and betrayal of a patient's trust (especially one so emotionally disturbed) is considered unforgivable by most psychotherapists. Mary was becoming so upset by his unreliability that her husband wrote a very angry letter to the therapist on his wife's behalf. 'The next session after that, my therapist was furious. Fifteen months later, I'm still a bit frightened that he could be as angry again towards me. I still feel his anger killed something in me. He accused me of manipulating my husband to write the letter, I felt I was being torn up by the roots.'

Such overdependency is also a problem when psychotherapy is curtailed. Jean saw an NHS therapist for two years, then her therapy had to stop because the therapist's contract (she was a junior doctor) was not renewed at that particular hospital. 'I don't blame the therapist, it was the system, the NHS, that stopped it. Therapy in itself creates such a need, it creates such a dependent relationship that there has to be the time allowed to work through that until you don't need such a relationship. You see, my therapist was my mother, my father, all sorts of important people to me, and I had to break off all those "relationships" at once.'

She has now referred herself for group therapy. 'I still need support but I don't want to go through the pain of that one-to-one therapy again. I don't want to be a patient for the whole of my life. But I do need the support which you can never get from friends, lovers, husbands. It can be very damaging to those relationships to want to delve too much. And to do that you need the structure of therapy.'

This woman was at least offered psychotherapy of a sort. Too many people, especially those designated 'working class', are not given such a choice by National Health Service workers and they usually have no idea where to find such help privately, even if they can afford it. Voluntary organizations, such as Marriage Guidance Councils or specialist youth counselling services, have gone some way to fill the gap, but government and local authority cutbacks in grants are already forcing them to reduce the number of clients they can help.

I will always remember one couple I interviewed – in South Wales – who, perhaps more than anyone else, reinforced my belief in the 'talking treatments'. It was a second marriage for both of them and they had just emerged from a very difficult few months. He had been seriously depressed, mainly because of unemployment and related financial difficulties, and they had barely communicated with one another. I was there to discuss their marital therapy, which they had received through a voluntary organization and which had helped them considerably.

I discovered that she had learned the importance of talking about problems the hard way. She had previously been married to a violent man who expected her to cope with small children single-handed and on very little money. Eventually she became depressed and went to her GP. He did not ask her why she felt like that and, not unlike many of us, she was reluctant to talk; he prescribed tranquillizers time and time again. She weaned herself off them after eighteen years. During that time, she had twice tried to commit suicide and had been admitted to the local psychiatric hospital. 'Even then,' she recalled, 'no one ever asked me what problems had pushed me into overdosing, they just stomach pumped me and prescribed more drugs.' She had been in contact with numerous professionals over many years and none of them had *talked* to her, or offered any support.

I do not believe that therapy or counselling are the answer to every problem, but I do believe that giving someone the chance to talk through their difficulties is showing them respect for their human-ness, their humanity, and, in cases such as chronic physical illness where physical treatments are essential, may speed, or at least encourage, recovery. In this so-called age of communication, let us not lose that essentially human skill of communicating with one another, especially when someone is in pain.

Resource guide

ANALYSIS

Association of Jungian Analysts
Flat 3
7 Eton Avenue
London NW3 3EL
01 794 8711

The clinic offers Jungian analysis with trainees under supervision but referrals can also be made to fully qualified members of AJA. An assessment is first made with an analyst who is a psychiatrist. Treatment is two or three times a week for at least a year, more likely two years or more. There is no NHS treatment. Analysis with a trainee ranges in cost from £2 to £8; with qualified analysts fees range from £15 to about £25. There are a few members outside London, in Surrey and Essex.

C. C. Jung Clinic (The Society of Analytical Psychology)
1 Daleham Gardens
London NW3 5BY
01 435 7696

Offers Jungian analysis. Much of the work is done by trainees, under careful supervision of experienced analysts. Patients are assessed first before a referral is made. Treatment is four times a week for a minimum period of two years. There is no NHS treatment and fees are not less than £2.50 per session. There is a Professional Practice Committee.

London Clinic of Psycho-Analysis
63 New Cavendish Street
London WIM 7RD
01 580 4952/3

Offers psychoanalysis with a Freudian/Kleinian orientation. Much
of the work is done by trainees (as the clinic is attached to the
major Institute, The British Psycho-Analytic Society) with careful
supervision. Many of the analysts are medically qualified. Patients
are assessed first before a referral is made to an analyst. Treatment
is five times a week for, on average, two to three years. Fees are
charged according to income but there are a few NHS vacancies.
There is a Professional Practice Committee.

For people wanting analysis outside London, these organizations
may be able to recommend analysts but there are not many outside
the south east of England.

COUNSELLING

Alton Counselling Service
Friends Meeting House
Church Street
Alton
Hampshire
Alton 83459

Offers counselling in all areas of need – relationships, be-
reavements, marital, family – on a one-to-one basis. Counsellors
are mostly trained by the Westminster Pastoral Foundation
courses, and their orientation is psychoanalytic or humanistic.
Clients are assessed before referral. Clients see their counsellor
once a week for an hour, on average for six to eight weeks. Set fees
are not charged but a contract is set up between client and
counsellor, in which the client agrees to pay whatever he or she can
afford.

Blackpool and Fylde Counselling Centre
Beaufort Avenue
Bispham
Blackpool
0253 56624/866976

Offers one-to-one and group counselling. No particular theoretical orientation. Clients seen once a week for an hour. Services are free though donations are welcomed.

British Association for Counselling
37a Sheep Street
Rugby
Warwickshire CV21 3BX
0788 78328/9

The BAC does not provide counselling direct, but does provide information about counselling resources on a broad front. These include information sheets and directories, available from the above address.

Carrs Lane Counselling Centre
Carrs Lane Centre
Birmingham B4 7SX
021 643 6363

Offers one-to-one counselling, 'mainly for the normal life-maturational situations' such as family and matrimonial work. The work is eclectic but largely client-centred and non-directive. Counsellors are trained at the Centre and supervised by professional practitioners. Most clients see their counsellor once a week, some only a few times, others for several months. There are no set fees but the Centre 'hopes for a donation'.

The Isis Centre
43 Little Clarendon Street
Oxford OX1 2HU
0865 56648

Offers individual, marital and family counselling plus some groups. There is 'an underlying acceptance of psychoanalytic principles'.

Nearly all clients are seen weekly and the average number of sessions is eight. All treatment is given on the NHS; a client qualifies by residing in the county of Oxfordshire. Counsellors have a range of qualifications and professional training.

Morpeth Centre for Psychotherapy
4 Market Place West
Morpeth
Northumberland NE61 1HE
0670 57434

Offers counselling and psychotherapy, for individuals and groups, using a person-centred model and some psychodrama. Most clients are seen once a week and duration varies from nine weeks to three years. No NHS treatment available.

The Norwich Centre for Personal and Professional Development
7 Earlham Road
Norwich NR2 3RA
0603 617709
10am to 12pm, and 1pm to 3pm

Offers one-to-one counselling, couple counselling and some groups occasionally. It takes the Rogerian, person-centred approach. Clients see their counsellor once a week, and it can last from four weeks to two years; the average number of sessions is eight. The basic fee is £12 per hour, but this can be negotiated in cases of hardship. No NHS counselling available. All the counsellors are trained with a range of qualifications and professional backgrounds.

The Tom Allan Centre
23 Elmbank Street
Glasgow
041 221 1535

Offers individual, family and group counselling from trained counsellors.

Westminster Pastoral Foundation
23 Kensington Square
London W8 5HN
01 937 6956

Offers counselling for individuals and some groups, plus marital counselling for couples. The theoretic orientation is eclectic: Jungian, Freudian and others. There is an assessment before referral. Sessions are usually on a weekly basis and may last weeks, months, even two or three years. Counsellors are either trained by WPF or on similar training courses. There are no set fees but everyone is expected to make some contribution, the average is about £6.50. WPF is probably the largest counselling service in the country and has 20 affiliates in other parts of London and the UK (including Chelsea, Highgate, Enfield, Wembley, Croydon, Chelmsford, St Albans, Southampton, Penarth). Although many of the counsellors have strong religious beliefs, clients do not need to and there is no attempt to convert people to a particular belief system.

FEMINIST THERAPY

Birmingham Women's Counselling and Therapy Centre
43 Ladywood Middleway
Birmingham B16 8HA
021 455 8677

Offers individual therapy and counselling. Therapists have a variety of orientations: psychoanalytic and humanistic but all basically feminist, seeing a woman's distress in terms of societal experience. There is always an initial assessment. Treatment is free. All the workers are qualified as social workers and/or counsellors.

Women's Counselling and Therapy Service
Top Floor
Oxford Chambers
Oxford Place
Leeds LS1 3AX
0532 455725

Offers psychodynamic psychotherapy from a feminist perspective. They also use some techniques from humanistic therapies, counselling and cognitive therapy where appropriate. There is an initial assessment. Therapy is usually once weekly for one to two years. Fees range from £3 to £15 but there are some free places. All the therapists are lay, but they are supervised by a psychoanalyst who is a psychiatrist.

The Women's Therapy Centre
6 Manor Gardens
London N7 6LA
01 263 6200

Offers individual long-term and short-term therapy, analytically orientated, and group therapy. It also runs a wide range of workshops which are more eclectic, using techniques from humanistic therapies. All the therapists have a professional training and the majority have a psychodynamic orientation – Freudian, objects relations, Kleinian, Jungian. New clients are always given an initial interview with a therapist to see whether the therapy is appropriate and whether the client and therapist think they can work together. Because of very limited resources, the Centre also has a referral network of therapists in London and other parts of the country. Individual therapy is once or twice weekly, and groups meet once a week. The time contract is agreed between therapist and client at the outset, and can either be open-ended or limited to one or two years. Fees are on a sliding scale, according to the client's income and circumstances. The therapists treat people with a wide range of problems but the Centre has developed a particular approach to working with women with eating problems.

The Centre may be able to refer clients to feminist therapists in other parts of the country.

GROUP PSYCHOTHERAPY

Many of the centres listed in the individual psychotherapy section also offer group psychotherapy:

Association for Group and Individual Psychotherapy
Arbours Association
The Clinic of Psychotherapy
Ealing Psychotherapy Centre

Institute of Psychotherapy and Social Studies
Lincoln Memorial Clinic
London Centre for Psychotherapy
Nafsiyat
North London Personal Consultation Practice
The South London Psychotherapy Group
Tavistock Clinic

Group-Analytic Practice
88 Montagu Mansions
London W1H 1LF
01 935 3103/3085

Offers group-analytic psychotherapy. Group sessions last for one and a half hours, once or twice a week. An assessment is made before referral to a particular group. For a once weekly group, the standard fee is £46 per month, calculated to cover forty sessions of treatment in any calendar year.

North London Centre for Group Therapy
6B Priory Close
London N14 4AW
01 440 1451

Offers psychoanalytically based group psychotherapy. Assessment is normally made by a consultant psychiatrist. Group therapy is once or twice weekly, and duration varies greatly. There are no NHS facilities and fees are by arrangement with the therapist.

INDIVIDUAL PSYCHOTHERAPY

Arbours Association
41A Weston Park
London N8
01 340 7646

The Arbours Association is perhaps best known for its crisis centre, which offers residential psychotherapeutic treatment. It also has a psychotherapy clinic which offers long-term and short-term therapy. Its orientation is both psychodynamic and 'sociodynamic (interpersonal') but within this framework, its therapists have their own special orientation – Kleinian, Freudian, and so on.

Many of the therapists have been trained through Arbours's own training programme but the majority will also have further qualifications from, for example, the Institute of Psychoanalysis and the Tavistock Clinic. Some are medically qualified, others have worked in social work or clinical psychology. Patients are assessed first before referral. Treatment is normally not less than twice a week, ranging from short-term therapy lasting a number of weeks to long-term therapy lasting a number of years. Fees range from £8 to £15, but low-cost sessions, from £3 to £6, are available.

There is a Professional Practice Committee.

Association for Group and Individual Psychotherapy
29 St Mark's Crescent
London NW1
01 485 9141

Offers individual analytically orientated psychotherapy. An assessment is first made by a medically qualified or senior member of the Association. Referrals are then made to a therapist working at the Association's headquarters or in the patient's locality. Treatment is usually twice a week, for two or three years on average. The fee for assessment interviews is £10 and for treatment it varies from £6 to £12 per session. Trainees on the Association's training course take on patients at a lower rate.

British Association of Psychotherapists
Secretary: Mrs Judith Lawrence
121 Hendon Lane
London N3 3PR
01 346 1747

The BAP is concerned with the training of analytical psychotherapists but it also offers a clinical assessment and referral service. This offers information and consultation to adults who may be interested in having psychotherapy, and referral when appropriate. The assessment is with a professionally trained and experienced psychotherapist; the cost for this consultation is £20. Referral can then be made to either a trained member of BAP or a therapist in training. The orientation of BAP members is analytic, covering Freudian, Kleinian and Jungian views. Some are medically qualified. Treatment is one, two or three sessions a week and duration varies considerably. Fees charged are usually within the range of £9 to £20 a session though some very experienced therapists charge more. It cannot offer NHS treatment but the assessor for the clinical service may refer someone on to a NHS clinic.

There is an Ethics Committee to deal with any complaints.

The majority of the BAP's members are in London but it does have some in other areas. They will cerainly try to refer someone within their area.

Camden Psychotherapy Unit
25-31 Tavistock Place
London WC1H 9SE
01 388 2071 extension 48

This unit offers psychoanalytical psychotherapy once weekly for up to two years. Clients are assessed before referral. The service is free to Camden residents. All psychotherapists have qualifications in psychotherapy or psychoanalysis. There is a medical consultant.

Clinic of Psychotherapy
Garden Flat
26 Belsize Square
London NW3
01 903 6455 (answering service)

This clinic offers psychoanalytic psychotherapy. Initial assessments are always carried out by one of the medically qualified staff before referral is made. The medical staff are psychiatrists and psychoanalysts; the non-medical staff are either psychoanalysts or have undergone training, usually with the British Association of Psychotherapists. Treatment is usually two or three times a week and can last up to several years. Fees range between £10 and £25. There is no NHS treatment. There is a Professional Staff Committee which can investigate complaints.

Ealing Psychotherapy Centre
St Martin's Rooms
Hale Gardens
London W3
01 993 5185

The Centre offers analytical psychotherapy. Patients are assessed before referral. Most of the psychotherapists have completed one of the recognized training courses but some are still training. Trainees are strictly supervised and have a restricted number of patients in therapy with them. Case discussions take place regularly with a medically qualified psychotherapist. Sessions range from one to four times a week; the average duration of treatment is three years. Fees range from £5 to £15; there is no treatment on the NHS.

Institute of Psychotherapy and Social Studies
5 Lake House
London NW3 2SH
01 794 4147

The centre offers psychotherapy with a psychodynamic and humanistic orientation, attempting to integrate both approaches. Individuals are assessed before referral. Therapy may be offered with trainees, who are carefully supervised. Treatment is twice a week for at least a year. Low cost therapy is available from trainees; there is no NHS treatment. Fees are charged according to means, ranging from £5 to £15.

There is a complaints procedure, as yet unused, and all staff members and trainees have to sign an ethical statement.

Lincoln Clinic and Institute for Psychotherapy
77 Westminster Bridge Road
London SE1 7HS
01 928 7211/261 9236

This is a training institute, so the Clinic offers psychotherapy with experienced clinicians and trainees. It offers analytical psychotherapy and 'focal psychotherapy' which is briefer, tending to focus on particular difficulties. Individuals are assessed before referral; £18 is the normal diagnostic fee but it can be reduced, according to means. Apart from the Institute's own trainees, all psychotherapists are qualified members or associate members of one of the other recognized training bodies such as the British Psycho-Analytic Society or the BAP. All patients come on medical referral, usually GPs and sometimes psychiatrists. Treatment ranges from once to three times a week; duration of treatment may be months or years, but the average is one to two years. Fees are £18 with senior clinicians, £5 to £12 with trainees; there is no NHS treatment.

There is a Professional Committee to investigate complaints.

London Centre for Psychotherapy
19 Fitzjohn's Avenue
London NW3 5JY
01 435 0873

The Centre runs its own training courses so it can offer low-cost training with trainees. It also has about 100 fully qualified psychotherapists, some practising at the Centre itself, others with consulting rooms in and around most parts of London. The orientation is analytical. Patients are assessed first by a medically qualified psychotherapist (£15 is charged for this) and a small panel of senior psychotherapists meet to decide on the referral. Fees range from £9 or £10 a session.

Nafsiyat
The Inter-Cultural Therapy Centre
278 Seven Sisters Road
London N4 2HY
01 263 4130

Psychodynamic techniques are used by the therapists but special account is taken of the cultural factors involved. Patients are assessed before referral. Treatment may last a few weeks, or months, or over a year, according to the patient's needs. Some patients are seen in their own home. The psychotherapy is free for patients living in the Islington area; a fee of £15 is charged to those people coming from other areas. There is a Professional Committee to deal with complaints.

North London Personal Consultation Practice
17A Templars Crescent
London NW3 3QR
01 349 9399

Offers brief and long-term psychoanalytic psychotherapy. Patients
are assessed before referral, for a fee of £40. All the therapists are
doctors, psychologists or social workers, and all have some qualification in analytic psychotherapy. Brief psychotherapy involves
ten to twenty sessions. Longer term varies from once to five times
a week, lasting months or years. Fees vary according to means,
frequency and type of treatment.

Scottish Institute of Human Relations
56 Albany Street
Edinburgh
031 556 6454

Offers psychoanalytically orientated psychotherapy. The initial
assessment costs £18 to £20 and sessions, which may be more than
once a week, at £17 per session. Some members of the Institute
work in Glasgow.

South London Psychotherapy Group
Honorary Secretary: 19 Broom Water
Teddington
Middlesex TW11 9QT
01 977 6303

Offers psychoanalytic psychotherapy. The assessment is normally
with the therapist who is likely to be able to offer the vacancy. The
fee for assessment is £15. Therapists are members or associate
members of the London Centre for Psychotherapy. Treatment is
one to three times a week, varying in duration. There is no NHS
treatment though an attempt would be made to refer to some NHS
treatment if this was thought necessary. Fees range from £8 to £20
a session.

Tavistock Clinic
Adult Department
120 Belsize Lane
London NW3 5BA
01 435 7111

Offers short-term and (a limited provision of) long-term individual psychotherapy, based on psychoanalytic principles. Patients are assessed first. The Tavistock Clinic is almost certainly one of the most eminent training bodies for psychotherapy in the country. All therapists have a specialist training in psychotherapy and are qualified psychiatrists, psychologists or social workers. Therapy is usually only once a week, and the average period of treatment is one to two years. It is an NHS unit and so no fees are charged. The Clinic's catchment area is approximately north London and the NHS's North East Thames Region.

For more information on individual psychotherapy outside London, see: British Association of Psychotherapists.

For NHS treatment you should ask your GP or call the Department of Psychology in the nearest general hospital. MIND is concerned that many areas seem to offer very little help of this kind, but MIND's regional offices (see below) or local associations (look in the local telephone directory) may be able to help. Community Health Councils may also have information about local therapists.

MARRIAGE GUIDANCE COUNSELLING

There are 160 Marriage Guidance Councils throughout the country, offering short-term and long-term counselling concerned primarily with marriage and relationship problems. Look in the telephone directory for your nearest branch. Fees are negotiable according to means, from about £5 to £15.
For further information:

The National Marriage Guidance Council
Herbert Gray College
Little Church Street
Rugby
Warwickshire
0788 73241

Catholic Marriage Advisory Council (Headquarters, but has branches throughout the country)
15 Lansdowne Road
London W11 3AJ
01 727 0141

Jewish Marriage Council
23 Ravenhurst Avenue
London NW4
01 203 6311

The Scottish Marriage Guidance Council
26 Frederick Street
Edinburgh EH2 25R
031 225 5006

Some of the counselling services listed also offer counselling for couples.

SEX THERAPY

Help for a wide range of sexual problems is offered at all Marriage Guidance Councils throughout the country, but a growing number have specialized counsellors offering sex therapy. If your local council does not have such a specialist, they should be able to refer you to the nearest one that does. Professional referral is preferred but it is not essential. Fees are negotiable. There is always an initial assessment interview.

The following services, to be found in various parts of the country, also offer specialist sex therapy, often on the NHS.

Brook Advisory Centres
Family Planning Association Clinics
Some departments of psychiatry and psychology have sexual
 dysfunction clinics or psychosexual clinics

The British Association for Counselling (address under counselling)
has a directory of agencies offering therapy, counselling and support
for psychosexual problems.

GENERAL INFORMATION

MIND nationally, regionally or locally (see your telephone directory for local associations) should be able to tell you of agencies and
individuals offering different types of therapy or counselling,
though they cannot make recommendations.

MIND
22 Harley Street
London W1
01 637 0741

Northern MIND
158 Durham Road
Gateshead NE8 4EL
091 478 4425

North West MIND
21 Ribblesdale Place
Preston PR1 3NA
0772 21734

South East MIND
4th Floor
24-32 Stephenson Way
London NW1 2HD
01 387 9126

South West MIND
Bluecoat House
Saw Close
Bath BA1 1EY
0225 64670

Trent and Yorkshire MIND
1st Floor Suite
White Buildings
Fitzallan Square
Sheffield S1 2AY
0742 21742

Wales MIND
23 St Mary Street,
Cardiff CF1 2AA
0222 395123

West Midlands MIND
Princess Chambers (3rd Floor)
52-4 Lichfield Street
Wolverhampton WV1 1DS
0902 24402

FEES

Psychotherapists in this country are unlikely to hit the super-tax bracket. Although any regular fees can seem costly, especially if sessions are more than once a week for several years, reputable therapists have sliding scales and often play at Robin Hood, charging according to means. I suspect that it is always worth discussing the possibility of a lower fee with a therapist. Some, for instance, will charge less to students and people involved in the helping profession.

The lowest fee I have heard about is for the latter group, at £5 an hour. The highest (usually charged by analysts for their psychotherapy) is £35. The average (with a qualified therapist) ranges between £10 and £15, possibly less if there are two or three sessions a week. The average with training therapists is between £5 and £10.

Analysis is probably the most expensive form of psychotherapy, ranging from £15 a session to £50, the highest I've heard of.

Glossary

Behaviour therapy

This form of psychotherapy is based on learning theory. So symptoms like anxiety or agoraphobia (fear of open spaces) are seen as the results of learning maladaptive habits, or ways of coping with certain situations or emotions, rather than the result of unconscious processes. As these habits have been *learnt*, so they can be *unlearnt*. The therapist takes a teaching role to help the patient learn more suitable, less painful ways of coping. Behaviour therapists are usually not concerned with the reason why a patient is suffering from a certain symptom, although some psychologists in the NHS have found they can successfully combine the behavioural and psychodynamic. Behaviour therapy has been found to be very successful with treating phobias and obsessional-compulsive behaviour, and with sexual dysfunctions, such as impotence.
The main techniques used are:

Desensitization, where once the patient has been taught to relax, he or she is exposed over a number of sessions to the thing or situation they fear, for example, a spider or flying in an aeroplane. They may be asked to imagine the object they fear, or they may be shown it in pictures.
Flooding, where the patient, with his or her consent, is confronted with the phobic object, or situation, until he or she becomes used to it and the anxiety level drops. Again he might also be taught useful relaxation techniques.

Cognitive therapy

This increasingly popular form of therapy is an offshoot of behaviour therapy and seems to be quite successful in treating depression.

It is based on the view that depression is a result of the way people think about and view the world; depressed people tend to have negative thoughts, they misinterpret or distort events and generally have a very pessimistic view of life. Cognitive therapists try to remove or ease the depression by helping the patient to change his or her attitudes and ways of thinking, by replacing negative with more positive thoughts. A patient might be offered about twenty treatment sessions, and between sessions would be expected to keep a diary of negative thoughts and the events or thoughts which led up to them. At each session these negative thoughts would be discussed and the patient would then be encouraged to replace them with more positive ideas. He or she would also be expected to develop activities which give him pleasure and, most importantly, increase his sense of personal achievement and self-esteem.

Humanistic therapy

Humanistic therapies include many types of therapy such as Gestalt, primal therapy, encounter groups, psychodrama, which developed so strongly in the 1960s and were part of the alternative society, the growth movement. They are still very popular in the UK as well as the USA, but as one of the practitioners explained, you no longer have to be a paid-up member of the alternative society to take part. Many therapists, working privately and in the NHS, mix the more conventional forms of psychotherapy with techniques taken from humanistic therapy.

Techniques often involve working on the body as well as the mind, and some therapies also lay great emphasis on the spiritual side of our natures. The prime aim of these therapies is to help people get in touch with their 'real self', and to fulfil their potential. Carl Rogers's techniques (see Chapter 7) demonstrate well this way of working. There is also more stress on change rather than adjustment to society's conventions, and humanistic therapists have a more optimistic view of human nature than, say, the Freudians.

Libido

Freud used this term to mean sexual and erotic drives. Jung widened it out to include also the desires and drives to be creative and to strive for fulfilment. When sex therapists talk about 'loss of libido', they are very specifically talking about loss of sexual desire.

Major tranquillizers

Also known as anti-psychotic drugs, tranquillizers such as Largactil and Stelazine are far more potent then the minor tranquillizers. These are used to treat schizophrenia mainly, though some depressed people may be prescribed them. They can be given in tablet form or as long-acting injections. They do *not* cure psychotic illnesses, but do remove most, if not all, of the symptoms. The side effects often associated with them include dizziness, dry mouth, blurred vision, and movement disorders such as uncontrollable twitching and distorting of face and limbs. The most severe is tardive dyskinesia, a form of brain damage, which cannot be easily treated.

Minor tranquillizers

Commonly used to treat anxiety and depression, though they may cause depressed feelings. Other side effects include drowsiness. Over the past few years, there has been increasing criticism of doctors' over-use of such drugs and, slowly, they are being prescribed less. They can be useful as a short-term crutch.

Psychotic illnesses

These include those serious mental conditions, such as schizophrenia and manic depression, where, for varying lengths of time and intensity, the person loses touch with reality. He or she may hear voices, or see visions, or imagine they are someone else. The cause of these illnesses is not yet known; the experts argue over whether the cause is likely to be totally biochemical in nature or whether factors involved are psychological, such as stress and certain types of families. Most sufferers are treated with drugs alone, mainly the major tranquillizers.

Notes

Chapter 1

1. Sigmund Freud, *Introductory Lectures on Psychoanalysis* (Harmondsworth: Penguin, 1982), p.41.
2. Derek Russell Davis, *An Introduction to Psychopathology* (Oxford: Oxford University Press, 1984), p.144.
3. Anthony Clare, *Psychiatry in Dissent* (London: Tavistock, 1980), p.15.
4. ibid., p.32.
5. Luise Eichenbaum and Susie Orbach, *Understanding Women* (Harmondsworth: Penguin, 1985) p.174.
6. Bertram Karon and Gary VandenBos, *Psychotherapy of Schizophrenia: the Treatment of Choice* (New York: Jason Aronson, 1981).
7. David Malan, *Individual Psychotherapy and the Science of Psychodynamics* (London: Butterworths, 1982), p.223.

Chapter 2

1. George Weinberg, *The Heart of Psychotherapy* (New York: St Martin's Press, 1984), p.173.
2. ibid., p.175.
3. ibid., p.4.
4. Sue Llewellyn, 'The Challenge of Feminist Psychotherapy' in *Changes* magazine.
5. Sidney Bloch, 'Accountability in Psychotherapy'. A lecture delivered at the Uffculme Clinic in June 1982 and printed in the *Midland Journal of Psychotherapy*, December 1982.
6. Hans Eysenck, *Decline and Fall of the Freudian Empire* (New York: Viking, 1985).
7. Morton Schatzman, 'Anti-Freud' in *New Society*, 13 September 1985.
8. Anthony Storr, *The Art of Psychotherapy* (London: Heinemann, 1979), p.161.

Chapter 3

1. Sigmund Freud, *Autobiographical Study* in the Standard Edition of *The Complete Psychological Works of Sigmund Freud* (London: Hogarth Press), volume 20, p.17.
2. Sigmund Freud and Joseph Breuer, *Studies in Hysteria* (Harmondsworth: Penguin, 1983).
3. David Malan, *op. cit.*
4. Paul Kline, *Psychology and Freudian Theory* (London: Methuen, 1984), p.6.
5. Michael Jacobs, 'Psychodynamic Therapy: the Freudian Approach' in *Individual Therapy in Britain*, ed. Windy Dryden (New York: Harper and Row, 1984).
6. Janet Malcolm, *In the Freud Archives* (London: Cape, 1984).
7. Sigmund Freud, *Five Lectures on Psychoanalysis* in *Two Short Accounts of Psychoanalysis* (Harmondsworth: Penguin, 1962), p.63.
8. ibid., p.71.
9. Dennis Brown and Jonathan Pedder, *Introduction to Psychotherapy* (London: Tavistock, 1979), p.46.
10. Sigmund Freud, *New Introductory Lectures on Psychoanalysis* (1933) in Standard Edition, *op. cit.*, volume 22.
11. Sigmund Freud, *The Interpretation of Dreams* in Standard Edition, *op. cit.*, volume 5, p.608.
12. Sigmund Freud, *Five Lectures on Psychoanalysis*, *op. cit.*, p.82.
13. Sigmund Freud, *Remembering, Repeating and Working Through* in Standard Edition, *op. cit.*, volume 12, p.150.
14. George Weinberg, *op. cit.*, p.142.
15. Sigmund Freud, *Five Lectures on Psychoanalysis*, *op. cit.*, p.8.
16. ibid., pp.81–2.
17. ibid., p.82.
18. ibid., p.79.
19. Julia Segal, *Phantasy in Everyday Life* (London: Penguin, 1985), p.44.
20. Anthony Storr, *Jung* (London: Fontana, 1973), p.44.
21. Luise Eichenbaum and Susie Orbach, *Outside In . . . Inside Out* (Harmondsworth: Penguin, 1982).
22. Michael Jacobs, *op. cit.*
23. Anthony Storr, *Jung, op. cit.*, p.19.
24. ibid., p.90.

25. William McGuire and R.F.C. Hull (eds.), *C.G. Jung Speaking* (London: Picador, 1980), p.165.
26. Anthony Storr, *Jung*, p.104.
27. Carl Jung, *Collected Works* (London: Routledge and Kegan Paul, 1958), vol 16, p.41.

Chapter 4

1. Anthony Storr, *The Art of Psychotherapy*, op. cit., p.151.
2. Sigmund Freud, *Lines of Psychoanalytic Therapy* in Standard Edition, op. cit., volume 17, p.164.
3. Joel Kovel, *A Complete Guide to Therapy* (Harmondsworth: Penguin, 1978), p.113.
4. Anthony Storr, *The Art of Psychotherapy*, p.56.
5. Sigmund Freud, *Recommendations to Physicians Practising Psychoanalysis* in Standard Edition, op. cit., volume 12, p.118.
6. Anthony Storr, *The Art of Psychotherapy*, p.64.
7. ibid., p.67.
8. Carl Jung, *Collected Works*, op. cit., volume 2, pp.338–9.
9. Anthony Storr, *The Art of Psychotherapy*, p.31.
10. Sidney Bloch, *What is Psychotherapy?* (Oxford: Oxford University Press, 1982), p.70.
11. Anthony Storr, *The Art of Psychotherapy*, p.31.
12. Sidney Bloch, ibid., p.70.
13. Anthony Storr, *The Art of Psychotherapy*, p.34.
14. David Malan, *A Study of Brief Psychotherapy* (New York: Plenum, 1975), p.8.
15. Anthony Storr, *The Art of Psychotherapy*, p.x.

Chapter 5

1. Marilyn Lawrence, *The Anorexic Experience* (London: The Women's Press, 1984), p.80.
2. Sheila Ernst and Lucy Goodison, *In Our Own Hands* (London: The Women's Press, 1981), p.268.
3. ibid., p.219.
4. Luise Eichenbaum and Susie Orbach, *Understanding Women*, op. cit.
5. Susie Orbach, *Fat is a Feminist Issue* (Feltham: Hamlyn).

Chapter 6

1. S.H. Foulkes and E.J. Anthony, *Group Psychotherapy: the Psychoanalytic Approach* (Harmondsworth: Penguin, 1973).
2. *MIND OUT*, December 1981.

Chapter 7

1. Carl Rogers, *On Becoming a Person* (London: Constable, 1961).
2. ibid.
3. Keith Oatley, *Selves in Relation* (London: Methuen, 1984), p.58.
4. Brian Thorne, 'Person-Centred Therapy' in *Individual Therapy in Britain, op. cit.*
5. Susan Oldfield, *The Counselling Experience* (London: Routledge and Kegan Paul, 1983), p.36.
6. Brian Thorne, *op. cit.*
7. Keith Oatley, *op. cit.*, p.59.

Chapter 10

1. Joy Melville, 'On the Couch' in *New Society*, 24 November 1977.

Further reading

Analysis

B. A. Farrell, *The Standing of Psychoanalysis* (Oxford: Oxford University Press, 1981).

Joseph Sandler, Christopher Dare and Alex Holder, *The Patient and the Analyst* (London: Karnac, 1982).

History

Henri F. Ellenberger, *The Discovery of the Unconscious: the History and Evolution of Dynamic Psychiatry* (New York: Basic Books, 1970).

Novels and Personal Accounts

Lisa Alther, *Other Women* (New York: Viking Penguin, 1985).

Marie Cardinal, *The Words to Say It* (London: Pan, 1984).

Sarah Ferguson, *A Guard Within* (London: Chatto and Windus, 1973).

Judith Rossner, *August* (Sevenoaks: Coronet, 1983).

D. M. Thomas, *The White Hotel* (Harmondsworth: Penguin, 1981).

Sex Therapy

Paul Brown and Carolyn Faulder, *Treat Yourself to Sex* (Harmondsworth: Penguin, 1979).

Anne Hooper, *The Body Electric: a Unique Account of Sex Therapy for Women*, (London: Virago, 1980).

W. H. Masters and V. E. Johnson, *Understanding Human Sexual Inadequacy* (Sevenoaks: Coronet, 1971).

Index

Nancy Friday

My Mother/My Self

Why are women the way they are? Why, despite everything, do we find so much of ourselves mysterious? Where do the dependence, the longing for intimacy, the passivity come from?

Drawing on her own and other women's lives, Nancy Friday shows compellingly that the key lies in a woman's relationship with her mother – that first binding relationship which becomes the model for so much of our adult relationships with men, and whose fetters constrain our sexuality, our independence, our very selfhood.

'Brilliant. Courageous. Moving. One of the most important books I have ever read about my mother, myself and my life.' WASHINGTON POST

'A book most women will want to read and every man ought to.' Michael Korda